# Birdwatcher's
# DAILY COMPANION

QUARRY

"The truth of the matter is, the birds could very well live without us, but many—perhaps all—of us would find life incomplete, indeed almost intolerable without the birds."

*- Roger Tory Peterson*

First published in the United States of America by
Quarry Books, a member of
Quayside Publishing Group
100 Cummings Center
Suite 406-L
Beverly, Massachusetts 01915-6101
Telephone: (978) 282-9590
Fax: (978) 283-2742
www.quarrybooks.com

**Library of Congress Cataloging-in-Publication Data**
Warhol, Tom.
  Birdwatcher's daily companion : 365 days of advice, insight, and information for enthusiastic birders / Tom Warhol, Marcus H. Schneck.
      p. cm.
  Includes index.
  ISBN-13: 978-1-59253-650-4
  ISBN-10: 1-59253-650-6
  1. Bird watching. I. Schneck, Marcus. II. Title.
  QL677.5.W337 2010
  598.072'34—dc22

                                                                            2010019106

  ISBN-13: 978-1-59253-650-4
  ISBN-10: 1-59253-650-6

  10 9 8 7 6 5 4 3 2 1

Design: everlution design
Illustrations: Judy Love
The illustrations on pages 28, 111, 187, and 222 were first published in *The All-Season Backyard Birdwatcher* (Quarry Books).
Tech Editor for days 76/77, 90/91, 186, 209/210, 251/252, 258/259, 265/266, 335/336: Karen Ruth

Printed in China

# Birdwatcher's
# DAILY COMPANION

## 365 Days
### of Advice, Insight, and Information for Enthusiastic Birders

Marcus H. Schneck and Tom Warhol

BEVERLY MASSACHUSETTS

QUARRY BOOKS

"I value my garden more for being full of blackbirds than of cherries, and very frankly, give them fruit for their songs."

– JOSEPH ADDISON, 1672–1719, English essayist, poet, and politician

# contents

# Introduction

Many birdwatchers are introduced to the pursuit by relatives or friends. Seeing the fervent interest this special breed of people gives to the brilliant yet fleeting avian denizens we share the world with often encourages others to see what they're seeing, and to experience what they're experiencing while engaged with nature. Some people may lose interest eventually, while others may also be bitten by the birdwatching bug.

The two authors of this book discovered birdwatching through different paths. Marcus's mother maintained an array of feeders in her backyard, aligned for prime viewing through the kitchen window, and a pair of binoculars and a field guide to the birds rested nearby, at the ready, throughout her life. From that vantage, she shared with her young son her excitement over the sight of the varied and colorful species, such as the mobs of grosbeaks that came south from the boreal forests of northern Canada in difficult winters. She also attuned his ears to the equally colorful sounds coming from the yard, such as the wide-ranging repertoire of imitations demonstrated by a resident mockingbird. Through this and many other details, she instilled an enthusiasm for birds, bird feeding, and birdwatching in this budding naturalist.

Tom came to birding somewhat later, in his twenties, while living in the Boston area. The intense attention his close friends John and Caroline devoted to the birds of the region inspired him to raise the binoculars and see a whole new world. Up to this point, Tom's attention had been largely focused on plants and mushrooms; this new pursuit opened his eyes not only to the colorful personalities of birds and the shared joy of correctly identifying species, but also to a whole new group of living organisms, which broadened his view of the workings of ecosystems.

The common thread of both Tom's and Marcus's experiences is recognizing and responding to others' enthusiasm for these endlessly entertaining, vital members of the world's biota, from blue jays at backyard feeders to rarer peregrine falcons roosting on cliff faces and skyscrapers. Their mutual interest led the authors to join forces and share their own passion for birds in as wide a way as possible—through this book.

As they benefited from their predecessors, they hope this compilation of hints, tips, and tricks will deepen and expand your birdwatching, whether in your backyard or on long-distance outings to special birding hotspots. They've explored a wide range of information that should prove handy both as a reference for those experiences and as a day-to-day infusion of new knowledge.

So place this book next to your kitchen window or whatever viewing portal into the world of birds you favor, and enjoy a bit of insight every day.

# How to Use This Book

This book is organized as a day minder, with entries creating a complete year's worth of information. Each of the year's fifty-two weeks has six entries.

You can start reading this book from the beginning, following the days of the week through the calendar year, reading one entry a day. You can also read from the middle of the book, the end, or skip around from week to week as inspiration strikes. The most important thing to remember is that you can use this book however you want. Dive in and enjoy birdwatching tips and information, from birds in mythology to birds in your backyard.

## A Birdwatcher's Year

 **MONDAY** is for bird-finding tips and techniques.

 **TUESDAY** gives you tips and tools for species identification.

 **WEDNESDAY** opens your mind to ideas for birding excursions and travel.

 **THURSDAY** helps you find and attract birds in your backyard.

 **FRIDAY** teaches you about birds in history and mythology.

 **SATURDAY + SUNDAY** offers ideas and instructions for birding projects and activities.

# Find the Habitat, Find the Birds

ALTHOUGH BIRDS IN GENERAL can be found nearly everywhere, not all birds can be found everywhere. There is considerable overlap among species, but each bird seeks to satisfy its own special mix of the four basic needs for life—food, water, shelter/protection, and space—with its own particular preference. For example, a field-hunting species such as the kestrel will tend to satisfy its needs in grassland and farmland environments, while a woodland/brushland species such as the bushtit will be found in a very different setting.

In addition, all living things attempt to satisfy those needs with the smallest expenditure of energy possible by traveling as little as possible each day. That works in the birdwatcher's favor, increasing the chance of finding a desired species when the search is concentrated on sites of its preferred habitat within its range.

However, a superficial examination of a habitat, such as a quick look from the side of the road, can be misleading. For example, it might look like a stream and flow like a stream, but it also might carry heavily polluted water that supports no benthic or fish life. Contrary to first impressions, a fishing bird, such as a heron, would not find much to hold its interest in that particular stream.

In nature, appearances are very often deceiving, and closer inspection is needed before useful information and direction can be drawn from initial observations.

› Tip

Although knowing the habitat preferences for a bird species can be very helpful in finding that species, that knowledge can also serve as a field identification tool. If you are questioning the identification of a bird that has been sighted, consider the habitat: If the sighting was made in an unlikely habitat for the species, it may indicate a flawed identification.

American kestrel (*Falco sparverius*)

# Wading Birds: Great Blue Heron
## (*Ardea herodias*)

A COMMON SIGHT in North America's wetlands is the great blue heron, standing still and patient in shallow water, keeping a watchful eye out for fish and crustaceans, or striding forward through the water on its long, lanky legs. It uses its long, spearlike bill to strike and grab its prey.

**PHYSICAL CHARACTERISTICS**: The great blue heron is North America's largest wading bird, averaging 46" (1.2 m) from the tip of its long bill to the tip of its tail. The bird's large, 6' (1.8 m) wingspan and elongated neck make it almost prehistoric in appearance.

The yellow bill of this bird contrasts nicely with the blue-gray feathers of its back. The light gray feathers of the neck are often streaked with black, rust-brown, and white. The long black plumes on the crest of the bird's head and its ruffle of gray feathers hanging at its chest add to the elegance that this graceful yet lanky bird exudes.

**RANGE**: This heron can be found all across North America—in the southern United States year-round and in the northern United States and Canada in summer. Some spend winter from Mexico to the northern part of South America.

**HABITAT**: A truly gregarious bird, the great blue heron can be found in nearly any type of aquatic habitat, from ocean shores to small freshwater ponds, where it dines on small fish, crustaceans, frogs, snakes, insects, small mammals, and even other birds. Nests of these birds can be found in colonies in the tops of dead trees in old beaver ponds.

**SONGS AND CALLS**: The harsh croaks of the great blue heron may fit the bird's size, but it belies the bird's elegant appearance.

**CONSERVATION STATUS**: Like other large birds, particularly raptors, great blue heron populations were affected by DDT poisoning, causing weakening of eggshells. The current population is sizable and strong.

Great blue heron (*Ardea herodias*)

# South America: Manu National Park, Peru

IF YOU'RE LOOKING TO exponentially increase the number of birds on your life list, then Manu National Park, in the southwest corner of Peru, is the place to do it. There are more birds within this 5,800-square-mile (15,000 square km) park than any other site in the world. About 1,000 birds can be found, and in large numbers, including the red-and-green macaws and various parrots and parakeets that visit a clay lick in the park. Fully one-third of South America's birds and one-tenth of the number of world species can be found here.

Comprising most of the Manu River watershed, as well as many tributaries of the Alto Madre de Dios River, Manu Provincial Park, designated a United Nations Biosphere Reserve, also sits at the confluence of three significant biogeographic regions: the Eastern Andes Mountains, the Western Andes Mountains, and the Southeast Peruvian lowlands. All this, plus the park, ranges in elevation from 1,200' to 13,000' (365 to 4,000 m), which means there are seven different habitat types along that gradient, from humid lowland forest to puna (montane grasslands).

The park itself remains nearly pristine—the tourist accommodations can be found in the adjacent Manu Reserve Zone. The Manu Wildlife Center and Lodge is a well-reviewed accommodation, offering package tours of the park, which include travel (plane and boat) from Cuzco. Twenty-two bungalows sit on the lodge's grounds, and nearby trails and viewing platforms in trees offer birding and other wildlife watching (ten species of monkey, tapirs) around the clock.

**BIRDS TO SEE**: The species list is long, so this is just a taste of the resplendent birds seen here: red-and-green macaw, paradise tanager, Peruvian recurvebill, Manu antbird, Orinoco goose, Andean cock-of-the-rock, Koepcke's hermit, golden-headed and crested quetzals, pearled treerunner, and capped conebill.

# The True Importance of Bird Feeding

BIRD FEEDING HAS BECOME a big enough hobby (and business) to generate several chains of stores that specialize in providing the seeds, feeders, and other gear and supplies demanded by the millions of participants. Even many of the big-box stores have acknowledged the money to be made by catering to the special interests of birders with expanded offerings on their shelves and even special departments. The fact that the bird-feeding supplies do not go into storage at the end of winter reflects the fact that it's a year-round hobby with year-round potential for sales.

But beyond the economic impact, is there benefit in bird feeding?

If we are completely honest with ourselves, we must admit that the benefit is largely our own. We feed the birds in our backyards so that we might get closer, longer, and more insightful looks at them and their behaviors. We enjoy expanding our tallies of birds we've attracted and observed. And we feel good about doing something extra for the wild things whose homes we may have supplanted with our structures.

The equation is mostly one-sided. Through our bird-feeding activities, some sick, injured, old, or genetically inferior birds might survive a bit longer or through an especially harsh period of inclement weather. However, bird feeding in general has very little impact on any bird species as a whole. We do not help bird species to thrive by keeping our feeders filled with fresh seed.

Some have suggested that a few species have benefited from backyard feeding. Some have speculated that the northern cardinal, for example, has expanded its range north in response to the bounty it has found in backyard feeders throughout its region.

Moreover, some negative impacts have been identified, usually in local groups of birds rather than across an entire species. For example, bird feeders tend to cause birds to congregate in unusually high densities in relatively small areas. Such conditions can lead to the hastened spread of disease among the birds, even to the point of temporary decimation of local flocks.

That is not to argue that bird feeding is a negative and should be discontinued. Rather, it's simply an acknowledgment that any action we take in relation to wild things has consequences, often more unintended than intended.

# The Raven: Symbol of Life and Death

THE CLOSE ASSOCIATION of corvids, especially crows and ravens, with humans has earned them both respect and disdain. Although the respect results from our appreciation of these birds' intelligence and cleverness, this same cleverness and opportunism bring them into conflict with us, as they raid crops and steal objects. So opportunistic are these birds that they are commonly seen feasting on the corpses of battlefields, earning them an association with death.

Along with the coyote, crows and ravens are often portrayed as tricksters in many cultural myths. The opportunistic nature of these creatures is likely what gives rise to these stories. The raven commonly appears in the mythology of the native peoples of the northwestern United States, where its dual nature—greed and creativity, trickster and wise one—is often featured in the same myths. The bird is considered a key player in tribal creation myths of the Tlingit, Haida, Tsimshian, Bella Bella, and Kwakiutl.

In European mythology, the raven is also closely associated with war and death. This connection has also given rise to the raven as a messenger of the Underworld. This connection with the unknown also accounts for the assignment of the gift of prophecy to the raven. The bird is often seen in many myths as white in color, but through some misdeed is turned black by some action or god.

One of the more interesting myths in European lore is that of Odin, ruler of the Norse gods, and his twin ravens, Huginn and Muninn, translated from Old Norse as "Thought" and "Memory," respectively. They are Odin's eyes and ears, flying around Midgard, the Norse gods' home, and bringing him news of any happenings.

The raven is featured as a creation of ill portents in more modern culture as well, evidenced by Edgar Allan Poe's 1845 poem "The Raven." In this poem, a distraught man who has lost his lover engages in a maddening interaction with a raven, whose only word, "Nevermore," sends and seemingly guides the man further and further into madness.

1883 engraving of Odin, ruler of the Norse gods, with his twin ravens

# Top Annuals for Birds

SOME TOP SEED-PRODUCING annuals that provide a fantastic show in the garden include the following.

- **Ageratum**, *Ageratum houstonianum*, grows to nearly 1.5' (46 cm) in moist, rich soil in full sun; blue, pink, or white flowers

- **Tickseed sunflower**, *Bidens aristosa*, grows to 3' (91 cm) in moist soil of average fertility in full sun to partial shade; yellow flowers

- **Cosmos**, *Cosmos* spp., grows to 6' (1.8 m) in well-drained, moist soil of average fertility in full sun; red, orange, yellow, pink, purple, and white flowers

- **Queen Anne's lace**, *Daucus carota*, grows to 3' (91 cm) in well-drained, average soil in full sun; white flowers

- **Sunflower**, *Helianthus annuus*, grows to 12' (3.7 m) in well-drained soil of average fertility in full sun; yellow to orange flower with a large, black center

- **Verbena**, *Verbena* spp., grows to 1' (30 cm) in well-drained soil of average fertility in full sun; pink, white, red, purple, and yellow flowers

- **Zinnia**, *Zinnia elegans*, grows to 3' (91 cm) in moist, well-drained, rich soil in full sun; flowers in nearly all colors

Zinnia (*Zinnia elegans*)

# Life in the Edge

THE EDGE, THE AREA where one type of habitat meets and mixes with another, usually offers a greater variety of bird species than either individual type of habitat.

To some that statement may be a revelation, but it has relatively common-sense underpinnings. Birds from both habitat types will frequent the blended habitat elements of the edge, but fewer will be inclined to move through the edge to their nonpreferred type of habitat.

Additional bird species are likely to appear in the edge, simply because of the greater diversity offered there. For some species, the edge is its own specific habitat type.

The attraction of the edge works at all levels of the food chain. Great diversity of plant life in the edge produces great diversity of seeds, nectar, and the like, which attracts great diversity of insects, which attracts great diversity of insect eaters, which attracts great diversity of larger predators.

Some edges are more clearly defined than others. The edge where a lake and a forest meet is fairly sharp, while the edge where a field and a forest meet is less so, with significantly more blending of the two habitat types.

> **› Tip**
>
> Although *edge* has for decades been the accepted term for the area where two habitats meet and merge, a new term being applied to the same concept is *ecotone*.

THE BIRDWATCHERS' DAILY COMPANION

**Great horned owl fledglings**

# Raptors: Osprey (*Pandion haliaetus*)

THE OSPREY IS ONE of the most distinctive birds of prey in the world. So much so that it is classified in its own taxonomic family, Pandionidae, within the order that includes all other raptors.

**PHYSICAL CHARACTERISTICS**: The osprey is a largish raptor, generally colored brown above and white below, with a white head and black cap and mask. The undersides of the wings are patterned in dark and light colors, with dark wrist patches. The osprey has special adaptations for catching fish, including scaled legs with spicules, or pointed scales, that aid in latching on to slippery fish. The outer toe on each foot can slide to the back of the foot to help with this.

**RANGE**: Considered a cosmopolitan bird, the osprey can be found throughout the world, on every continent except Antarctica. These birds breed in Canada, the eastern seaboard of the United States, northern Europe, and Siberia. They winter in Central and South America, as well as in sub-Saharan Africa, parts of Southeast Asia, and coastal Australia.

**HABITAT**: With a diet consisting primarily of fish, ospreys are naturally associated with waterways, from inland freshwater lakes and rivers to ocean shores; they have a preference for clearer, slow-moving water. They perch on exposed dead trees, utility poles, cliffs, and even buildings near water.

The osprey's hunting behavior is extraordinary. The raptor hovers over the water, beating its wings while keeping its body steady in one spot, as it scans the water for fish. Then, the osprey plunges completely into the water, with wings stretched back. Its oily feathers help to repel the water and allow the bird to lift off before absorbing much water.

These raptors construct large nests in tall trees, on cliffs or abandoned buildings, as well as on nesting platforms that humans construct for them—an increasingly common phenomenon.

**SONGS AND CALLS**: The osprey will vocalize during display for territorial and mating purposes. These calls range from high-pitched, short, sharp whistles and chirps to more throaty notes.

**CONSERVATION STATUS**: The osprey has a large worldwide population, although in some areas, populations have declined in past years and the bird is still struggling to return to previous levels. The International Union for the Conservation of Nature (IUCN) has listed the bird as Least Concern.

Osprey (*Pandion haliaetus*)

# South America: Abra Patricia–Alto Nieva Private Conservation Area, Peru

PERU IS A FASCINATING country both biologically and culturally, and this northern part of it has only recently been opened to ecotourism. A newly created road over the Andes via the Abra Patricia pass created a unique opportunity to explore the avifauna of the Yungas cloud forest. This forest is located midslope along the eastern flanks of the Andes, in a zone between the highlands and the eastern lowland forests. New species are discovered here regularly to add to the current total of 317. An ecotourism lodge has been located here at the 6,690-acre (27.1 square km) Abra Patricia–Alto Nieva Private Conservation Area, established by the American Bird Conservancy.

**BIRDS TO SEE**: Two enigmatic species most birders search for at Abra Patricia are the rare marvelous spatuletail, a hummingbird with an incredibly long tail, and the recently discovered but as yet unstudied long-whiskered owlet, a resident of moist dwarf forests. This secretive owl is so unique that its discoverers placed it in its own genus. Other rare species recorded here include the ochre-fronted antpitta, ash-throated antwren, royal sunangel, bar-winged wood wren, and Lulu's tody-flycatcher. Tanagers and hummingbirds are common. The cloud forests are also wintering grounds for North American breeders such as the blackburnian warbler, Swainson's thrush, and alder flycatcher

# Watching for a Quick Getaway

MOST BIRDS, particularly songbirds, are fairly low on the food chain. Plenty of other critters, wild and domestic, are waiting to make a quick meal out of any unwary bird.

Aware of being constantly under threat, birds find comfort in always having an escape route. That is true whether in the most remote forest or in our backyards, and offers us yet another element that we can add to enhance the attraction of our properties for the birds.

Escape cover, such as a thick bramble patch, cluster of evergreen shrubs or trees, or brush pile, should be close to every feeder and water source. "Close" means about 8' (2.8 m) from the feeder or water source. Any closer would provide hiding cover for potential predators.

When they perceive a threat, the birds can flit into the escape cover, from where they will be able to safely assess it and, if necessary, await its departure.

Escape cover is an important habitat element for all birds, but it is especially crucial for vulnerable, ground-feeding birds.

> ⟩ Tip

The route between feeding area or water source and escape cover is far from a one-way street. Subordinate birds will perch in the escape cover to wait their turn at the food or water while dominant birds take their fill.

# The History of Bird Protection and Conservation I: The Early Years

THE CONCEPT OF BIRD conservation began in the United States in the late 1800s, spearheaded by George Bird Grinnell, who started the first incarnation of the Audubon Society, and Augustus Hemenway, who started the Massachusetts Audubon Society, one of the oldest conservation organizations in the United States. Their efforts galvanized support against the slaughter of millions of Florida birds for the fashion trend of feathers in women's hats, mostly heron and egret feathers.

These pioneering conservationists had a friend in the White House with Teddy Roosevelt as president. This helped the passage of the Lacey Act, which prohibited the interstate trade of wildlife killed in violation of state laws, and the Audubon Model Law of 1901, which outlawed plume hunting in Florida.

In an effort to engender public support of bird protection and to assess bird populations, Frank Chapman, curator of the American Museum of Natural History, initiated the first Christmas Bird Count in 1901. This hugely successful wildlife census continues to this day and has provided invaluable data on U.S. bird populations. (To participate, check with your local or national Audubon Society chapter or other local bird group.)

These efforts also gave birth to the National Wildlife Refuge system when Pelican Island was named by President Roosevelt as the first Federal Bird Reservation. During Roosevelt's administration, fifty-one Federal Bird Reservations were created.

# Grow Your Own Seeds

YOUR AVERAGE BACKYARD flower bed can be an abundant source of food for birds.

Sunflowers are an obvious choice for anyone thinking of growing and harvesting seeds for feeding to birds. However, many other common flowers produce seeds that will be attractive and useful to birds. These include cosmos, four o'clocks, marigolds, petunias, and zinnias.

For the truly daring bird gardener, some common wildflower species—a.k.a. weeds— will grow well in a backyard flower bed and produce crops of seed even better than many of the domesticated varieties. These include chicory, dandelion, foxtail, goldenrod, horsetail, milkweed, thistle, and many other wild species. Planted in an ornamental pattern,

like conventional garden flowers, the wild counterparts perform similarly, providing a wonderful display of color followed by loaded seedheads for the birds.

At the end of the growing season, let the seedheads dry on the plants. Then, you can harvest them or leave them on the stem, where the birds will find and feast on them.

To harvest the seeds from a seedhead, carefully place a plastic bag around the seedhead, then close the bag tightly and shake the stem vigorously. Take care not to shake the plant too much until the collection bag is in place and ready. Covering all the seedheads on a plant before shaking the plant will ensure that you capture most of the available, dry, loose seeds.

# Gaining Binocular Speed

BINOCULARS ARE ESSENTIAL for a fully enjoyable birdwatching experience. Without a good pair of binoculars, a birdwatcher will miss much detail, and much will pass by unseen.

However, many birdwatchers, even experienced birdwatchers, never master the ability to quickly sight their binoculars on their intended targets. Many a special bird sighting passes before they even get the bird in their lenses.

Practice is the key to developing this skill.

Begin with the binoculars dangling from their strap around your neck or held casually at your side, whatever is your usual manner of carrying them in the field. Select a large but obvious and stationary target at medium range. Repeatedly raise the binoculars to your eyes and level them on the target.

After you've gotten the hang of sighting the large target, select a second, smaller, but still obvious and stationary target. Repeat the raising and sighting procedure several times, until you can quickly find the target through the binoculars each time you raise them.

Now, move on to a less obvious but still stationary target, and repeat again, until you are satisfied with the skill level you've developed.

Finally, switch to a large but moving target, such as a car passing on a roadway or a plane flying across the sky. Repeat the procedure until you can get a moving object quickly in your lenses.

Now, you might be ready for the birds.

# Raptors: Bateleur (*Terathopius ecaudatus*)

THE WORD *BATELEUR* is French for "tightrope walker." This eagle received this name because of its habit of tipping its wings in flight, as a tightrope walker dips the ends of his or her balance pole when walking a wire.

**PHYSICAL CHARACTERISTICS**: A dramatically colored eagle, the bateleur sports plumage that is mostly black above, except for gray shoulders and a chestnut-colored back and upper tail. The bare skin of the face, cere (bare skin at the top of the bill), bill, and legs are usually red in color but can flush deeper when the bird is excited. There is also an uncommon color morph where cream-colored feathers replace the chestnut back. The female has gray flight feathers, which makes it easy to distinguish the sexes. The undersides of the wings are white.

**RANGE**: The bateleur is restricted in its range to Africa south of the Sahara Desert and the southwestern corner of the Arabian Peninsula, specifically the countries of Saudi Arabia and Yemen.

**HABITAT**: This mighty eagle makes its home in open country, notably savannas, thornbush, and open woodlands, where it hunts a wide variety of prey, from mice to antelope and including reptiles, birds, and insects. It also commonly eats carrion (dead animals).

Large nests are made from sticks high in trees. As with other large birds, and especially raptors, the brooding stage takes nearly a year, from hatching to fledging. The young stay with their parents for several months learning to hunt before heading off on their own.

**SONGS AND CALLS**: Usually silent, the bateleur makes up for it when it does call, with a loud barking *kow-aw*.

**CONSERVATION STATUS**: BirdLife International classifies the bateleur as Near Threatened because it has seen significant declines in the past four decades. This has been attributed to habitat loss, shooting, and incidental poisoning.

Bateleur (*Terathopius ecaudatus*)

23

# South America: Pantanal—
# Brazil, Bolivia, and Paraguay

ONE OF THE MOST species-rich areas on the planet, the Pantanal, covering an area of approximately 66,000 square miles (170,000 square km) in Brazil, Bolivia, and Paraguay, is a huge wetland system (actually an inland delta) with seasonal inundations of 6.5' to 16.5' (2 to 5 m) of floodwaters. The world of the Pantanal floods from November to March and slowly dries up as it drains into the Paraguay River and other smaller tributaries until the low water levels are reached between April and September. This is the prime time for birders to visit, as most of the bird life—indeed, most animal life—becomes concentrated in the remaining pools.

The richness of this region is nearly incomparable, approached only by the most highly diverse regions of Africa. Estimates of the number of birds found here range from 500 to 700 species. Two protected areas lie in the northern part of the region: Pantanal National Park and Taiamã Ecological Station. Visitors can stay at the Pantanal Wildlife Center (just off the Transpantaneira, the main highway in the region) which also offers boat and horseback tours of the wildlife. This center is about a two-and-a-half-hour drive from Cuiabá, Brazil, the nearest city with an airport.

**BIRDS TO SEE**: The fish that become stranded and concentrated in the smaller and smaller pools are a ripe food source for the various larger wading birds such as roseate spoonbills, Jabiru and wood storks, and great and snowy egrets. Other wading birds include herons (capped, whistling, striated, and rufous tiger) and ibises (bare-necked and buff-faced). Other distinctive birds include the flightless rheas and tinamous. Waterfowl are plentiful, with whistling-ducks being common. Many raptor species feed here, including black, turkey, and yellow-headed vultures; black-and-white hawk-eagles; Aplomado falcons; crested caracara; and, crane, savanna, Harris's, black-collared, and roadside hawks. Fifteen species of parrots utilize the Pantanal woodlands, as well as cuckoos, woodpeckers, parakeets, sparrows, wrens, becards, kingfishers, tanagers, flycatchers, kiskadees, antbirds, antshrikes, antwrens, and many, many others.

# The Range of Feeding Possibilities

BIRD-FEEDING STORES and big-box stores offer an ever-widening choice of feeders. Although many of those feeders appear to share features, some are better adapted than others for serving the needs of and attracting particular types of birds.

Hanging feeders, particularly the tube type with short perches at the feeding holes, are highly attractive to the smaller birds that prefer to perch while feeding and can be bullied off the feeders by larger, more aggressive birds. These include finches, chickadees, cardinals, titmice, and siskins.

So many popular backyard species prefer niger, or thistle seed, that the bird-feeding industry has developed several versions of a specialized niger feeder. The feeders all feature perches above the feeding holes, which targets the unique ability of popular species, especially the goldfinch, to feed while hanging upside down. They evolved that ability to eat seeds from the flower head of a preferred wildflower, the thistle.

Mesh-bag feeders also accommodate the special feeding behavior of the goldfinch, allowing the bird to hang from the mesh while pulling niger seeds through the holes of the mesh.

Many species of larger birds also perch to feed, but need wider perches to allow them to snug their larger frames up to the feeding holes. For many of these, such as the jays and the grosbeaks, hanging tube feeders will suffice, but bin feeders may offer more comfort while feeding. Bin feeders feature a large seed-holding area that gradually gravity-feeds the seed to feeding holes below the bin. They usually have perches that run the entire length of the feeder to accommodate more than one bird at a time, and can be hung or mounted atop a pole for more stability.

Many birds prefer to feed on the ground, and many others that prefer to feed at an elevated position will feed on the ground when the opportunity presents itself. The simplest way to feed those birds is to just scatter seed on the ground. However, a more protected and easier-to-clean situation can be created by spreading the seed on the top of a large, flat rock, or a board on the ground or on short legs.

### Feeders Preferred by Some Common Backyard Birds

# Mythical Birds: Thunderbird

ALTHOUGH MOSTLY associated with Native American mythology, the figure of the Thunderbird can be found in many cultures. Some historians trace the mythical creature to a belief that woodpeckers were bringers of rain and storms. This view stems from the drumming these birds make when boring with their beaks into wood for insects. The sound can echo loudly in deep woods and be reminiscent of thunder. Cultures from all over Europe have evidence of this association.

Other birds have also been connected with thunder and storms. In China, the pheasant was believed to bring rains with its movements, and people imitating the bird in dances were believed to do the same. Tribes in northern Siberia and Manchuria believed that a swan caused thunder.

Depictions of a large, powerful bird thought to be inspired by eagles are found commonly in many North American cultures. It has also been suggested that an ancient, extinct, giant bird, *Aiolornis incredibilis*, is the source of the myths. The belief in the Thunderbird is widespread among indigenous people of the Pacific Northwest in Canada and the United States. The Thunderbird is commonly viewed as a giant bird; the beating of its wings brings thunder and clouds, and the blinking of its eyes spawns lightning. The Tlingit people believed the Thunderbird was so large it carried a lake on its back that spilled over as it flew and caused rain. The Nuu-chah-nulth thought the Thunderbird served the great spirit as a messenger and dwelled on a mountain; the Kwakwaka'wakw people believed there were many Thunderbirds and that they could assume human form.

The Thunderbird is featured prominently in the art of the Northwest Coast indigenous people, especially on totem poles and masks.

# Neat Hedges Are Good for Birds

THE IDEA MAY SEEM contradictory, but a heavily pruned hedge actually provides more benefit to birds than the same plants would if left without pruning year after year.

Pruning produces a denser hedge that for birds results in not only improved shelter and cover, but also more berries on the new growth.

When left on their own, most hedge plants, including the broad-leafed deciduous and the evergreens, will eventually grow into shrubs or small trees, losing the dense growth of small, new twigs and branches that are so beneficial to birds.

Each family of hedge plants, and often each species or cultivar, has its own ideal amount of pruning. For hollies, for example, removing at least one-third of new growth each year will produce the densest growth. In contrast, the oldest branches should be removed annually from viburnums.

In addition, many hedge plants require males and females of the species to be in close proximity to one another for the pollination needed to produce berries. What constitutes close proximity varies by plant species and local landscape conditions.

# Reading the Beak

THE BEAK OF A BIRD can tell us a lot about what and how that bird eats. We can then use that information as a compass to guide us to the prime locations for finding and observing that bird.

Like a well-equipped handyman's workbench, the world of birds is filled with specialized tools, each one designed for a specific task. Adaptive evolution has supplied birds with a wide array of food-gathering tools to fit the various niches of the ecosystem.

**Short, thick, conical beaks**, such as those of finches and sparrows, are designed for cracking open seeds and extracting the kernels inside the hulls.

**Thin, slender, pointed beaks**, such as those carried by warblers and wrens, are used to pluck insects from twigs, bark, and leaves and from plant litter on the ground.

**Long, heavy, chisel-like beaks**, the tool of woodpeckers, are built for drilling holes into trees to get at insects that live under the bark.

**Long, delicate, tubular beaks**, such as those of hummingbirds, often are associated with even longer tongues and a penchant for sipping nectar from flowers.

**Large, heavy, slightly curved but conical beaks**, such as those of crows, provide their owners with the ability to take advantage of a wide range of foods.

**Long, flat, fringed beaks**, the equipment of many ducks and other waterfowl, are designed for straining food from water.

**Sharp, hooked beaks**, such as those threatening tools carried by hawks and owls, are used to catch, kill, and rip apart live prey.

**Long, pointed, spearlike beaks**, such as those of herons and kingfishers, also are designed for catching live prey, but from a spearing and gulping-down approach.

While there is considerable overlap and some exceptions, the ecosystem that supplies the food source for which a beak has evolved often can be expected to host the birds with that beak.

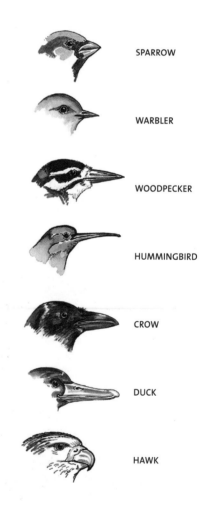

SPARROW

WARBLER

WOODPECKER

HUMMINGBIRD

CROW

DUCK

HAWK

# Raptors: Peregrine Falcon
## (*Falco peregrinus*)

FORMERLY KNOWN AS the duck hawk, the peregrine falcon has become a symbol of the environmental movement. It is known as the fastest bird in the world and the bird with the widest distribution of any other vertebrate in the world.

**PHYSICAL CHARACTERISTICS**: This "hooded" falcon has the appearance of a serious hunter. With a dark blue-gray back and cap and a downward-pointing stripe along the cheek, it almost seems dressed like a medieval executioner. The upper feathers of the tail are barred with pale blue-gray and dark blue-gray. The underside, including parts of the head not covered by dark feathers, can be whitish, grayish, or cream-colored with brown horizontal streaking in adults and vertical streaking in immature birds. The short, hooked, yellow-green bill is typical of falcons. Yellow legs and feet end in powerful talons.

**RANGE**: The peregrine falcon can be found on every continent except Antarctica, but is noticeably absent in areas such as the Sahara Desert, central Pacific islands, the steppes of East Asia, New Zealand, and Iceland. Many populations in warmer climates tend to be resident, while northerly breeding populations move south over great distances to their wintering range, a roundtrip of as much as 15,500 miles (25,000 km).

**HABITAT**: The peregrine prefers locations with cliffs or tall trees for nest sites, with good access near open areas for hunting. Cities are also increasingly playing host to peregrines; with their preference for tall sites for nesting and perching, they have taken to using skyscrapers.

These falcons have a strong preference for other birds as a food source, which they often take from the air. Their hunting prowess is renowned. They will "stoop" down onto a bird by folding their wings and dropping at incredible speeds, usually killing the prey animal on impact.

29

**SONGS AND CALLS**: Most often heard is the harsh *kak kak kak kak*, repeated for long periods, usually in defense or alarm.

**CONSERVATION STATUS**: Because of a serious decline in North American populations due to the widespread use of pesticides and their effect on this and other species' eggs, there are greater densities of peregrine falcon populations in Europe. The species was extirpated in the United States and southern Canada east of the Rockies. Aided by the federal government's species recovery plan and several nonprofit groups, many captive-bred individuals were successfully released into the wild. Now the North American population is steadily increasing.

# South America: Manaus, Brazil

A CONSTANTLY EVOLVING avifauna list awaits birders in the Amazonia region of Brazil, perhaps the most biologically diverse region in the world. So much territory, much of it unexplored, likely harbors new species to add to an already incredible list of 950 recorded species. The capital of the Amazonas state, Manaus, at the confluence of the mighty Rio Negro and Rio Solimoes, is an ideal spot to launch an excursion. From here, visitors can take boat tours up the two large rivers or land treks into the rainforest.

**BIRDS TO SEE**: Various forest habitats each support their own bird life and all of these can be easily explored from a base in Manaus. The forest habitat along the rivers and on their islands supports Klage's and Cherrie's antwren; Snethlage's tody-tyrant; olive-spotted hummingbird; Zimmer's woodcreeper; Castelnau's antshrike; gray-chested greenlet; dark-breasted, Parker's, scaled, and red-and-white spinetails; brownish elaenia; blackish-gray antshrike; and pearly breasted conebill.

Two observation towers found in the nearby terra firme forests can bring an untold number of species to a life list. These include crimson fruitcrow, pompadour and Guianan red-cotingas, several macaw species, jacamars, Guianan toucanet, racket-tailed coquette, red-billed pied tanager, and if lucky, the harpy eagle.

A boat trip up the Rio Negro takes visitors to Jaú National Park, one of Brazil's largest conserved areas, for birds such as the bar-bellied woodcreeper and chestnut-crested and Yapacana antbird.

**Birdwatching tower**

# The All-Important Choice of Seed

NO ONE TYPE OF FOOD, or even mix of food, will always attract the most bird species under all conditions in all areas. The natural world has too many variables for that to be possible. And most of us live in highly developed, human-dominated landscapes that have intensified those variables.

Black-oil sunflower seed may be the closest thing backyard birders have to a universal food for our feathered friends. More species of songbirds relish black-oil sunflower than any other type of seed.

But hummingbirds do not eat black-oil sunflower seeds, or any of the seeds we normally offer in our feeders. Mockingbirds eat seeds only as a last resort, when their normal food sources of berries and insects have been depleted in their home range.

Obviously, even the highly praised black-oil sunflower seed cannot be all things to all birds. The best options for those of us interested in attracting maximum bird diversity and maximum bird numbers into our backyards are simple:

• A seed mixture, including a healthy amount of black-oil sunflower seeds

• Various seed mixtures in multiple feeders

• Various types of seeds offered in different feeders

> Tip

One important method of reducing negative impacts on birds in your backyard is to keep the feeders and the ground beneath the feeders as clean as possible. Regular emptying and washing of the feeders is a great start. Removal of debris, seed husks, bird droppings, and the like from beneath the feeders ensures cleanliness of the feeding area.

Always wear rubber or vinyl gloves when cleaning areas and equipment frequented by birds. It's important to place a barrier between you and anything the birds might be carrying.

# Pale Male, New York City's Avian Superstar

THE STORY OF THE RED-TAILED HAWKS Pale Male and Lola has excited birders and nonbirders alike. Few took notice of Pale Male when he first arrived in New York City in the early 1990s. But gradually, birders took more notice when he and his first mate, First Love, nested on a Fifth Avenue apartment building across from Central Park. Pale Male has mated with three females in the city, and they have raised an estimated twenty-six chicks.

After being injured, First Love was captured and taken for rehabilitation. In the meantime, Pale Male took another mate, dubbed Chocolate. After Chocolate died, First Love, having been healed and released, returned to Central Park and her mate. Unfortunately, First Love died from eating a poisoned pigeon in 1997. After another successful pairing with Blue, Pale Male mated with Lola in 2002, and they have gone on to raise several successful clutches, all

from a nest built on ornamental stonework on a different building, a residential co-op.

And then came the hullabaloo. The co-op's board had the nest and the building's pigeon spikes removed, but the birds were being so closely followed by the birdwatching community that the nest's removal caused worldwide protest. After much discussion, the board agreed to replace the nest and spikes. However, it appears that the placement of the new spikes caused failed nestings. Bird experts determined that the spikes beneath the nest protruded through the nesting material, preventing the mother from rolling the eggs, necessary for proper development. These spikes were removed and the birds have gone on to reuse the nest site.

A book and a film have been made about the famous hawks, and they continue to be monitored intensively by area birdwatchers.

# Designer Birds for Everyone

A CUSTOM-DESIGNED backyard bird community is within our reach. It's just a matter of considering the possibilities, and the requirements of achieving those possibilities.

The one big qualifier in this is that we're dealing with nature, and only species provided by nature are possible. For example, if your backyard is not large enough to redefine what a backyard is, and it lies in close proximity to a major body of water, your chance of attracting eagles is extremely limited.

Begin the design process with a list of the ten or twelve bird species currently in the greatest abundance and the most frequency in your

backyard. Note the species you would like to see more often and in greater numbers.

In a new column, note the species that your neighbors attract that you would like to add. For each species, include an idea on why they may be attracted to those neighboring properties but not yours. Maybe your neighbor has some thoughts on what he or she is doing right.

Working with your "most wanted" backyard bird lists in hand, comb through the many pages of this book, and others on attracting birds into the backyard, to discover possible ways to attract the birds you want to share your habitat.

**Carved roundels in Central Park, New York City**

# Benefits of Joining a Bird Club

A LOCAL BIRD CLUB is a treasure-trove for a birdwatcher. Membership brings close and regular contact with more experienced birdwatchers with much amassed knowledge of the local topography, best birding spots, bird populations, seasonal changes, and much more. Membership also offers camaraderie, opportunities to share retellings of special birdwatching experiences, and potential companions for future field experiences.

Locating a nearby club has never been easier. A simple Internet search will turn up all the needed information to make initial contact and learn of upcoming meetings, which, by the way, often feature first-rate speakers and fascinating programs.

Many local clubs also are a potential route to local conservation projects in need of new volunteers.

# Shorebirds and Relatives:
# Arctic Tern (*Sterna paradisaea*)

LIKE OTHER TERNS AND GULLS, the Arctic tern spends most of its time around and over the ocean. However, the Arctic tern performs a feat that no other bird approaches. It performs a migration of approximately 20,000 to 25,000 miles (32,000 to 64,000 km) in about three to four months, from its Arctic breeding grounds to its Antarctic wintering habitat. It travels southward along the west coasts of Europe and Africa, and for its return trip, it follows the South and North American coastlines. Its unusually long life span—approximately thirty years—means the Arctic tern puts in a lot of miles in its lifetime.

**PHYSICAL CHARACTERISTICS**: The Arctic tern's plumage is very similar to other terns. Subtle differences include more overall gray on its back and wing backs, with just a slight edging of black, and generally more pale gray on its undersides (instead of white). The bird also has shorter legs than other terns. A black cap of feathers sits atop its head, and a long, all-red bill and legs in breeding season are prominent. (Other terns usually have a black tip to their red bills.)

**RANGE**: The Arctic tern's range is circumpolar, meaning along the north latitudes around the globe. The species breeds on shores and in marshes, nesting on the ground in colonies, where it communally defends its nest quite aggressively. Its long migration takes it to the shores of Antarctica. Between its breeding and winter habitat, it spends more time in daylight than any other animal on Earth.

**HABITAT**: The coastlines of the mainland and islands in the Arctic and Antarctic seas, as well as inland lakes in the tundra, form this bird's preferred habitat. It feeds primarily on fish, crustaceans, and insects during breeding and primarily on ocean fish during its long voyage between habitats. The Arctic tern hovers above the water scanning for fish, and then plunges straight down very rapidly into the water to grab its prey.

**SONGS AND CALLS**: The Arctic tern's common call is a harsh, strident *keyyuurr*. A more chittering note is uttered when the bird is agitated.

**CONSERVATION STATUS**: Arctic terns are subject to a wide variety of disturbances that affect the nesting success of the species. These disturbances, such as nest displacement by gulls, hunting of eggs and birds by humans, loss of nesting habitat, and poisoning by pesticides, have caused the bird to be listed at various levels of concern depending upon the jurisdiction. The IUCN lists it as Least Concern.

Arctic tern (*Sterna paradisaea*)

# South America: Los Llanos, Venezuela and Colombia

BIRDERS WITH A PENCHANT for wading birds and waterfowl need look no further than this vast wetland region of Venezuela and Colombia. Comprising fully one-third of the country of Venezuela, the region is the floodplain for the major Orinoco River. Traditionally used as cattle ranching country, Los Llanos now supports large areas of agriculture as well. Hemmed in by mountains on three sides, this region is a vast grassland bowl emptying into the Atlantic Ocean. The southern section, which receives more water and is home to cattle ranches that also serve as accommodations for traveling birders, is the easiest and most fruitful part of Los Llanos to visit.

**BIRDS TO SEE**: More than 300 species of birds use the Los Llamos area as feeding grounds. Many species are here for the winter season and congregate in the shrinking pools of water. So, large numbers of birds can be seen if you visit during this time. Wading birds, including storks, herons, and ibises, are widespread. Shorebirds such as sandpipers, and grassland songbirds such as dicksissels and bobolinks, flock in great numbers here for winter.

The list of birds includes twenty species of herons, most notably the exceedingly rare zigzag heron, and seven species of ibis, including green, sharp-tailed, and buff-necked ibises. To be expected, ducks are here as well, including whistling-ducks, cormorants, and gallinules. Also found here are dara, wattled jacana, roseate spoonbill, jabiru stork, wood stork, white-faced whistling-duck, fulvous whistling-duck, snowy egret, rufescent tiger-heron, black-collared hawk, scarlet macaw, and hoatzin.

These swollen populations of songbirds, shorebirds, and wading birds share the abundant food with and, in some cases, are the food for birds of prey. Snail kites and slender-billed kites feed on crustaceans in the wetlands, while ospreys and black-collared hawks feed on fish. The lesser yellow-headed hawk cleans up after these hunters, scavenging what dead meat it can find.

# Seed Choice Guide

STUDIES CONDUCTED by Aelred D. Geis developed the following data on seed type preferences among common bird species.

- Mourning doves were the only species that showed any interest in buckwheat, a common filler in bird seed mixtures.

- Another common seed mixture component, canary seed, was more attractive to mourning doves than buckwheat. House sparrows found it about half as attractive, while song sparrows preferred it more.

- Cracked corn was most attractive to white-throated sparrows and common grackles. Mourning doves and blue jays also showed some interest in cracked corn.

- Golden, or German, millet, which is smaller than white proso millet, is attractive to the same species, but at lower levels of interest. Mourning doves and sparrows in particular liked the golden millet.

- Oats, either whole or hulled, were eaten by very few species, notably the European starling. The common grackle finds it somewhat attractive, too.

- Starlings found peanut hearts much more attractive than black striped sunflower seeds, while several species preferred peanut kernels, including blue jays, scrub jays, and tufted titmice.

- Rape seed, a major ingredient in domestic canary food, and rice were not attractive to any wild bird species, and only mourning doves and house finches showed any interest whatsoever in rape seed.

- Mourning doves and white-crowed sparrows were the only species interested at all in rice.

- Safflower, which often is whispered as the secret seed for attracting cardinals, when first offered to the birds was only about 30 percent as attractive to the species as black striped sunflower seed.

- Milo, or sorghum, which is a major ingredient in many commercial bird-feeding mixtures, was relatively unattractive to nearly all bird species. (Most sorghum produced today has been genetically engineered to have a high tannin content to make it "bird resistant.")

- Black striped sunflower seed was preferred by most of the highly sought-after songbirds. The smaller the seeds, the better.

- Hulled sunflower seeds and broken sunflower kernels were relished by American goldfinches, house finches, white-crowned sparrows, and white-throated sparrows.

- Thistle, or niger, seed is generally the most attractive seed for American goldfinches and purple finches.

- Of all the birds visiting the test feeding sites, only tufted titmice, grackles, and blue jays did not show a preference for black-oil-type sunflower seeds. New, smaller varieties of black-oil-type sunflowers have been introduced into the bird-feeding industry, making that variety more attractive to more birds.

- Wheat was eaten by several species, including mourning doves, house sparrows, and white-throated sparrows, but didn't approach the attractiveness of white proso millet or black striped sunflower seed for any species.

Although the study was set up with four very widespread sites to determine if birds in different regions have different seed preferences, no such regional differences were detected.

# Vultures in Parsee and Tibetan Buddhist Burial Rituals

BIRDS OF PREY PLAY prominent roles as symbols in many cultures and religions throughout the world. However, in two cultural traditions, vultures play a key, physical role. The practice is thought to have arisen as the result of the lack of other resources for the disposal of mortal remains. In areas where there is largely only rocky ground and little wood to spare other than for warmth and cooking, using the carrion eaters' natural tendencies to dispose of loved ones became the principal funerary rite.

Tibetan Buddhists believe that after death the body is simply a vessel for disposal, and the soul will be reborn into a new physical manifestation. In their *jhator*, or sky burial ritual, a person's remains are carried to a high mountaintop where the vultures feed on them. In what may seem to nonpractitioners a gruesome part of the ritual, the bodies are dismembered by family members and the bones are crushed to ensure complete disposal. In their respect for all life, Tibetan Buddhists believe that in this way the body is not wasted as it is used to sustain other living creatures.

The Parsees are one of two groups of Zoroastrians, members of one of mankind's oldest faiths. Parsees still practice their beliefs in Iran and in parts of India, but the Indian population is by far the largest. One of the tenets of the religion holds that upon death, the body becomes contaminated with evil. Disposal of the body via burial in earth, via fire, or in water is thought to pollute these sacred elements.

Parsees believe that vultures were created by God to dispose of dead bodies. Towers of Silence have been built, surrounded by gardens in which the loved ones mourn. The towers are raised platforms with high walls open to the sky. Bodies of men are placed in an outer ring, women in an inner ring, and children in the center. The exposure to the sun and, of course, vultures gradually eliminates the flesh of the dead. The birds are believed to carry the deceased person's soul to the heavens. After as long as a year of exposure to sun and wind, the bones are moved to the center and are processed with lime to assist their gradual decomposition. The resultant particles are washed away via rainwater through sand and charcoal filters.

Unfortunately, a severe decline in the numbers of vultures (99.9 percent as of 2008) has caused a crisis in the Parsee community. (This is thought to be due to the widespread use of an anti-inflammatory drug, diclofenac, in cattle. The vultures that eat the dead livestock build up the chemical in their systems and eventually die.) Many bodies are not entirely consumed, leading to incomplete rituals and, perhaps more practically, an increasing stench and health problem. Some Parsee are lobbying for leaders to allow cremation, while others are attempting captive breeding of the vultures with the hope of increasing the birds' populations so as to continue the current tradition.

Black vultures

# Top Perennials for Birds

BEYOND THEIR NATURAL BEAUTY and color, many common perennials for the garden also can be relied on to provide ample crops of seeds for hungry backyard birds. Among these are the following.

- **Wild columbine**, *Aquilegia canadensis*, grows to 3' (91 cm) in well-drained soil of average fertility; red and yellow flowers

- **New England aster**, *Aster novae-angliae*, grows to nearly 3' (91 cm) in moist soil in full to partial shade; purple, pink, or white flowers

- **Leopard lily**, *Belamcanda chinensis*, grows to 3' (91 cm) in well-drained, fertile soil in full sun; orange flowers

- **Lance-leafed coreopsis**, *Coreopsis lanceolata*, grows to 2' (61 cm) in well-drained, fertile soil in full sun; yellow flowers

- **Globe thistle**, *Echinops ritro*, grows to 4' (1.2 m) in well-drained, poor-quality soil in full sun; purple or pink flowers

- **Fireweed**, *Epilobium angustifolium*, grows to 5' (1.5 m) in moist, well-drained soil in full sun; pink flowers

- **Red-hot poker**, *Kniphofia uvaria*, grows to 5' (1.5 m) in moist soil of average fertility in full sun; bright red spiky flowers

- **Scarlet monkey flower**, *Mimulus cardinalis*, grows to 1' (30 cm) in moist, rich soil in full sun; red flowers

- **Wild bergamot**, *Monarda fistulosa*, grows to 4' (1.2 m) in moist, well-drained soil of average fertility in full sun; pink to lavender flowers

- **Evening primrose**, *Oenothera spp.*, grows to 6' (1.8 m) in average soil in full sun; yellow, pink, or white flowers

- **Wild blue phlox**, *Phlox divaricata*, grows to 1.5' (46 cm) in rich, well-drained soil in partial shade; blue, purple, or white flowers

- **Orange coneflower**, *Rudbeckia fulgida*, grows to 3' (91 cm) in moist soil in full to partial sun; yellow to orange flowers with black centers

- **Purple coneflower**, *Rudbeckia purpurea*, grows to 4' (1.2 m) in moist, well-drained soil in full sun; pink to purple flowers with brown centers

- **Black-eyed Susan**, *Rudbeckia spp.*, grows to 6' (1.8 m) in well-drained, fertile soil in full sun; yellow flowers with brown centers

- **Scarlet sage**, *Salvia splendens*, grows to 1' (30 cm) in well-drained, fertile soil in full sun; red flowers

- **Showy sedum**, *Sedum spectabile*, grows to 2' (61 cm) in well-drained soil in full sun; pink to red flowers

- **Ironweed**, *Vernonia noveboracensis*, grows to 7' (2.1 m) in moist, fertile soil in full sun; violet flowers

# Follow the Thunder

SOMEONE WAS RUNNING a lawnmower in the forest that day. A lawnmower?

That's what it sounds like when a male ruffed grouse starts "drumming."

The 17" (43.2 cm) bird climbs atop his favorite log and begins beating the air with his wings. Slowly at first, but quickly increasing, the action produces a drumroll-like thumping noise that sounds much like a motor running in the distance.

It can be heard a quarter-mile (0.4 km) away or more, which is what the grouse wants. He's telling other male grouse in the area that this is his territory, and signaling his availability to any female grouse in the vicinity.

A "drumming log," which may be a log, an exposed tree root, rocks, or simply a mound of dirt, is used again and again by the same male grouse. Ideal drumming logs are old and covered with moss. They often are the trunks of trees that have fallen naturally and still have some roots attached.

The "log" may be worn from repeated use, though the grouse does not strike it with his wings. It is just the stage for his performance. Another telltale sign of a drumming log is a pile of grouse droppings at one end.

The log is usually 10" to 12" (25 to 30 cm) above the ground and found in moderately dense brush. The grouse likes to see about 60' (18 m) in all directions while he drums.

Drumming occurs year-round, whenever the snow is not deep enough to bury the "log," but it becomes more frequent and prolonged in spring, when the male is seeking a mate.

In the range of the ruffed grouse, likely spots to hear them drumming are the south sides of mountains and the heavily forested valleys between forested mountains. Tangles of wild grape vines, thickets of laurel, and clusters of small evergreens are favorite grouse haunts.

The sound of drumming is created in the same way that lightning produces its thunder. Beating wings create a vacuum. The rapid expansion of air surrounding the vacuum creates a sonic shock wave that produces the sound.

# Songbirds: Ruby-Crowned Kinglet (*Regulus calendula*)

THE DELIGHT OF OBSERVING the diminutive ruby-crowned kinglet forage among apple trees for insects—flitting from one branch to the next, hovering above a cluster of leaves—is wholly rewarding.

**PHYSICAL CHARACTERISTICS**: Due to its small size of just 3.5" to 4.3" (9 to 11 cm) and its habit of flitting quickly among tree branches, the ruby-crowned kinglet's plumage of dull olive green above and pale dusky yellow below makes the bird very difficult to spot. However, the bird's size is one of its identifying characteristics, as well as two prominent white wing bars and white eye ring. If you're lucky, during breeding season the male will display its vibrant red crest attempting to entice females of the species.

**RANGE**: The ruby-crowned kinglet breeds in the boreal (spruce-fir) forests of North America, mostly in Alaska and Canada, but also extends into the Northern Rockies and northern New England in the lower United States. It spends the nonbreeding, summer season in the southern United States and Mexico.

**HABITAT**: For its breeding habitat, this bird prefers old-growth coniferous and mixed coniferous and deciduous forests. This habitat allows easy access to the kinglet's food source: insects and their larvae and eggs. The bird feeds by gleaning, rooting out the insects from leaves and bark, as well as hovering and gleaning from leaves and flowers.

As a forest dweller, the ruby-crowned kinglet nests in trees in small nests made of feathers, lichen, mosses, grasses, spider webs, and other fine materials. Remarkably, this little kinglet has one of the largest broods of any North American bird; up to twelve eggs are laid.

**SONGS AND CALLS**: These little birds have a rich, varied, and loud song that seems startling from a bird so small and inconspicuous. The song is broken into several repeated *tsee* notes, followed by deeper *tur* notes, which is then followed by a series of higher-pitch strings of notes. Calls are lower-pitched, singular, and abrupt.

**CONSERVATION STATUS**: The ruby-crowned kinglet is considered common in its range. However, as with so many species, there is some evidence that the species is declining, particularly in the east of its range. The IUCN lists it as Least Concern.

Ruby-crowned kinglet (*Regulus calendula*)

# South America: Santa Marta, Colombia

LOCATED ALONG THE Caribbean coast of northern Colombia, the El Dorado Bird Reserve sits on the Sierra Nevada de Santa Marta Mountain, a massive peak isolated from the nearby ranges which make up the northern extensions of the Andes Mountains. This reserve was protected in 2008 because of the amazing diversity of the area, but particularly because of the avifauna. Many endemics occur here, and new species are still being discovered and described. The 1,700-acre (6.9 square km) reserve was developed by Fundación ProAves, American Bird Conservancy, and Conservation International. They have used this model of sustainability to bring attention and protection to the area, with an ecolodge and restaurant serving tourists.

At 18,947' (5,775 m) in elevation, the Sierra Nevada de Santa Marta hosts a large number of habitats, from tropical beaches at its base to glaciers atop. It is an island of endemism (twenty species!) in a sea of diversity—Colombia boasts nearly 1,900 avian species. A newly discovered owl, the Santa Marta screech owl, apparently roosts near the ecolodge, and the Santa Marta parakeet, Santa Marta brush finch, and Santa Marta antpitta are all found only on this mountain.

**BIRDS TO SEE**: Other specialties of the area include rusty-headed and streak-capped spinetails, Santa Marta sabrewing, bearded helmetcrest, Santa Marta toucanet, and Santa Marta tapaculo. Black-fronted wood-quail, white-tipped quetzal, strong-billed wood-creeper, gray-throated leaftosser, golden-breasted fruiteater, black-hooded thrush, and white-lored warbler can all be seen near the lodge. The area is also an important wintering ground for many North American migrants.

# Zapped Bird Food

AN ECONOMICAL WAY to feed birds with your backyard insects (see Days 139 + 140) is to gather insects during the warmer months and preserve them in your freezer for year-round feeding.

An electronic bug zapper is a quick way to collect lots of bugs on summer evenings. Just station a tarp or blanket under the zapper and empty the fried contents into a freezer bag every now and then. On a "good" night, a zapper might down a few hundred insects. However, a bug zapper is an indiscriminate killer, and some research suggests that most of the devices kill more beneficial and nonharmful insects than mosquitoes and gnats.

A greener method of insect gathering is to coat tree branches and tree trunks with a sugar-water solution. A mixture of four parts water to one part sugar, blended well, will attract most insects. Paint the solution on the tree in the morning; leave it for a few hours and in early afternoon collect the accumulated insect life. Just scrape the bugs from the tree with a butter knife and into a freezer bag. To remove the sugar, add a bit of water to the bag, swish the contents around, and pour the mixture through a strainer. Return the insects to the bag and freeze them.

These insects will be the most common and most abundant species, leaving plenty of their kind in the ecosystem.

# The Eagle in Myth, in Legend, and as Symbol

IT IS NO SURPRISE that eagles—those large, majestic soaring raptors—have made their way into countless cultural myths. Eagles accompany both the Roman god Jupiter and the Greek god Zeus, for whom the eagle carries thunderbolts. This led to the belief among Greeks that eagles could not be hurt by lightning. Farmers buried eagle wings in their fields to keep storms away.

Several Greek stories relate how gods and humans assumed the form of eagles. In one, Zeus takes the form of an eagle to carry off the beautiful, mortal man, Ganymede, to be cupbearer to the gods. Another tale tells how King Merops was turned into an eagle by the goddess Hera. It was believed that one of these mythic eagles flew into the night sky and became the constellation Aquila, named after the Latin word for eagle.

Many mythical creatures were inspired by eagles. One of the most well-known and widespread creatures was the griffin, a protective creature with the head and wings of an eagle and the body of a lion. Many variations on this theme can be found. For example, the ancient Assyrians believed in Ishtar, a creature associated with immortality and the sun. It had the opposite features of the griffin, with the head of a lion and the body of an eagle. Eagles are also cited often in the Christian Bible, which sometimes refers to them admirably and sometimes derisively.

Images of the eagle are still ubiquitous today, including as symbols for nations, such as the United States and Mexico. The assumed tough, aggressive nature of the eagle makes it a favorite of sports teams as well. The first lunar lander, piloted by Neil Armstrong, was named the Eagle. And of course, the most obvious symbols of eagles we see every day are on money from many nations.

**Griffin statue, London, England**

# Stage Right: Bird Enters

LIKE A WELL-PLANNED staging of a theatrical performance, placement of bird feeders around the outside of a home can be a superbly crafted production or an awkward presentation that leaves everyone not quite satisfied. Feeder placement is a study in theater-in-the-round, but with the actors—the birds—as a distinct audience.

Audiences for each production of A Midsummer Feeder's Dream include humans (both inside and outside), and dogs and cats, which have their own reasons for watching birds at feeders.

As with any good theater's layout, the experience for the various audiences should be considered in feeder placement. And of course, different audiences have differing importance to the production.

Unlike human theaters, however, the bird-feeding theater-in-the-round must first consider the desires of the actors. The birds must be attracted to the feeders or there will be no performances. That means the birds must be able to see the feeders from some distance, at least as far as the nearest good perching trees and shrubs; they must be able to fly to the feeders; and they must be able to fly away from the feeders, often in an excited rush.

Within those basic criteria, then, the designer of the backyard-feeder theater must decide the next most important audience: those inside the home or those outside the home. Some properties allow enough space and orientation to serve both audiences, but many more do not.

If the primary audience is to be outside the home, such as passersby on a sidewalk or roadway, the feeders should be oriented from that perspective. Shrubs, small trees, and vines closest to the home serve as the stage scenery. The feeder setup is designed for curb appeal and for the aesthetic benefit of the neighborhood.

If the primary audience is the residents of the home, who will be doing much of their viewing from inside the house, the orientation focus switches to the opposite direction. The shrubbery around the house now must be viewed as obstacles to be avoided in planning the line of sight for viewers.

And if the upcoming performances are planned for viewing from inside the house, an important question is: What is the best window for birdwatching? Many backyard bird-feeding stations have been positioned to offer the best vantage point for viewing from a kitchen window. But that may be a holdover from the days when the birdwatcher in the home was primarily the wife and mother, who could then enjoy "her birds" while she "did the dishes" every evening.

Today, however, standing over the kitchen sink may no longer be the most comfortable location in the house. As you stage-manage the design of your personal bird-feeding theater-in-the-round, consider the appeal to the audience—you and others in the home who share your enthusiasm for the birds of the backyard—of every possible window, room, and seat.

With these considerations in the plan, you can avoid any less-than-favorable opening-night reviews.

# Bird Tracking for Beginners

A FEW GOOD BOOKS have been published on the subject of bird tracks. The best among them offer photos or detailed sketches of tracks for the bird species they cover. Much can be learned about identifying bird tracks and tracking birds from those books, but no book can substitute for firsthand, in-the-field tracking.

And there's no better place to begin than your own backyard. You know the landscape, the birds that frequent it, and the spots they use most heavily. Finding tracks and identifying the species that made them should be easier on your home turf.

A fine way to get started in tracking is to clear an area under your bird feeders of all grass and plant matter, leaving only a depression of a few feet (about 61 cm) in diameter. Coat that depression with a half-inch depth (about 1.3 cm) of fine, dry sand. (Think of it as installing a Zen sand garden beneath your feeders.)

With the sand raked smooth, leave the feeding area and watch it from some spot where you won't cause the birds to stay away. When you spot the first birds hopping across the sand, note the species and whether they're male or female. Return to the feeders to inspect the tracks. Take careful note of the tracks the birds made in the sand, which serves as a tracking slate of sorts.

Note the size of the tracks, their configuration, their placement in relation to one another, and the distance between them. A digital camera can help you to remember the tracks, and you can write your notes, such as sizes, directly onto printouts of those photos.

Repeat the process again and again, until you've considered the tracks of many of the species that visit your feeding area.

Heron footprints in sand

# Nightjars: Whip-poor-will (*Caprimulgus vociferus*)

WHIP-POOR-WILLS are part of an unusual bird family called the nightjars, formerly known as goatsuckers. These birds are insect eaters, and they often frequent farms with livestock to feed on the plentiful insects there. Likely because of this association with livestock, a mistaken belief that the birds sucked milk or blood from goats arose.

**PHYSICAL CHARACTERISTICS**: These compact birds are beautifully patterned to match the coloring of the forest floor on which they nest and rest during the day. Their black throats and, on the males, white outer tail feathers are diagnostic features. However, these birds are rarely seen, because of their cryptic coloration and their nocturnal habits. Small bills attached to a gaping mouth fringed with fine feathers are efficient tools for feeding on insects.

**RANGE**: Whip-poor-wills are found in the eastern United States north of the far southern states during breeding season. They migrate to Central America for the winter, nonbreeding season.

**HABITAT**: As suits their camouflage plumage and their preferred prey, whip-poor-wills are found primarily in mature hardwood forests in the eastern United States; a population is also found in the pine-oak woodlands of the mountains of the southwestern United States. They feed primarily by aerial gleaning, taking insects on the wing; they also dart out from perches to catch prey, much like the flycatcher species.

The birds nest on the dry leaves of the forest floor, relying on their camouflage to keep them hidden from predators. They time their egg-laying so that the eggs will hatch about ten days before the moon is full; this ensures plenty of light for the parents to gather insects for their voracious young to eat.

**SONGS AND CALLS**: Rarely seen, the whip-poor-will is often heard; its unmistakable call is the source of this bird's name. The accent is on the first and last syllables, and the bird will often call for hours on end throughout the night, delighting some and frustrating others.

**CONSERVATION STATUS**: The whip-poor-will has seen some small declines in recent decades. Speculation as to causes includes removal of understory habitat in forests as a result of grazing and removal of habitat due to human development. Some populations have seen increases due to abandonment of agricultural lands. The IUCN lists the species as Least Concern.

*49*

Whip-poor-will (*Caprimulgus vociferus*)

# South America: Tierra del Fuego National Park, Argentina

THIS PARK AT THE end of the world, lying just north of the town of Ushuaia on Isla Grande in far southern Argentina, protects the south-ernmost extremes of the Andes Mountains. Glaciers are still active here and meet the sea. Rivers cut deep valleys in the 3,300' (1,000 m) -tall mountains. The foothills are covered in Andean-Patagonian forests, which are composed of mostly Nothofagus, or southern beech trees, a family native to South America and Australasia. About ninety species of birds have been recorded in the park. Visitors can stay in the town and take light rail to the park entrance.

**BIRDS TO SEE**: Forested areas of the park support the beautiful Magellanic woodpecker, one of the largest in the world, as well as the white-throated treerunner, Austral thrush, Austral parakeet, Austral pygmy owl, thorn-tailed rayadito, and black-chinned siskin. In wetland areas of the park, species such as ashy-headed and upland geese can be found. Birds along the coastal shoreline include the flightless steamer duck, blackish and Magellanic oystercatchers, and great grebe. Departing the park and traveling up the Beagle Channel may yield species such as Magellanic penguins, red-faced rock and blue-eyed imperial shags, Chilean skua, southern fulmar, and petrels (Magellanic diving, white-chinned, and southern giant). Birders looking for rare birds will want to seek out white-bellied seedsnipe, a swamp-dweller, and yellow-bridled finch.

# Feeling Gritty

BIRDS DO NOT have teeth. With the exception of raptors, which do some ripping of their prey before swallowing, birds gulp their food pretty much whole, leaving the tearing and shredding to an organ called the *gizzard*. The bird swallows its food, which first moves into the *crop*, where it is moistened. From there, except in very small birds, the food passes into a stomach known as the *proventriculus*, where it's mixed with digestive juices and moved along into the gizzard. That muscular organ, often lined with grit, grinds the food into a digestible form.

That's why birds eat grit in the form of everything from fine sand to bits of eggshell to crushed seashells. And they'll be happy to find that grit offered to them in a convenient location right next to your feeders. Put out a plate or tray or flat rock and heap the grit upon it.

If you decide to use eggshells as a form of grit, bake them at 250°F (121°C) for twenty minutes or so before offering them to the birds. That will destroy any salmonella bacteria the shells might harbor and prevent the spread of the disease to the birds at your feeders.

Smash the eggshells or seashells into bits as small as you can, or buy the finest grade of sand you can find.

# Bird Sayings, Part I: Skylarks, Loons, and Catbirds, Oh My!

MANY CULTURES around the world consider the bluebird to be a positive force and symbol, representing happiness, good fortune, and the coming of spring, hence the enduring phrase, the "bluebird of happiness." Dead bluebirds were said to represent the loss of innocence or growing up.

*Skylarking* is a term meaning to engage in playful or childish antics. It is sometimes connected with mischievous acts. The word comes from the display habits of the skylark, a European bird that flies straight up in the air and then whirls around, calling as it descends. Doing something "on a lark" also refers to spontaneous activity.

Although loons themselves might not be deranged, their haunting calls have caused people to liken the sound of a loon to the cries of an insane person, therefore the phrase "crazy as a loon" in common usage. The "crazy" theme extends and may be partially derived from the use of the term by Shakespeare as a shortened form of *lunatic*, a word which has its own roots in luna, the moon. A lunatic was said to have been driven mad by the power of the moon.

The vociferousness of crows is certainly the origin of the phrase "something to crow about." The bird's nasal calls can be likened to complaining. And "eating crow" refers to the humiliation incurred for having to apologize for making a grievous mistake. Crow is not considered a very palatable bird.

A person who keeps a close eye on something can be said to "watch like a hawk" or have an "eagle eye," referring to the keen eyesight of raptors. Having a "voice like a nightingale" clearly refers to someone with an excellent singing voice; the bird's songs are particularly beautiful.

One can be said to be "sitting in the catbird seat" when he or she is on the top of his or her game or feeling very lucky. The phrase has its roots in the southern United States, where the catbird is common and can often be seen prominently singing from the top of a tall bush, the better to be seen and heard, advantageous for mating purposes.

The term *jaywalking* means crossing a street against a traffic signal, but the word has its origins from country folk being called jays. When they visited the city, they were usually overwhelmed by traffic and unsure how to get around.

*51*

# The Good, the Bad, and the Natural

NOTHING IN NATURE is one-sided. Nothing in nature is all good or all bad. Nothing we do in our backyard habitats will have only an upside. Everything we do for nature will have unintended consequences, such as drawing responses and presence from species not desired right along with the targeted and desired species.

That's a truism which, once learned and kept in the forefront of your mind, will serve everyone who sets out to shape the nature of his or her backyard.

It leads to questions such as: If I add a brush pile at the back of my property to provide small, ground-hugging songbirds with escape and protection from predators and shelter from the elements, what other wild things will find that brush pile to their liking and make my backyard habitat part of their home range? What undesirable consequences might those beneficiaries of the new brush pile bring with them? As my vegetable garden is only a few dozen feet from the spot where I would like to place the brush pile, will the new habitat feature attract wildlife that will damage my garden?

Think like an investor in all new backyard habitat features. There is always an income and expense ledger, a benefits versus liabilities equation, a set of columns for pluses and minuses. As with any investment, whether it is money in the stock market or a new habitat element in the backyard, a preinvestment assessment can avoid later losses.

# Lose Focus to Gain Perspective

A LACK OF FOCUS can be a good thing in birdwatching. We're not talking about a lack of dedication or enthusiasm for the pursuit of birdwatching. We're talking about a physical lack of focus in the birdwatcher's vision.

From an unfocused vantage point, your eyes are able to take in much more over a larger area than when you are focused on just one point. Your eyes will pick up tiny movements across the landscape, most of which previously went unnoticed. Slight movements of well-camouflaged birds in the undergrowth suddenly will appear magnified and highlighted.

And nearly anyone can learn how to do this visual "unfocusing."

Start by focusing intently on a distant target, maybe the horizon or a far-off tree line. Without moving your eyes, try to switch to your peripheral vision, or the portion of your vision around the edges. Maintain your focus on that distant target, but try to take in the rest of the information that your eyes are gathering. Then, when you begin to take in the periphery, allow your eyes to gradually lose focus entirely.

At this point, those tiny movements you may have missed previously will begin to be evident.

Achieving this unfocus usually takes a lot of practice. Allowing our eyes not to be focused runs counter to our instincts, both ancient instincts of survival and modern instincts. For that reason, maintaining a state of unfocused vision also will be challenging.

# Owls: Little Owl (*Athene noctua*)

THE LITTLE OWL is one of the most common and widespread owls in the world and is often seen around towns and cities. These owls had an image makeover in recent decades. They were long derided by farmers as pests that preyed on farm animals. However, extensive research determined that the bulk of the little owl's diet consists of insects. So, these birds actually benefited farmers by ridding their crops and barnyards of pests that caused damage to their plants and animals.

**PHYSICAL CHARACTERISTICS:** The little owl has a compact body, flat head, and short tail. Its brown back is spotted with white, and its white breast is streaked with brown. The facial disks that are common to all owls and help focus sound to an owl's ears are not as prominent in this species. This may be because the little owl relies on sight more than hearing for hunting. The little owl is often active during the day in open areas. The bird has an undulating style of flight unusual for owls; wing beats are alternated with glides, much like woodpeckers.

**RANGE:** The little owl is widespread and common within its range, which includes most of Europe, Central Asia, North Africa, and East Asia.

**HABITAT:** The little owl prefers open habitats, such as grasslands as steppes, as well as near human dwellings, such as in villages and even more urban areas. It can often be seen perching on wires, posts, and buildings.

This common owl feeds on a wide variety of prey, including small mammals, birds, amphibians, reptiles, and insects. It nests in tree cavities or holes in rock faces, and is sometimes seen nesting in buildings.

**SONGS AND CALLS:** The call of the little owl is a single, high-pitched note, repeated.

**CONSERVATION STATUS**: A widespread and common bird within its range, the little owl population is considered healthy, although some sources list it as declining.

Little owl (*Athene noctua*)

# North America: Texas Coastal Bend, United States

THE SOUTHEAST COAST OF Texas along the Gulf of Mexico is known as the Coastal Bend, and is home to a staggering array of bird species. The barrier islands and other coastal habitats serve as breeding grounds and as migratory stop-over spots for many species traveling along the Eastern, Mississippi, Central, and Rocky Mountain flyways. All of these routes become funneled at this point on the continent, with 510 of the 650 U.S. and Canadian breeding bird species spending time there. Not only is the number of species impressive, but the number of individual birds is dizzying—tens of thousands of hawks and hundreds of thousands of ducks make their way along the Bend during migration. In addition, many tropical birds wander up to the Gulf Coast.

Corpus Christi is considered a good starting point for most birding trips in the area. On its Great Texas Wildlife Trails website, Texas Department of Parks has organized the various regions of Texas into groups, with loop trips that guide travelers around key birding areas. Printable maps and short descriptions of the sites and species are very helpful for trip-planning.

Many local, regional, state, and federal parks dot the coast, each with their own habitats and species, providing great opportunities for birdwatchers. With 70 miles (112 km) of beaches and 130,434 acres (527.8 square km) of land, Padre Island National Seashore, stretching from Corpus Christi to Brownsville, is the largest undeveloped barrier island in the world. Habitats here include coastal dunes, grasslands, and the Laguna Madre, a hypersaline lagoon. The largest number of birds can be found in early spring or during fall and winter.

**BIRDS TO SEE**: Harris's hawk, white-tailed hawk, white-faced ibis, scissor-tailed flycatcher, Hudsonian godwit, magnificent frigatebird, lesser nighthawk, northern gannet, clapper rail, roseate spoonbill, and many, many others can all be seen here.

Aransas National Wildlife Refuge, southeast of the city of Victoria, comprises 58,000 acres (234.7 square km) of prairie, oak savanna, oak woodland, primary bay, freshwater marsh, and pond habitats. It boasts the second highest bird species count of any wildlife refuge in the United States—an amazing 406 species! The world's only natural flock of whooping cranes winters at the refuge.

**BIRDS TO SEE**: Some of the highlights at Aransas include groove-billed ani, golden-fronted woodpecker, common pauraque, Sprague's pipit, buff-bellied hummingbird, white-tailed kite, crested caracara, Inca dove, seaside sparrow, painted bunting, and marbled godwit.

**THINGS TO DO**: Many towns along the Bend have taken advantage of the interest in their wonderful bird life by hosting birding festivals throughout the year. Here are a few to start the trip-planning.

• Late February: Visit Port Aransas to see the wintering population of whooping cranes during the town's Celebration of Whooping Cranes.

• Early April: In time for the spring migration, the Galveston FeatherFest on Galveston Island offers activities for the whole family.

• Mid-September: See the staggering number of migrating ruby-throated hummingbirds during the Hummer/Bird Celebration in Rockport.

# What Makes a Habitat?

IN CREATING A HABITAT to attract birds to your backyard, you must satisfy the following four basic elements, which all birds (and all living things) require to survive and propagate the next generation of their species.

• **Food**: For a bird to remain in a given area year-round, it must find sources of food year-round. Those sources might vary from season to season, but the bird needs to find something nutritious every day of its life.

• **Water**: Water is most often overlooked by birders wanting to attract birds to their backyards. There seem to be streams, rivers, ponds, lakes, and mud puddles everywhere, so what's the big deal? Well, when we look deeper, we find there are considerable periods of the year when water can be in short supply. Among those times is the depth of winter, when natural sources of water might be frozen solid and unavailable to birds.

• **Shelter and protection**: This protects birds from enemies and the elements, and gives them a place to nest and rear their young. For many birds, the same trees, shrubs, and herbaceous plants satisfy the joint need. Other birds have specialized needs, particularly when it comes to nesting and raising their babies.

• **Space**: This element was included on the primary list only recently, but has been identified as one of the most important. Even with all the other elements satisfied, a bald eagle is generally not going to be a backyard bird. It needs more seclusion than the typical backyard will supply. As we humans convert ever larger tracts of the natural world to our uses, space for birds and other wild things carries an even higher premium.

Several bird species, and other species of wildlife, might satisfy their basic needs from the same sources in one location. In nature it's usually impossible to do something to benefit just one species without impacting a number of other species. That can be a nice benefit for those wanting to create a habitat for a range of species, with one new plant or one new water source or one new feeder satisfying the needs of and attracting multiple bird species.

# Cultural Uses of Bird Feathers

BIRDS HAVE BEEN revered by many cultures and thought to contain special powers. Live birds have been kept for ceremonies and parts have been used as decoration, as talismans, and for casting spells and healing.

Bird feathers have long been used as adornment by the people of many cultures. It is thought that primitive peoples believed the feathers conferred power upon them, since birds had the ability to fly and were likely thought to travel up to the gods. Cave paintings often depict humans with feather decorations.

More recent history has documented many cultures, such as Native North and South Americans, South Pacific Islanders, and African tribal peoples, who use feathers in elaborate headdresses, masks, robes, and costumes. The stark black-and-white plumage of the caracara was used in the clothing and decorations of the Inca rulers.

In the Amazon basin, the Shavante people used the primary flight feathers of the Cooper's hawk on their arrows because they knew this bird to be a fast flier and expert hunter. Some tribes, notably in South America and the southwestern United States, kept birds as pets so that their feathers could be harvested for their use.

In most cases, the males of a tribe wear the feather adornments, conferring power and status. This practice mimics the use of colorful plumage in nature, where the males are more colorful. Feather plumes were also used as a mark of status in many European societies starting in the sixteenth century. The elaborate use of the plumes increased markedly in the nineteenth century. The harvest of birds for trade nearly caused mass extinctions of many species, including egrets and birds of paradise.

# A Sweetener by Any Other Name…

THE WIDESPREAD INTEREST in feeding hummingbirds in our backyards on simple blends of sugar and water has led to a great deal of experimentation in mixtures of other substances for the tiny birds. If sugar works, why not:

Artificial sweeteners? Do we really think a bird already facing extremely high energy demands just to survive needs to go on a diet?

Honey? There's a reason so many experts advise parents against giving honey to their infants. Honey can carry the bacterial spores of the *Clostridium botulinum* bacteria, more commonly known as what causes botulism.

Brown sugar? Manufacturers produce both white and brown sugars for a reason. The brown varieties have molasses in them, and molasses is another sweet substance not needed in hummingbird nectar, either as part of brown sugar or as molasses.

Simple, white table sugar will get the job done. It's cheaper than any of these other sweeteners and, when mixed at one part sugar to four parts water, closely approximates the nectar of wildflowers on which the hummers naturally feed.

# Nests in Winter

MIDWINTER THROUGH early spring is prime time for scoping out the favored nesting sites of birds that you want to observe later in the year. Leaves are off the deciduous trees, and even the evergreens are a bit thinner after a winter's worth of bashing by the elements. Most birds' nests from last spring and summer, however, are still in place and even identifiable as to the species that built them.

A good field guide to bird nests will greatly enhance this experience. Choose a top-quality guide for your region. In addition, binoculars or a spotting scope will make close-up examination of nests in tall trees and particularly thorny shrubs a bit easier.

And good, warm clothing, in layers, will give you time to stay in one spot, focused on identifying each nest before moving on.

Move through your backyard, a local park, your neighborhood, or other area of birding interest, examining every tree, shrub, and patch of weeds as closely as possible. Some nests, such as that of the ruby-throated hummingbird, are tiny and well camouflaged, and only close observation will reveal their locations.

Take a pad and pencil along to record the nests you find and their exact locations. (A GPS unit can aid a great deal in this part of the effort.) You'll then be able to investigate the same locations this spring and summer to see if the same species of birds, maybe the same birds, are using the same locations again.

# Swifts: Alpine Swift (*Apus melba*)

A BIRD COMMONLY seen in the cities of Europe and Africa as well as over mountainous terrain or nesting in shoreside bluffs, the alpine swift, like other swifts, spends most of its life on the wing. These birds never perch, but cling to cliff faces and building walls in their concealed nesting and roosting sites.

**PHYSICAL CHARACTERISTICS**: The largest swift in the world, the alpine swift boasts a wingspan of 8" (20.3 cm). Its pale underside distinguishes this species from other European swifts. The white belly is broken only by a brown breast band, the same color as the back, wings, and short, forked tail.

**RANGE**: The alpine swift's breeding range extends from southern Europe west to the Himalayas and India and south into eastern Africa. The birds migrate long distances to their wintering range in southern Africa.

**HABITAT**: As the name suggests, alpine swifts nest in colonies at high elevations in mountain cliffs and caves as well as in coastal bluffs. Their nests are constructed of feathers, sticks, mosses, and plant material, adhered to the rock with saliva. They also nest on buildings in cities.

The open areas that this swift prefers enable the bird to practice its preferred method of hunting insects: aerial gleaning.

**SONGS AND CALLS**: The alpine swift utters a chittering, whistling call similar to that of other swifts and swallows.

**CONSERVATION STATUS**: With a large population, the IUCN lists this bird as Least Concern.

Alpine swift (*Apus melba*)

# North America: Florida, United States

PROBABLY NOWHERE ELSE in North America is a visitor able to see such a wide variety of species as in Florida. It is the only part of the continent where the subtropical climate intrudes, specifically in southern Florida. This allows many species not found anywhere else in the country to extend their range northward for the breeding season.

From the "Space Coast" around Titusville and Cape Canaveral down the east coast to the Keys and the Everglades and on up the Gulf Coast, there are numerous spots to visit. The Florida Fish and Wildlife Conservation Commission has pieced together the Florida Birding Trail, which encompasses 489 sites along a 2,000-mile (3,220-km) route. Visitors can use the commission's map and guides to piece together their own tour, based on location, amenities, and/or species.

The barrier islands near Titusville include Canaveral National Seashore and Merritt Island National Wildlife Refuge, wonderful places to spend a day or even a long weekend and only a short drive from Orlando and Daytona Beach. More than 300 species of birds utilize the saltwater estuaries and marshes, coastal dunes, pine flatwoods, scrub oak, hardwood hammocks, and other habitats that make up these public lands. The Space Coast Birding and Wildlife Festival occurs in late January every year. Noted speakers and guides accompany birders on hikes to see the dense concentrations of species that frequent the area at this time of year.

**BIRDS TO SEE**: The endangered wood stork and roseate tern, as well as the threatened Florida scrub jay are found at Merritt Island. The refuge is also a good location to see the American alligator and the West Indian manatee. Other bird species include bald eagle, osprey, peregrine falcon, reddish egret, tricolored heron, brown and white pelicans, roseate spoonbill, black skimmer, and a host of peeps and other shorebirds.

Subtropical species can be found throughout the Everglades National Park system, which comprises 1.5 million acres (6,070 square km) of southern Florida. Many foot and canoe trails thread through the park. Some of the best ones for viewing freshwater species include the Anhinga Trail, Eco Pond, and Shark Valley. Canoeists will delight in plying their way along Shark Bight near Flamingo at the very southern tip of Florida, or on the Gulf Coast in Chokoloskee Bay, where they can see large numbers of wading birds on the mud flats and shallows and ducks in the open water. Birdwatchers can hire guides in the park for trail walks and boat trips.

**BIRDS TO SEE**: With more than 360 species recorded in the Everglades National Park, visitors are sure to see plenty of new and exciting birds on their trip. The six species of heron (including green-backed, tricolored, black-crowned night, and yellow-crowned night), four species of egret (great, reddish, snowy, and cattle), and four species of ibis (white, scarlet, white-faced, and glossy) may be the most commonly seen. But there are plenty of ducks, shorebirds, and forest birds, and even eight species of pigeons and doves.

Twenty-two species of raptors include snail kite, white-tailed kite, golden eagle, Swainson's hawk, northern harrier, and black vulture. Subtropical specialties include short-tailed hawk, mangrove cuckoo, smooth-billed ani, groove-billed ani, Bahama mockingbird, Bahama swallow, and tropical kingbird. This is also the only place to see the endangered Cape Sable seaside sparrow.

Home to the largest intact mangrove swamps in the United States, J.N. "Ding" Darling National Wildlife Refuge on Sanibel Island in the Gulf of Mexico off Cape Coral and Fort Meyers is a major migratory stopover for birds.

The refuge is located in the subtropical climate zone of Florida, and it boasts nearly 300 bird species. The best time to visit the refuge is between December and March, when the birds are most abundant.

**BIRDS TO SEE**: Roseate spoonbill, white ibis, wood stork, mottled duck, swallow-tailed kite, mangrove cuckoo, and gray kingbird can be seen here, among many others.

# Uninvited Guests

THE BIRDS HAVE abandoned the feeders. A big hawk is hanging around the neighborhood. You saw it grab a little bird under your feeders. The impact of hawks on backyard bird feeding is an regular issue for many birdwatchers.

It's completely natural, if sometimes a bit bloody and disconcerting to some birders, for predators to take advantage of such a rich abundance of prey and to make spots of such abundance part of their regular, daily hunting territory.

Some common hawk species have adapted to the modern, human-dominated landscape of the suburbs and even cities. The Cooper's hawk, sharp-shinned hawk, red-tailed hawk, and American kestrel are among them. The Cooper's hawk, in particular, specializes in preying upon birds. At the same time, backyard bird feeding concentrates large numbers of prey species in small spaces, often in unnaturally open areas with very little escape cover (better known as lawns).

The most effective action in backyards where it's possible is to add some escape cover, such as planting evergreen shrubs, near the feeders or by moving the feeders closer to existing escape cover. And then, just enjoy the whole of nature that comes to the backyard, including the predator-prey interactions.

Where such changes are not possible, or not desired—or the sight of a hawk taking a bird is just too upsetting—a short interruption of feeding likely will solve a backyard birder's problem. Without full feeders for a couple of weeks, the feeder birds will disperse, causing the hawk to alter its daily rounds in search of more fertile feeding grounds. After the hawk hasn't been spotted for several days, resume normal feeding.

One thing you cannot do is to harm the hawk. Beyond the fact that offing the hawk will have no lasting impact, it also is illegal to harm, harass, or otherwise disturb hawks.

# Falconry

ONE OF MANKIND's oldest positive relationships with birds is via the sport of falconry. The earliest known record of falconry is from the eight century B. C. E. in Assyria, but many ancient cultures—including Japan, China, Korea, Persia, and Arabia—have a long history of utilizing birds of prey for assisted hunting. The practice didn't spread into Europe and the Christian world until around the fifth century C. E. At the height of falconry's popularity, the raptors were not only commonly used for hunting, but also became a fashionable adornment, worn on the arms to court, to church, and even into battle.

The same birds that were so revered, respected, and utilized during falconry's peak in Europe were later slaughtered and treated as vermin when the invention of guns made hunting with birds obsolete. The birds were seen as competition for game. In much of the world, the practice of falconry has since been relegated to a few small clubs.

However, in regions in the Middle East, falconry is still firmly rooted in the culture, even though the goals of providing food are less a necessity than in ancient times. Familial and tribal bonds are maintained through hunting trips. Concern over the continuation of the sport has been sufficient to prompt conservation efforts, captive rearing of falcons as opposed to wild-caught birds, and avian veterinary research.

Some of the most commonly used species are peregrine falcons (historically, the most important species), gyrfalcons, sakers, and Harris's hawks, now the most commonly bred species for falconry. This hawk's natural habit of communal hunting makes it the perfect species for the sport. Technically, those who hunt with species other than falcons (hawks and eagles) are called *austringers*. Falcons are usually used in more open country, while the accipiters (Cooper's hawk, sharp-shinned hawk, and goshawk) are used in forested areas. Incredibly, Mongolians hunt on horseback with golden eagles for large quarry such as foxes and wolves.

# Sounds Like a Plan

THE DEAD OF WINTER, or any doldrums, when most activities, both natural and man-made, are at an ebb, is prime time for planning the year's bird habitat.

First take an inventory of what plants and features you already have on the ground. What were your successes in the past year? What were your failures? What did you plan to accomplish but never got around to starting?

Then, draw a map of your property. Work at a scale, such as 1" (2.5 cm) equaling 1' (30.4 cm). Outline the boundaries and general shape of the property. Sketch in your home, garage, and all outbuildings, and the paths, sidewalks, and walkways.

On each building, note ground-level windows and doors. Birdbaths, mini ponds, brush piles, and the like are next. Move on to trees, shrubs, gardens, flowerbeds, and such.

With that list and map in hand, you should ask the following questions: What, if anything, from that list do I want to carry over onto a new plan for the coming year? And where on the map can I place it?

Start a new list of plans for the coming year, with some tentative calendar points for starting each project. Using a different, lighter color, sketch on the map your corresponding projects and planned additions for the year.

# Clues from Nest Building

BIRDS IN THE PROCESS of gathering nesting material are prime candidates for some careful spying by the birdwatcher wanting to find the nest site. They obviously are engaged in putting together the object of your search, and before they've actually laid eggs they likely will be a bit less cautious about concealing their activities.

Of course, nesting material varies widely by species. A good field guide, complete with information about preferred materials and nest location for each species, is a valuable aid in this process. But few birds carry materials such as leaves, grass, hair, string, and the like for any purpose other than nest building.

Observe the birds and the spot where they are carrying the materials from a discreet distance. Although they may not be as secretive about their activities as they will become later, they also do not want to locate their nest in a spot that feels threatened by some large predator. (You know you have no predatory intentions, but the birds do not know that.)

Patience and distance are the keys to locating the future sites of the nests, which you will visit regularly throughout the nesting period to steal glimpses of the growing birds.

**A green finch gathering nesting material**

# Game Birds: Gambel's Quail
## (*Callipepla gambelii*)

THE GAMBEL'S QUAIL is well known in its small range in North America. It travels in coveys, or small flocks, and spends much of its time on the ground, scampering under dense vegetation when disturbed.

**PHYSICAL CHARACTERISTICS**: Gambel's quails are noted for their scampering and their plumage. The male wears a chestnut-colored cap above a white eyebrow and topped with a short black "topknot" of feathers that overhangs its face, which along with its bill and bib are all black lined with white. All this stands out against its mostly gray back and breast. A cream-colored lower breast sits above another black feather patch on the abdomen just above the legs, and its flanks are chestnut interspersed with white feathers. All these colors are enhanced by a simple gray back and chest.

Females lack most of the black coloration, and they have small topknot plumes. The gray back extends to the head with subtle variations around the eyes and bill.

**RANGE**: The Sonoran Desert is home for the Gambel's quail, its only native fowl-like bird; it also occurs in parts of the Chihuahuan and Mojave deserts. This range includes much of southern Arizona and northwestern Arizona into southern Utah, parts of western Colorado, central and southwestern New Mexico, southeastern California and Nevada, and along the northwestern coast of Mexico. The species has been introduced elsewhere, including the Hawaiian islands.

**HABITAT**: Like other desert species, Gambel's quails stick closely to waterways, such as river corridors, washes, and seeps. These sites must have dense brush for cover from both the sun and predators, and the birds can be found at elevations of up to 5,000' (1,650 m). Unlike other quail species, these quails prefer to spend the night perched above ground in a bush or small tree.

Gambel's quails are largely vegetarian, feeding mostly on seeds, especially those from mesquite trees; they glean these from the droppings of cattle and wildlife, as the husks of the seeds are too hard for them to open unaided. They will also eat leaves of grasses and herbaceous plants, as well as berries when they are available. When nesting, they will take advantage of the more plentiful insects in spring and summer.

The nest of this species is usually on the ground, well protected beneath a dense shrub or even within a clump of cactus. Simple in design, nests are scrapes in the ground lined with twigs, leaves, grass, and feathers.

**SONGS AND CALLS**: Although Gambel's quails do not have songs per se, they utter a variety of calls, based on need. Growling, trilling, or sharp *took* calls are used when feeding or locating food. Males begin the mating season with a *kaa* or *cow* call to advertise availability. The most commonly heard call is the assembly call—*ka-KAA-ka*—which stimulates birds to gather when separated.

**CONSERVATION STATUS**: Although populations of Gambel's quail fluctuate considerably due to the amount of precipitation received in winter and the success of their hatchlings, the species is considered stable.

Gambel's quail (*Callipepla gambelii*)

# North America: Bay of Fundy, New Brunswick and Nova Scotia, Canada

BORDERED ON THE NORTH by New Brunswick and on the east and south by Nova Scotia, the Bay of Fundy, with the greatest tidal change in the world, is perhaps the most important migratory stopover for millions of birds of about 360 species that travel along the Atlantic flyway. With numerous sites, hiking trails, and whale watch and seabird boating tours plying the bay, this truly is a birder's paradise. Portions of the bay, Shepody Bay and Minas Basin, are part of the Western Hemisphere Shorebird Reserve Network.

Many sites around the bay are great for birding, from coastal locations to the islands in the bay. The massive tides in the Bay of Fundy draw out as much as 56' (17 m) of seawater from the upper basins, exposing acres of mud flats. Shorebirds are drawn to these sites, such as at Irving Nature Park, to feed on the rich invertebrate life buried in the mud. Grand Manan Island, near the bay's mouth, plays host to nearly 400 bird species, while Machias Seal Island not far away is a nesting ground for Atlantic puffins, terns, and razorbills.

Visitors can go ashore this uninhabited (except for two lighthouse keepers) island, but be careful not to disturb the nesting birds.

The dense salt marshes at Mary's Point Sanctuary, at the head of the bay, are feeding grounds for hundreds of thousands of shorebirds, including many species of sandpipers. A boardwalk system traverses the Tantramar marshes, also at the head of the bay. These man-made marshes were built some 200 years ago, but they are now home to large numbers of ducks, hawks, and songbirds.

**BIRDS TO SEE**: Semipalmated sandpipers, greater yellowlegs, black-bellied plover, sanderling, willet, ruddy turnstone, red knot, shearwaters (greater, sooty, and Manx), Atlantic puffin, common and thick-billed murre, Pomarine and parasitic jaeger, common snipe, peregrine falcon, bald eagle, American and least bittern, herons (great blue, little blue, green, and tricolored), snow goose, tundra swan, tufted duck, king eider, harlequin duck, and many others can all be seen here.

# Successful Invaders

BACKYARD BIRD-FEEDING enthusiasts facing ever-increasing seed and suet costs can begin to hope for a migration by the massive flocks of house sparrows that seem to spend their days wolfing down every bit of food they can find at the feeders. Unfortunately, no such respite will be coming.

The house sparrow is a year-round resident of most of North America. An introduced, invasive, exotic species, the house sparrow tends to live in close proximity to man and will continue to show up at your feeders as long as you continue to fill them with seed.

Natives of Europe, the first few dozen in North America were released in Brooklyn, New York, in 1851. By 1900, the species had proliferated and spread west and north to the Rocky Mountains. Additional releases were later made in San Francisco and Salt Lake City.

The house sparrow is primarily a ground forager and can be somewhat controlled in the backyard by limiting large, flat perching areas at the feeders and restricting the amount of unused seed that falls from the feeders to the ground.

# Mythical Birds: Phoenix

ONE OF THE MOST ubiquitous mythological characters, the phoenix appears in nearly ever major culture, with the core theme of rebirth intact. Although depicted in Egyptian mythology originally as a heron, the phoenix has also been represented as an eagle, but more commonly as a generic large bird of bright, fiery colors.

The myth of the phoenix holds that this long-lived bird is essentially immortal, only passing from this life by its own actions and being reborn. At the end of its 500-year life cycle, the phoenix builds a pyre of sticks and ignites itself in it, only to rise from the ashes of its former self. In the Egyptian legend, the bennu bird (as the phoenix was known in this culture) gathers up the ashes and encases them in a myrrh egg, which it carries on the wing to the Heliopolis, the city of the sun.

The rebirth of the bennu bird was closely associated with the rising of the Nile, which signals the flooding of the fields, enriching them for planting.

The word *bennu* was changed in ancient Greece to *phoenix*, which refers to the colors purple-red and crimson. Greek writings about the phoenix place the bird's origin in India. The legends there tell of rebirth by fire into a wormlike creature, which grows feathers and becomes full-grown within three days. Persia's version of the phoenix was the huma, a benevolent and peaceful bird whose touch brought good fortune, and who feeds only on carrion and embodies both male and female natures. This is similar to the Chinese belief that the *fenghuang*, their form of the phoenix, embodies yin and yang.

**Salt marshes at the Bay of Fundy in Nova Scotia, Canada**

# On the Bluebird Trail

FEW BIRD SPECIES have benefited from the boom in birdwatching enthusiasm over the past several decades as much as the bluebird. A downward spiral in the species' population has been halted and even reversed in many areas through the installation of thousands upon thousands of man-made bluebird boxes, which provided the cavities for nesting that the bluebirds had been losing to other, often exotic, species.

A great many of the bluebird boxes went into backyards throughout the bluebird's natural range, but large numbers also found their way into a new phenomenon, the bluebird trail, in parks, industrial development areas, farmland edges, and other public and semipublic lands. A bluebird trail is a route along which boxes have been erected every 100 yards (91.4 m) or so, which is about as close as bluebirds like

to nest in proximity to one another. Regular maintenance includes cleaning out old nesting materials as soon as the nestlings have been fledged from each box; preventing competing species, such as European starlings and house sparrows, from taking over the nest boxes; and making repairs as necessary. Many also prefer to maintain a regular schedule of travels along their bluebird trails to keep accurate records of the successes of the bluebirds that use the boxes.

The great surge in development of bluebird trails has slowed in the past few years, after many amenable sites had gotten their trails. However, fewer enthusiasts are now seeking to install new trails, leaving plenty of opportunity for newcomers wanting to develop and maintain new trails, maybe someone like you.

# Nesting Sites: Keep the Pressure Off

TOO MUCH DISTURBANCE too close to an active nest often will cause parent birds to abandon the site and even their still-dependent nestlings.

Observation of the nest requires a somewhat unobscured line of sight to the nest site, but not one that has been artificially cleared of vegetation. After locating the nest, the careful birdwatcher should scout the perimeter of the area to find the spot that already offers a great view from a distance and will afford a great viewing experience without pressing the birds too closely.

If the spot is not easily remembered from some natural landmark, a small guiding mark might be deployed to direct a return visit. A small flag attached to a tree or shrub can be used to mark the spot. If it's small and discreet enough, it is unlikely to attract less caring humans or to lead anyone with crude intentions to the actual nest site.

More care must be taken to avoid leading natural predators to the site. No trail should be carved from the underbrush or walked into the soil through too-often-repeated visits. Approaching from different angles also will tend to throw off creatures that might try to follow the birdwatcher's trail out of simple curiosity and hope that it will lead to some reward.

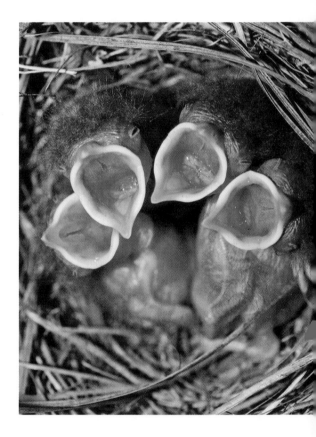

# Raptors: Harris's Hawk
## (*Parabuteo unicinctus*)

THE ONLY NORTH AMERICAN raptor to hunt communally and the only raptor to hunt with advanced cooperation, the Harris's hawk is unusual for other reasons as well. A native of hot desert and savanna, this species is also known to have repeated nestings throughout the year. Because of its cooperative nature, this species of hawk is well suited for falconry.

**PHYSICAL CHARACTERISTICS**: A member of the *Buteo* genus of hawks, the Harris's hawk is a bulky, large-bodied and broad-winged bird. The striking plumage colors of both males and females include a dark brown to black head, back, breast, and lower wings, with upper wings, wing lining (underneath), and thighs a cinnamon-rufous color. The hawk's bright yellow bill with black tip and feet stand out sharply against these other colors.

**RANGE**: The Harris's hawk can be found mostly in northern Mexico, extending into the United States in southern Arizona, southeastern New Mexico, Texas, and into Louisiana. A subspecies known as the bay-winged hawk is resident in South America.

**HABITAT**: A bird of prey of dry desert and savanna, the Harris's hawk requires several perches in its habitat in order to hunt.

These hawks live communally; family sizes from just a single pair to as many as seven hawks have been noted. The species may practice monogamy or polyandry (one female to many males) and sometimes polygyny (one male to many females).

They feed mainly on large mammals such as hares and rabbits, ground squirrels, and wood-rats, birds such as quails and roadrunners, and even lizards. A group of hawks may use one of three different types of hunting techniques: converging on their prey all at once; one bird flushing prey while others attack; or a relay chase, with fresher birds taking over the lead chase position. All of the hawks share the kill, with the dominant bird feeding first.

Nests of the Harris's hawks are built in trees or tall cacti of sticks and lined with fresh leaves. A mated pair may build as many as four nests, in case of damage to the one they're using.

**SONGS AND CALLS**: The call of the Harris's hawk is a harsh, high-pitched *irrr* note.

**CONSERVATION STATUS**: Harris's hawks at their nests are easily disturbed by humans. Populations of this hawk are also impacted by habitat loss, as well as electrocution on power lines where they sometimes perch. The species has not been formally protected, although many researchers have called for assigning them this status.

Harris's hawk (*Parabuteo unicinctus*)

# North America: Gaspé Peninsula, Quebec, Canada

SITUATED JUST 2.2 miles (3.5 km) off the southern coast of Quebec's Gaspé Peninsula is Île Bonaventure, which hosts one of the largest breeding colonies of northern gannets in the world. The island is literally covered with these birds, as well as other nesting seabirds. The best way to see the colonies is from a boat, and several tour operators are available for hire. Trails on the island also allow viewing of boreal forest species. Between June and July is the best time to go, since the colony activity is greatest then, but the birds are present throughout summer. Visitors can stay in nearby Percé.

A trip to the Gaspé also gives birders the opportunity to visit the coastal towns, stunning coastline, and boreal forest and muskeg (flooded peatlands) sites in the Parc de la Gaspésie, with their host of breeding waterfowl and songbird species, as well as possible sightings of woodland caribou, moose, and deer. Forillon National Park on the northeast tip of the peninsula supports more seabirds along the coastal cliffs, as well as up to twenty-six raptor species during migration. Whale watch cruises and sea kayak trips are also available from this point.

**BIRDS TO SEE**: The seabird colonies of Bonaventure are dominated by the northern gannets, with more than 100,000 birds. Other breeding species with large populations include black-legged kittiwake and common murre. Also using the island are black guillemots, great black-backed and herring gulls, great and double-crested cormorants, razorbills, Leach's storm-petrels, boreal chickadees, and blackpoll warblers.

# Niger (or Nyjer): A Worthwhile Investment

NYJER, ALSO KNOWN AS *thistle*, *niger*, and *Guizotia abyssinica*, is an annual, native wildflower in Ethiopia. It is raised under cultivation there and used in East Africa, India, and the West Indies as a source of vegetable oil. About half of the vegetable oil used in Ethiopia is derived from nyjer, which is 35 percent to 40 percent oil. The seed, which is relatively high in calories, is also is ground into an edible paste and eaten directly or pressed with honey into cakes.

Nyjer is a member of the sunflower family, but is most closely related to the popular garden plant cosmos. The flowers look like yellow cosmos atop 6' (1.9 m) -tall stems.

Nyjer is popular for its ability to attract finches. When it was first introduced into the bird-feeding trade about fifty years ago, most of the seed was marketed simply as *niger*. The misnomer of *thistle* probably was attached to nyjer because the import looks similar to the native, preferred seed among species such as goldfinches that also is considered a noxious weed.

In 1998, the Wild Bird Feeding Industry trademarked the name *nyjer* to battle the incorrectly perceived association with thistle and to avoid offensive mispronunciation of the word *niger*. However, many in the industry still refer to the seed as *niger*.

# The History of Bird Protection and Conservation II: Dust Bowl to Duck Bowl

AFTER INITIAL SUCCESSES during the early years of bird conservation initiatives in the United States, the first sweeping federal and international legislation to protect migratory birds was passed in 1913 with the Weeks-McLean Act. Not only was spring hunting outlawed nationally, but so was the sale and purchase of wild bird feathers, which effectively ended the plume trade. The law was strengthened after World War I with the Migratory Bird Treaty Act of 1918, in which the United States entered into agreement with Great Britain, which then administered Canada, to afford protection to birds migrating between the two North American countries.

The efforts to pass these treaties were one of the first real and effective cooperative actions between the nascent environmental movement (in the form of the Audubon Society) and sportsmen's groups. Both were alarmed at the rapid decline in bird populations and pressed their legislators to enact protective measures.

Partly to deal with the environmental crisis created by the intensive farming practices of the 1920s, which dried up many wetlands across the U.S. Midwest, the Migratory Bird Conservation Act of 1929 was passed. This act provided funding for the National Wildlife Refuge system to assist in the acquisition of lands and the creation of habitats, primarily for wetland bird species, such as ducks and shorebirds. The cooperation that this attention and funding generated helped organize the refuge system into a very effective conservation initiative. However, when it became clear that the amount of appropriated funds was insufficient, the Migratory Bird Hunting Stamp Act was passed. This extracted fees from hunters via the purchase of duck stamps, which hunters had to place on their hunting licenses.

Although the U.S.'s Great Depression severely reduced membership funding for the National Audubon Society, the publication of Roger Tory Peterson's *Field Guide to the Birds* (see Day 124) helped attract attention once again to birdwatching and the society.

# Soda Bottle Goldfinch Feeder

A STANDARD (2 L) soda bottle can be easily converted into a niger feeder for use by birds such as American goldfinches, which can hang upside-down to feed (see Day 32 for more about birds who prefer niger).

Remove the label from the bottle, wash it out, and allow it to dry completely. Next, with a large nail or an awl, poke holes into the sides of the bottle:

one pair of holes directly opposite one another about 3" (7.6 cm) from the neck of the bottle

one pair of holes (again opposite one another but perpendicular to the first) about 2" (5.1 cm) below the first set

one pair of holes (again opposite one another but spaced at 45 degrees to both of the first sets of holes) about 3" (7.6 cm) below the second set.

Insert 6" (15.2 cm) pieces of ¼" (6 mm) dowel through each set of holes.

Considering the neck of the bottle to be the top of the feeder, use a sharp knife to cut a ¼" (6 mm) blade-wide, vertical slit about 1" (2.5 cm) beneath each protruding dowel section.

Tightly twist one end of a long piece of heavy-gauge wire around the neck of the bottle, below the lowest lip edge of that neck.

Fill the bottle with niger seed, screw on the cap, and use the loose end of the wire to hang your new feeder in a spot where the birds will find it.

There will be a lot of niger seed in the bottle that the birds will be unable to access. To mix the seed and distribute the old seed with the new, shake the bottle vigorously to blend the seed every time you refill the feeder.

# Winged Creatures of the Night

MANY SPECIES OF BIRDS migrate during the day, including the big showy travelers such as geese, hawks, and shorebirds. But many others, particularly songbirds, migrate at night.

A growing number of birders have been tapping into this phenomenon to listen to the nighttime calls of passing birds, and even to watch them through spotting scopes and binoculars pointed at the moon.

The nighttime flyers lift off soon after dusk and fly for the next eight to ten hours, coming back down just before dawn to feed and rest throughout the next day or next few days.

There are some advantages to covering long distances at night. Primary among them is the general pattern of calmer and more stable skies during the hours of darkness, when stronger winds generally fade. The night also usually offers cooler temperatures than the day, which can be important to birds that experience moisture-sapping rises in body temperature of several degrees while working hard to fly. In addition, the migrants may find a slight reduction in predator activity during the night, although some researchers have observed bird-eating hawks after dark.

Songbirds on the migratory move have a different vocabulary than during their daylight activities, generally comprising short, high-pitched call notes that sound a lot like the chirp of a cricket to the untrained ear.

However, researchers are beginning to differentiate among the calls of the different species. A team from the Cornell Lab of Ornithology in Ithaca, New York, has a firm handle on the night-flight calls of about three dozen species and has a pretty good reading on another thirty or so species. For example, the red-headed woodpecker calls out as queeer, the red-breasted nuthatch as *aah, aah, aah*, the dicksissel and indigo bunting with a buzzy note, and the chipping sparrow with a short and high *tseep*.

The birds use their call notes to remain in contact with their traveling companions through the dark skies.

# Kingfishers and Relatives: Laughing Kookaburra (*Dacelo novaeguineae*)

AS ITS NAME SUGGESTS, the call of the laughing kookaburra is this Australian bird's most prominent characteristic. Its call, usually uttered at dawn and dusk, has caused the bird to be alternatively named the "Bushman's alarm clock."

**PHYSICAL CHARACTERISTICS**: The laughing kookaburra is the largest bird in the kingfisher family, measuring an average of 18.5" (47 cm) from tip of bill to tip of tail and weighing as much as 17.5 ounces (500 grams). The bird is drabber than other kingfishers, a group known for being colorfully plumaged. The laughing kookaburra has a mostly buff-colored breast and head, with dark brown wings and back, streaked with pale blue. A dark, wide eye stripe sits above the bird's prodigious bill, which is dark above and pale below.

**RANGE**: The laughing kookaburra is endemic to the Australian continent, and is resident in the eastern and southeastern parts of the country (Queensland, New South Wales, and South Australia). A population has been introduced into the southwestern corner of Western Australia and on the island of Tasmania.

**HABITAT**: Again defying kingfisher commonalities, the laughing kookaburra does not frequent waterways or eat much fish. Rather, the bird makes its home in forests and woodlands, where it hunts small mammals, reptiles, amphibians, and insects. The bird darts down to grab its prey with its bill, then carries it back to its perch where it will beat it against a tree branch to soften it for swallowing.

The laughing kookaburra uses tree cavities for nest sites, as well as termite mounds built in acacia trees or on the ground. The species often functions in a family group, with several previously reared young assisting with brooding (nest sitting), feeding, and territorial defense.

**SONGS AND CALLS**: The laughing kookaburra has a loud rattling call, much like a laugh. It begins with a tamer chuckle, builds to a hearty laugh, and then ends with the same chuckle.

**CONSERVATION STATUS**: The province of New South Wales has given the laughing kookaburra protected status. Threats to the species include deforestation and pesticides, ingested through their prey.

Laughing kookaburra (*Dacelo novaeguineae*)

# North America: Plum Island, Newburyport, Massachusetts, United States

FOR YEAR-ROUND BIRDING, one can do no better on North America's eastern seaboard than Plum Island. A barrier island lying between the outlets for two major rivers, the Merrimack to the north and the Ipswich to the south, Plum Island is in the town of Newburyport and also contains the Parker River National Wildlife Refuge. The refuge is the best place to view the birdlife among its 3,000 acres (12.1 square km) of salt marsh and 6.5 miles (10.5 km) of beach. Add to this a dune-beach complex, maritime forest, and freshwater impoundments and you have a recipe for very high avian diversity.

Migration brings huge numbers of shorebirds, which use the shorelines and river mud flats to hunt for invertebrates, crustaceans, and mollusks. Many birders also brave the sometimes biting wind and snow of winter to catch sight of unusual waterfowl and raptors. Visitors can stay in nearby Newburyport, Ipswich, Essex, or other towns and experience the North Shore's hospitality and cuisine while on their trip.

**BIRDS TO SEE**: More than 350 species of birds use the refuge throughout the year. Spring brings floods of migrants, such as wood warblers, vireos, thrushes, flycatchers, raptors (American kestrel, sharp-shinned hawk), and shorebirds, including the endangered piping plover, which nests at the refuge. Woodcocks perform their showy mating rituals in open areas. Purple martins arrive in spring to spend for breeding season. During summer, northern harriers quarter low over the dunes.

Birds begin their southward migration in July and continue doing so through September, with later migrants, such as peregrine falcons, seen here through November. Tree swallows congregate in the tens of thousands to bulk up on bayberries before the long journey. Great blue herons and great egrets can be seen in the marshes and impoundments. Winter may be quieter, but many birders still come for a chance to catch a glimpse of short-eared owls, rough-legged hawks, and the semi-regular snowy owls, as well as the abundant waterfowl, including oldsquaw, bufflehead, common and Barrow's goldeneye, common and hooded merganser, loon, grebe, and scoter.

**Semipalmated sandpipers at Parker River National Wildlife Refuge**

# Starlings Be Gone

Although we feel special kinship with our backyard birds, sometimes some of them can wear out their welcome. Starlings, in particular, can gather in bothersome numbers at certain times of the year.

Often a pesky flock of the buzzing birds will be particularly attracted to roosting habitat ranging from a stand of bamboo to a wooded lot on the crest of a hill. If that roosting habitat happens to be around your home or if your home lies on the flock's favored route to that roosting habitat, your love for these birds might be tested.

Although habitat manipulation, such as thinning the bamboo or woodlot, would be the most effective solution, it is not always a possibility.

Fortunately, many types of frightening devices are available that may get the job done. These devices range from the more invasive exploding shells, gas exploders, and alarm calls, to much less invasive concepts such as hawk and owl decoys and silhouettes, big-eye balloons, and flashing lights. Always try the less invasive devices first.

Frightening devices usually require a week of effort to reach maximum effectiveness. And those that rely on visual impact must be moved frequently to avoid having the birds grow accustomed to and familiar with them. Changing the location of the device makes the birds uneasy, which helps them decide to move.

Starlings are easier to scare off when they are in flight than when they are already roosted, where they feel a certain measure of protection. To take advantage, make sure your frightening devices are in place at least a half-hour before the birds normally begin to gather in the evening and at least a half-hour before they normally leave the roost in the morning.

However, be aware that convincing the starlings to vacate the stand of bamboo will encourage them to find a new roosting spot nearby. The problems associated with their congregational roosting will relocate with them. If they are also scared off their new roosting spot, they likely will return to the original location.

European starling (*Sturnus vulgaris*)

# Swallows, the Harbingers of Spring

SWALLOWS HAVE OFTEN signified the arrival of spring and summer. "One swallow does not a summer make," goes the old saying. They are often one of the first birds to return after winter, and they are usually seen in large numbers and very close to, if not inside, human habitations.

Farmers and people in general held the birds in such high regard not just for their symbolism of warm weather and the beginning of the crop cycle, but also because they feed on large numbers of insects. Many cultures worldwide have celebrated the bird's arrival.

Remarkably, in most cases the same species was being lauded—namely, the barn swallow, which has one of the widest ranges of any bird species. *Hirundo rustica* has a deep navy-blue back, white underside, and rusty-colored throat. It earned its common name because of its predilection for nesting in the rafters of farm buildings, where it constructs its nest of mud lined with grass and feathers and attached to a vertical wall just below an overhang, to help shield it from predators.

The ancient Greeks celebrated the arrival of the birds in spring, and this practice was continued until the beginning of the twentieth century. Festivals are still held today to mark the arrival of the swallows. One of the most famous is held in San Juan Capistrano, California, where the St. Joseph's Day Return of the Swallows is held in mid-March.

# Homemade Bird "Doughnuts"

A DELICIOUS TREAT for birds is a homemade "doughnut" packed with seeds, nuts, and fruits.

First chop a variety of fruit into very small bits: apples, apricots, blueberries, cranberries, currants, grapes, pears, raisins, and others, in any form, fresh, frozen, or dried. For a variation, switch the fruit with finely chopped nuts, such as peanuts, walnuts, almonds, and others. And for a major variation that might not be for the squeamish, replace the fruits with chopped insects, such as mealworms, crickets, grasshoppers, grubs, beetles, and others.

Next, thoroughly mix 2 cups (460 g) of whole wheat flour, 1 cup (230 g) of cornmeal, ½ tablespoon (7 g) of baking soda, and 1 tablespoon (14 g) of sand. (Obviously this recipe is not intended for human consumption.)

Mix the chopped fruits, nuts, or insects—or a combination of two or all three—into the dry ingredients, blending to evenly distribute.

Finally, blend in 1 cup (237 ml) of water and ½ cup (118 ml) of melted bacon fat into the batter.

Spoon small balls of the mixture onto a baking tray with raised sides and press the balls flat, to about ½" (1.3 cm). Cut a small circle from the center of each, shaping the portions you remove into additional balls.

Bake at 350°F (177°C) for 13 to 16 minutes. Allow them to cool and harden. Loop string, yarn, fishing line, or wire through the ring to hang or attach them to outdoor structures.

# Birds of Salt Marshes and Mud Flats

SALT MARSHES AND mud flats are those coastal areas flooded by the tidal action twice each day with food-rich water that leaves much of that food behind when it withdraws. Diverse invertebrates make their home in that highly variable environment.

On so many levels, it's a target-rich environment for wading birds, whose light stature and spread feet enable them to race across the muck and mud that would suck down anything heavier. When the water covers the area, the ducks and seabirds jump on the shallow-water opportunities at the same rich source of edibles.

Regardless of tide, some community of birds is active on the salt marches and mud flats throughout the daylight hours.

It is not a hospitable environment for humans, except at its grassy edges or by watercraft in its channels. Blinds set up in either of those situations will provide close-up access for viewing the birds. Floating blinds, particularly on small craft, carry the added benefit of mobility. They are easily maneuvered into optimum position, closer to the birds or to position the sun at your back rather than in your face. The position of the sun is a primary concern in this shimmering environment, where details of small birds can easily be blurred.

# Shorebirds and Relatives:
# Wilson's Snipe (*Gallinago delicata*)

AN ATYPICAL SHOREBIRD, Wilson's snipe prefers woody, marshy habitat to the shorelines of rivers and oceans that other sandpipers prefer. This bird is well known for its elaborate in-flight spring mating displays, but little is known about the species because they are difficult to locate.

**PHYSICAL CHARACTERISTICS**: The plumage of Wilson's snipe is a striking tapestry of browns, tans, white, and black. But in the bird's habitat, observers have little time to notice the pattern, as the snipe flushes quickly from cover, where the feather pattern blends in seamlessly with the forest floor. All that may be noticed is the orange-feathered tail.

Up close, the bird is awkward looking and plump, with a small head, large round eyes, and exceptionally long bill. The eyes, set far back on the side of the head, allow the bird to remain vigilant to any predators that may be attacking while it is digging for worms in the muddy banks of a marsh or stream. The bill probes the mud, using the sensory pits on its surface to detect movement of earthworms or other subterranean prey.

**RANGE**: The breeding range of Wilson's snipe in the Western Hemisphere extends throughout much of Canada and into the northern edges of the United States, notably northern New England. The bird winters in much of the rest of the United States, Central America, and northern South America. The Eurasian range extends throughout much of northern Europe and Asia, except northern Siberia, while the winter range extends as far south as central Africa.

**HABITAT**: The common snipe frequents bogs, marshes, fens, swamps, and streams, where it will wade in the water and probe in the mud for larvae, earthworms, and crustaceans.

The Wilson's snipe nests on the ground under cover of sedges or other swamp or streamside vegetation. It forms its nest of coarse and fine grasses in a shallow, scraped depression, where it lays usually four eggs.

**SONGS AND CALLS**: When flushed from cover, the Wilson's snipe will utter a rasping *scaap* call. During breeding season, the territorial and mating sound of the male snipe is not a call at all, but a winnowing sound made with the tail and wings during aerial displays.

**CONSERVATION STATUS**: The population of the Wilson's snipe is large in North America. The bird is commonly hunted.

Wilson's snipe (*Gallinago delicata*)

# North America: Cape May, New Jersey, United States

POSITIONED AT THE southernmost point of New Jersey, at the mouth of the Delaware River, Cape May is vital to migrating birds on the Eastern flyway, and birders know it. Almost 400 species have been recorded here. The dunes, fresh and saltwater marshes, meadows, ponds, and beaches of Cape May offer a wide diversity of habitats for migrating, breeding, and resident birds. As many as 100,000 individual warblers have been seen in a single morning, and hundreds of thousands of seabirds pass through each season. And, in an event unmatched around the world, an estimated one million shorebirds come in May to feed on the eggs of spawning horseshoe crabs on the beaches. The Cape May Bird Observatory assists birders on their hunts and offers programs and seminars.

**BIRDS TO SEE**: Birders flock here for spring and fall migrations, when they might see 22,000 raptors in a single day. Species include red-shouldered, broad-winged, Cooper's, and sharp-shinned hawks; American kestrel; peregrine falcon; merlin; bald eagle; and osprey. Shorebirds include red knot, ruddy turnstone, dunlin, sanderling, whimbrel, greater yellowlegs, black-bellied plover, and semipalmated sandpiper. Waterfowl including several species of duck and geese and the red-throated loon. Waders include great blue and little blue herons, great and snowy egrets, and glossy ibis. Migrating warblers like yellowthroat, black-and-white warbler, redstart, bluewinged warbler, ovenbird, and white-eyed vireo. Endangered piping plovers and least terns nest here as well.

# Can Spring Be Right around the Corner?

AH, THE FIRST ROBIN of late winter/early spring! What a comfort to know that the last lingering grip of winter is about to be broken. But is that what those orange-breasted birds really signify? As much as we might wish it, not all robins are the heralds of spring.

Although some robins migrate during the winter, many others do not. Numbers vary from year to year, depending on how harsh the winter weather and how scarce food is.

But some of them have stayed all along, living a nomadic lifestyle that occasionally brings them into view throughout the winter. They travel in flocks of a dozen all the way up to a couple thousand, seeking whatever fruit might still be available on trees and shrubs to substitute for their normally insect-centered diet. They'll also investigate every brushy woodland edge, thicket, and seep, where there might be some lingering insect life.

A similar thing can happen during a dry summer. Nearly all the robins may disappear from our lawns, as they flock together to roam damper spots in more heavily forested areas.

The birds that appear in our backyards in late winter also could be late migrants from northerly climes, forced to make a mini migration by advancing winter conditions.

For a true harbinger of spring, we need to wait for birds that truly did move south in the fall. When we spot *large* numbers of robins, consider that a sneak peak of spring.

# Evolution of Birds I: *Archaeopteryx*, from Lizard to Bird

THE CONCEPT OF EVOLUTION was hugely controversial in its day. In 1861, just two years after Darwin published his *On the Origin of Species*, a discovery was made in a German limestone quarry that would both bolster Darwin's hypothesis and add to the controversy his book had ignited. A birdlike dinosaur, complete with feathers, showed for the first time a definitive link between two distinct and once-thought unrelated groups of animals.

The first specimen of *Archaeopteryx lithographica*, dated to approximately 145 to 150 million years ago, was an incomplete fossil missing the head and most of the neck, but enough of the skeletal structure and feathers were preserved to make for interesting study. Subsequently discovered, more complete fossils found in the same quarry gave additional support to the claims of reptile ancestry for birds. *Archaeopteryx* clearly exhibits features that are both reptilian (small teeth; a long, bony tail; and three fingers with claws) and avian (feathers, wings, wishbone, and partially reversed first toe) in nature.

After many years of study and reconstruction, most scientists agreed that this creature was an ancestor of modern birds (although not a direct one; this was just one step on the way), capable of some form of flight. But it was the particular kind of flight that was hotly debated. Two camps formed. Some researchers believed that *Archaeopteryx* flew from above, alighting from trees or cliffs and gliding. Others posited that the bird was a ground dweller and flew from this vantage point, flapping its wings to attain short bursts of flight. Skeletal research seems to confirm the former theory, since the creatures were not capable of lifting their wings above their backs, a movement necessary for flapping, self-elevating flight.

More fossil finds are continuing to fill in some of the gaps in knowledge about *Archaeopteryx's* place in evolution. Late twentieth century discoveries in the Gobi Desert of feathered dinosaurs fill in some of the back story, suggesting that feathers may have evolved for warmth rather than flight, and that they later evolved to be used as flight aids.

Fossil of an *Archaeopteryx lithographica*

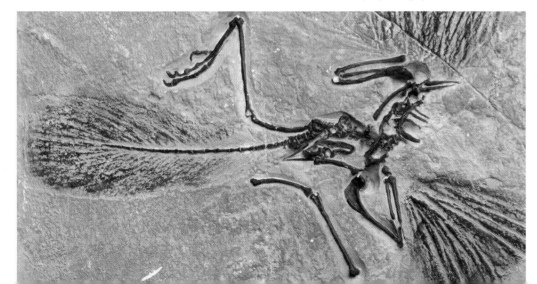

# Making Your Own Mini Pond

ALTHOUGH A WIDE VARIETY of heavy-duty, plastic mini ponds are available commercially, you can make your own simple mini pond at home easily and inexpensively.

Place a lid from a 30-gallon (114 L) trash can on a flat surface. Align a yardstick about 2" (5 cm) in from an edge and mark a straight cutting line. Now the circular lid has one flat edge.

Align the plastic lid from a 15-gallon (57 L) trash can with the cut edge of the large lid and mark the points on the edge of the smaller lid where it meets the cut-out area meets the edge of the smaller lid. Cut a similar straight edge along the side of the 15-gallon (57 L) lid, from one point that you just marked to the second. Keep the top of the lid beneath your cut attached to the lid.

Again align the cut edge of the smaller lid with the cut edge of the larger lid, slipping the part of the top of the smaller lid you kept attached under the larger lid. The pattern of the two lids should be a figure eight, with one loop of the eight smaller than the other. With the larger lid overlapping the small, attach the two with thermoplastic hot glue and heavy staples (the type applied with a carpenter's staple gun) through the larger lid into the smaller one beneath it.

Cut two sections of chicken wire fencing, one larger than each lid. Position the fence pieces over the two lids, with each section of fence overlapping the other lid just a bit. Press the fence down into the lids, allowing the edges to turn up along the sides of the lids. Connect the two pieces of fence where they overlap with wire, and press that as flat as you can.

Mix a batch of instant concrete—as much as it looks like it will take to fill the two lids—and pour it into the lids. Press it down into the lids and into the fence pieces, and mold it up along the sides of the two lids to form connected platelike bowls, with the centers about 1" (2.5 cm) deeper than the edge of the sides and the connection point about ½" (1.3 cm) deeper than the edge of the sides.

Cover the concrete mold with a sheet of plastic and let it cure for seven days, without touching it. At the end of that week, fill the mold with water to the brim and let it sit for another full day.

With the help of at least one other person, carefully carry the mold outside, near the spot you want to place your new mini pond, and even more carefully turn it over. Slowly and gently press down on the plastic lids to push out the concrete mini pond.

Carefully turn over the mini pond, move it into its final position, and settle it onto the surface of the soil. Fill the mini pond with water and wait for the birds to find it.

# New Hummingbird Opportunities

INCREASING NUMBERS of hummingbirds appear to be hanging around throughout the cold season rather than migrating to warmer climates. Some experts believe new wintering groups for some species of the tiny birds are developing new, closer migration destinations that future generations will be programmed to use.

Some regions are already treated to nearly a dozen different species on the pass-through portion of their migration flights. And hummer enthusiasts are now employing various techniques to encourage the birds to drop down temporarily from their high-altitude flights. Those techniques have ranged from maintaining large beds of plants that produce red flowers at just the right time of year, to spreading sheets of red plastic around their nectar feeders.

But in more recent years, those birders have found reason and reward to attempt attracting the hummers year-round, and wildlife agencies now recommend that it's a good idea to keep one feeder filled with nectar all year.

# Shorebirds and Relatives:
# Killdeer (*Charadrius vociferus*)

ONE OF THE MOST adaptable and widespread plovers in North America, the handsomely plumed killdeer can be found in a variety of habitats, not just near shorelines like other plovers. Killdeer are entertaining to watch, both on the ground where they run rapidly on long legs, stop suddenly and bob their heads, and run again, and in the air, where their long, narrow, pointed wings allow for rapid flight and tight maneuverability. If you live near killdeer, you'll know it, as they frequent mowed fields in parks, parking lots, and other open areas. Also, they call for long periods of time and even at night.

**PHYSICAL CHARACTERISTICS**: Like other ringed plovers, the killdeer (both male and female) has a brown back and upper wings, and a white underside. However, instead of a single black band running horizontally across its breast, the killdeer has two bands. A white collar and eyebrow break up the brown of the bird's head. The upper part of the tail is rufous in color, most visible in flight. Its narrow, black bill is useful for probing the ground and shorelines for insects.

**RANGE**: Due to human conversion of forestland to open habitats, such as farms, lawns, and parks, the killdeer's range expanded in North America during the twentieth century. The species breeds across nearly the entire continent, except far northern Canada and Alaska. The killdeer's winter range overlaps with the breeding range, beginning about halfway down the United States and extending through southern Mexico. Its exclusively wintering range includes the rest of Mexico, Central America, and northern and western South America.

**HABITAT**: The killdeer prefers open areas in both breeding and wintering ranges. These include everything from natural sites such as mud flats, sandbars, and meadows to human-created environments such as agricultural fields, athletic fields, golf courses, parking lots, and gravel rooftops. The bird hunts for its preferred prey, including earthworms, beetles, grasshoppers, crustaceans, and even small frogs in meadows and fields.

Killdeers make their nests on the ground with little cover, in cultivated fields, along roadsides, or even on rooftops. Sometimes the site is elevated, perhaps to protect against flooding and to provide a better view to see potential predators. The nest itself is a scrape in the ground, lined with white objects, such as rocks, bone, shell, and pieces of plaster and plastic, perhaps used as a method of camouflaging the eggs.

**SONGS AND CALLS**: The most common killdeer call is the onomatopoeic call, *killdeer*. This is used commonly in flight. Other calls include *dee*, *dee-dit*, and *seep*.

**CONSERVATION STATUS**: Although subject to the same threats as most other birds—pesticides, hunting (illegal), and collision with vehicles, buildings, and towers—the bird's range is quite large, as is its population.

Killdeer (*Charadrius vociferus*)

# North America: Point Pelee National Park, Ontario, Canada

BIRDERS ARE KNOWN to flock to natural funnels or points of land to view the concentration of species that naturally fly over them during migration. Most land-dwelling bird species tend to avoid open water during their twice-yearly long-distance movements as doing so provides few places for respite and also lacks *thermals*, or rising plumes of warm air that aid them in their flight.

One major location for such a collection of birds is Point Pelee National Park in the Canadian Province of Ontario. This spit of forested land jutting into Lake Erie was made into a national park in 1918 at the urging of birders and hunters. But it is not a well-kept secret; thousands of birders descend upon this rural part of Canada for the month of May to see an unparalleled collection of warblers, tanagers, and other songbirds on their way to their breeding grounds. All of these birds will be in their breeding plumage and perching in trees not yet flush with spring leaves. This provides an excellent opportunity for birders to compare and contrast the species, unobstructed by the late spring leaves.

**BIRDS TO SEE**: As many as thirty-nine species of warblers alone have been spotted at Point Pelee. The birds move through at different times of the month. Early May brings blackburnian, black-throated blue, Cape May, cerulean, chestnut-sided, common yellowthroat, golden-winged, magnolia, northern parula, orange-crowned, and perhaps even prairie and hooded warblers. Lincoln's sparrow, bobolink, gray-cheeked thrush, indigo bunting, and scarlet tanager are some of the other species making their appearance at this time. Mid- to late May brings bay-breasted, blackpoll, Connecticut, and Wilson's warblers, as well as other species such as alder flycatcher, ruddy turnstone, least bittern, sedge wren, and whimbrel. Hawks, ducks, and other species will appear throughout the month (and before and after).

# Was That a White Crow?

WHITE CROWS, which can be confusing because they are in such contrast with the natural coloring of the species, turn up every now and again, leading to a flurry of reports and discussion throughout the birding community.

According to Kevin McGowan, a scientist with the Cornell Lab of Ornithology in Ithaca, New York, who has been studying crows since 1988, about 1 percent of crow nestlings he bands each year have some white in their feathers and about 4 percent have white spots on other parts of their bodies. He said he spots about the same amount of variation in crows he observes in large foraging flocks.

That would mean completely white crows occur in far less than 1 percent of the population, and a truly albino crow is even rarer.

A partially white animal that normally is not white is not an example of partial albinism. Even a fully white crow is not necessarily an albino. Albinism includes other genetic results in addition to the white pigmentation, such as pink eyes.

# The Story of Eagle and Falcon

BIRDS OF PREY are important to many cultures worldwide, because of their hunting prowess, strength, and seeming fearlessness. Many cultures even worship them as gods or as major forces of nature. Australian aborigines show great respect for these birds, but they don't revere them as deities. The tribal structure of the aboriginal peoples is divided into moieties, or two-tribe divisions, in which each tribe is known by a totem, often a bird and sometimes a raptor. These people also often feature birds, as they do other animals, in stories that serve as important tribal lore and as guides for proper behavior.

One aboriginal story tells of two brothers, Eagle and Falcon, who hunted kangaroos together. After tracking some of these creatures to a cave, Eagle went in to scare them out, telling Falcon to wait at the entrance to catch any that escaped. But once inside the cave, Eagle became selfish and sent only the thin ones out, keeping the fat ones for himself. This angered Falcon, who set a fire at the mouth of the cave. When Eagle flew out, his feathers were scorched. This taught Eagle a lesson for being selfish. The aborigines say this is why the wedge-tailed eagle, a common species in Australia, has black feathers and why falcons often pester eagles, chasing them out of their territories.

# Accepting Squirrels

MOST PEOPLE WHO provide bird feeders in their backyards would prefer that squirrels leave their feeders to the birds. Many of those people could even be said to despise squirrels.

However, squirrels do not hold a similar enmity for those people who so loathe them.

As wild and natural creatures, squirrels are simply doing what comes naturally, seeking out and using the most accessible and abundant sources of food. In backyards stocked with bird feeders, those sources of food usually are the feeders.

So, the squirrels visit the feeders several times each day, often to the annoyance of the humans maintaining those feeders and paying for the seed in them. Short of very drastic measures, it's a situation that will continue as long as humans continue to fill feeders with seeds.

For those willing to accept the natural world, with all its upsides and downsides, and to adapt to the forces at play, diversion is often the simplest squirrel countermeasure.

Find an out-of-the-way spot in the backyard and maintain small piles of dried corn cobs there. The corn will attract the squirrels like a magnet, usually drawing most of their attention away from the feeders.

If you want to thwart the squirrels' attempts at carrying off the cobs of corn, try attaching them to stakes, permanent landscape features, trees, shrubs, and the like with heavy-gauge wire.

# Avoid Triggering Threat Avoidance

ALL LIVING THINGS "live" to avoid being captured, killed, and eaten. Species lower on the food chain, such as most songbirds, need to put most of their energy into risk avoidance.

Birds are on near-constant watch for any clues of an approaching predator. Sometimes that watch is a shared responsibility, such as in a mixed winter flock of chickadees, nuthatches, woodpeckers, and others, or in a flock of geese feeding in a field of grain. Some members of those flocks will always be on the alert, ready to spread alarm to everyone if a threat arises.

At other times, one bird will be the lone sentry, which can generate a nervous attitude in the bird and an increased preference for thicker cover.

A birdwatcher who knows how to avoid triggering the flight response in birds will have an edge: staying low; dressing in dull, muted tones; moving slowly; and keeping the noise down.

In addition to allowing the birdwatcher to see more birds, these techniques also will allow for viewing the birds while they are more relaxed and going about their business as usual.

# Shorebirds and Relatives: Eurasian Oystercatcher (*Haematopus ostralegus*)

THIS SPECIES OF oystercatcher is the national bird of the Faroe Islands, an autonomous province of Denmark. As a shorebird, it spends most of its time along the coast, and it pries open shelled animals with its long bill.

**PHYSICAL CHARACTERISTICS**: The bright red eyes and bill are common to many of the world's oystercatchers. The Eurasian species also has reddish legs. Plumage colors include a black head, breast, upper back, and tail, as well as a white underside, lower back and rump, and tail. The tail has a dark band at the edge.

**RANGE**: This bird has a wide range encompassing most of Europe and parts of Western and Central Asia, and also along the coast of East Asia. It is the only species of oystercatcher in this region, but four different races of the species are considered to be within its range.

**HABITAT**: Salt marshes, as well as sandy and shingle beaches on islands and along estuaries and large rivers, are the preferred breeding habitat. Prior to the early twentieth century, the species did not inhabit inland shores on large lakes, but it has since expanded its range to these habitats.

The Eurasian oystercatcher more often dines on many other species of mollusks other than oysters, as well as crustaceans, insects, and worms.

The species is a colonial nester; it nests in large groups of its kind, mostly on bare ground or within clumps of short grasses and sedges. It excavates a shallow scrape in the ground that it lines with random debris.

**SONGS AND CALLS**: Like other shorebirds, the Eurasian oystercatcher utters a loud piping call.

**CONSERVATION STATUS**: A wide range and large populations have kept the Eurasian oystercatcher off any threatened or endangered lists.

# North America: Aleutian Islands, Alaska, United States

THE ALEUTIAN ISLAND CHAIN stretches for 1,200 miles (1,900 km) from Alaska into the North Pacific Ocean. Much of the vegetation on the islands is grasses, herbs, and shrubs. Part of the chain is designated a unit of the Alaska Maritime National Wildlife Refuge, and for good reason: More than ten million seabirds nest on the island each year.

The Aleutians are clumped into four sets of islands: the Fox, Andreanof, Rat, and Near. Some of the islands are occupied by native Aleuts, where they run commercial fishing ports. Most people live on Unalaska, in the Fox group, closest to the mainland. Traveling on the islands is most easily done via the Alaskan Marine Highway System, a system of ferries that travel from as far south as Bellingham, Washington, to the Aleutians. Travelers can also fly by jet to Dutch Harbor on Unalaska Island, where a hotel offers accommodations.

**BIRDS TO SEE**: Kittiwakes, murres, murrelets, pigeon guillemots, auklets (seven species),

# Journaling for Insight and Memory

A BIRDING JOURNAL is a common tool for bird-watchers, and it is best started sooner rather than later in one's birding career. It's both a birder's long-term memory and the collected notes of a citizen scientist. Everything from the weather to the mood of the journal keeper to insights into bird behavior can be found in the pages of a well-kept journal.

Although great writing is not a requirement in a birding journal, honesty, time, and directed effort are. Even astute observation is not a requirement, but it's an ability that will develop over time through the simple process of keeping a journal.

Begin noting your experiences and observations in a notebook or journal as soon as possible and try to make entries on a regular basis: at a minimum, whenever you spend time watching birds. If you decide against making daily entries, you may eventually regret that later in your birding career.

Sketching the birds and their habitats is important, too. Fight your natural shyness over any perceived lack of drawing ability. Make your sketches as good as you can. Your ability will develop over time (and you will later cherish those first attempts). Use colored pencils to add key details to your sketches, too.

Don't fret over perceived "quality". Write anything and everything in your journal. As a beginner, you won't know which entries will be valuable later, and the simple act of recording daily observations will bring gradual and remarkable improvement.

Take your journal on all your outings. At home, keep it next to your favorite observation window, along with a working pen or pencil. That way, you'll always be ready to write.

# Mythical Birds: The Roc

THE ROC, OR RUKH, is an ancient mythological creature of immense proportions said to be able to carry off an elephant. The giant bird of prey appears in the legends of many cultures, from China to Europe (one researcher traced the story as far back as the second century C. E.), but the myth was certainly popularized in *The Arabian Nights* from the fifteenth century, and so it appears in many stories from Arabia and North Africa. Marco Polo describes how the bird would, after grabbing an elephant, carry it to a great height, drop it back to Earth, and then swoop down to feed upon the dead, broken body.

Many myths speak of sailors coming upon islands on which giant eggs are found. One of the Sinbad the Sailor stories from *The Arabian Nights* tells of how Sinbad was stranded on an island on which he discovered an immense egg.

Realizing that this must be from a giant bird, he hides himself beneath the egg. When the roc comes to sit on the egg, Sinbad attaches himself to the bird's leg in the hopes of being carried off the island. Instead, the roc travels to a diamond-filled ravine where the local inhabitants throw carcasses to attract the birds, as the natives themselves are unable to get to the diamonds because of numerous poisonous snakes. The birds carry off the diamond-studded carcasses to their nests, from which the natives can gather the diamonds.

Modern researchers have suggested that the myth of the roc grew from sailing expeditions to islands on which were discovered large, flightless birds never seen before, such as elephant birds from Madagascar. It is supposed that sailors thought these birds were the young of a much larger bird. Another supposition is that prehistoric large birds are the source of the legends.

Nineteenth-century illustration of Sinbad the Sailor in *Arabian Nights*

# Toys for Jays and Crows

MEMBERS OF THE crow family, such as crows, blue jays, and gray jays, are among the most intelligent of birds. That brain power gives them a natural curiosity that encompasses all small, shiny objects in their environment. They will investigate all such objects, often snatching them up and flying off to some special hiding place.

We can "play" with them by placing objects such as old beads, metal safety pins, shiny coins, small pieces of aluminum foil, bits of broken mirrors, and similar items in spots frequented by the birds, such as on the ground under our feeders. Then we just sit back, watch, and wait for the birds to appear. When they do, there will be a flurry of excited activity as the birds "steal" their newfound treasures.

Later, with binoculars in hand, we can stroll the woods and thickets, where the birds seemed to be secreting off to with the shiny baubles, and try to spot the beads, mirror bits, and such.

# Birds by Habitat: Coastal Habitats

AN ESTUARY IS A body of water where saltwater from the ocean and freshwater from a river (or rivers) come together. Estuaries provide a unique and sensitive environment, heavily used by a wide range of shorebirds, wading birds, and waterfowl.

Among the species commonly found in estuaries are the belted kingfisher, brant, Canada goose, canvasback, gadwall, great blue heron, green heron, herring gull, lesser yellowlegs, marsh wren, northern shoveler, osprey, red-breasted merganser, red-winged blackbird, ring-billed gull, ruddy turnstone, semipalmated plover, short-billed dowitcher, surf scoter, tree swallow, tundra swan, and yellow-rumped warbler.

Beaches, from dunes to simple flats of sand, are much more than great places for swimming. Among the species commonly spotted on beaches are American oystercatcher, black skimmer, boat-tailed grackle, Bonaparte's gull, common tern, fish crow, herring gull, horned lark, laughing gull, oldsquaw, peregrine falcon, piping plover, ring-billed gull, sanderling, semipalmated plover, spotted sandpiper, surf scoter, and white-winged scoter.

Rocky shorelines and cliffs along the shore commonly are home to Atlantic puffin, black-legged kittiwake, black scoter, common eider, double-crested cormorant, great black-backed gull, harlequin duck, herring gull, northern gannet, oldsquaw, razorbill, surf scoter, and white-winged scoter.

# Rails: Virginia Rail (*Rallus limicola*)

BECAUSE OF ITS SHY behavior and preference for marshy habitat, the Virginia rail is rarely seen and little studied. Although classified as a game bird species, this wetland bird is rarely hunted.

**PHYSICAL CHARACTERISTICS**: Virginia rails are somewhat fowl-like in appearance, with large feet and a stout body. However, the structure of the body has evolved with its habitat, resulting in large feet for walking on wetland vegetation mats and a compressed body (side to side) for easily slipping between plant stalks. Their long bill is their hunting tool, used to probe the mud.

The plumage of this rail helps it to blend with its surroundings. A black-and-brown streaked back sits above chestnut-colored wings and a rust-colored neck. A bright red pair of eyes is set in gray cheeks. Males and females have the same plumage.

**RANGE**: During breeding season, the Virginia rail makes its home in the northern tier of the United States, as far south as Virginia in the east and southern California in the west. The winter range for this species includes coastal southeastern U.S. states, southern Arizona, and northern Mexico.

**HABITAT**: Freshwater marshes are the Virginia rail's habitat of choice, with key elements being shallow water; dense, low vegetation for cover; and plenty of prey. They probe mud flats and shallows with their long, narrow bill, picking out insects and their larvae, spiders, snails, fish, slugs, and worms.

Virginia rails build their nests very close to water in dense wetland vegetation such as cattails, and they use these plants for their nest materials. They also bend overhanging tall plants to make a canopy over the nest for additional cover.

**SONGS AND CALLS**: The most commonly heard call of the Virginia rail is the grunt, given by a mating pair during courtship. Among other calls is a *kid-dik* sound made by males in spring.

**CONSERVATION STATUS**: Like other wetland species, the Virginia rail has experienced a dramatic loss of habitat over time, but researchers now consider the current population stable.

Virginia rail (*Rallus limicola*)

# North America: Alaska Chilkat Bald Eagle Preserve, Haines, Alaska, United States

NOWHERE ELSE IN North America can a birder be treated to such large numbers of the amazing bald eagle than at Alaska's Chilkat Bald Eagle Preserve. The preserve protects the habitat necessary to maintain populations of salmon and the bald eagles that feed on them.

Geology, geography, hydrology, and biology come together to create the unique conditions that bring the eagles here in numbers exceeding 3,000 from October through February. The glacial meltwater that pours into the Tsirku, Kleheni, and Chilkat rivers from spring through autumn collects at the rivers' confluence, forming a reservoir that maintains a temperature above freezing throughout the winter as it drains into the downstream reaches of the Chilkat River, keeping that water body open as well. The salmon that spawn in these waters from summer through early winter eventually die after completing their mating task. The open water allows the congregating eagles to easily access the dead fish, a favorite food source for the species.

**BIRDS TO SEE**: Some 200 to 400 bald eagles make their home in the Chilkat Valley year-round. However, most people come here for the congregations, and the town of Haines holds the annual Bald Eagle Festival in November to celebrate this event. In addition to the eagles, about 260 species of other birds have been recorded in the Chilkat Valley. Birds likely to be seen during a visit for the congregation include rock ptarmigan, blue grouse, green-winged teal, greater and lesser scaup, surf and white-winged scoter, harlequin duck, old squaw, common and red-breasted mergansers, common loon, marbled murrelet, American wigeon, great blue heron, mew and herring gulls, sharp-shinned hawk, and great horned owl, among others.

Bald eagles at Chillkat Bald Eagle Preserve

# The Question of Feeding Year-Round

"SHOULD I KEEP my bird feeders filled year-round?" asks every backyard birder eventually. Not only can maintaining a daily supply of seeds become pricey, but there's also the concern that a year-round food supply might impact birds' natural patterns. In addition, many wildlife agencies now encourage wildlife enthusiasts, particularly those living in areas where backyard feeding activities might lead to conflict with wildlife, to temporarily discontinue their feeding activities and even remove their feeders at especially critical times of the year.

However, the more food we provide, the closer (and longer) the birds will stay near abundant food sources. Feeding in spring and summer can encourage the birds to reveal territorial and mating activities that do not occur in fall and winter. In addition, spring and summer is the time of bright mating colors for many bird species. And spring and summer are the seasons when most birds are producing and tending to their young, activities many species will bring into our backyards with even slight encouragement.

In general, extending the feeding season, even to year-round, will not cause healthy birds to change their natural activities, such as the timing of migration. They will continue to follow nature's clock and maintain their normal seasonal schedule. Only sick, injured, old, or genetically inferior individuals will alter their seasonal plans because of a food source.

# The History of Birdwatching

BIRDWATCHING HAS ITS roots in the common, human act of collecting. People began gathering eggs and harvesting bird skins for collections in the late 1700s. Unfortunately, this meant most birds didn't survive mankind's latest pastime.

Birdwatching for the simple enjoyment of the task came about after the public became more concerned about the rapid decline in bird numbers, and legal efforts were made to offer birds protection. The rise of citizens' groups aligned with these efforts also helped popularize the activity.

Technology also played a key role in the rise of birdwatching. As portable optics were invented and made widely available, this sent more people out into the field to observe nature. Opera glasses were the first easily obtainable device, and the first field guide produced, *Birds through an Opera Glass* by Florence Bailey, was published in 1889.

By the early 1900s, with increasingly improving optics and widely available cameras and bird guides, all that the burgeoning population of bird seekers needed was a way to get around to see more species. This came, of course, in the form of the automobile, which enabled birders to easily travel outside their local area to start collecting bird sightings, adding them to life lists. The people who practice this form of birding are now called *twitchers*.

# Doing Our Part

ALTHOUGH MOST other outdoor enthusiasts buy licenses and pay fees to engage in their pastimes, and some birding venues are beginning to charge, birdwatchers largely have a free activity with free access to lands bought and maintained by other outdoor groups, often those accursed hunters and fishermen. In some places, taxes fund some of the much-needed work to preserve and improve our natural world. But across most of the birding landscape, we are taking a free ride.

We need to change that. Like hunters and anglers did decades ago, we birders need to ask our elected officials to tax the gear and accoutrements of birdwatching and to commit the tax revenue to conservation work. The governments should add a license structure to our activities and commit revenues from sales of those licenses to conservation work.

It's only fair, if we want to continue to call ourselves conservationists. And it's a matter of expediency if we want to keep unspoiled natural landscape available for birdwatching.

And until we have those taxes and licenses in place, we need to find other, real ways to make our contributions. Most wildlife agencies, who rely heavily on the sales of hunting, fishing, and boating licenses for support, now offer alternative routes for others to make contributions. Anyone truly committed to our natural world must step up to these needs and donate at least as much as our hunting and fishing counterparts are paying each year for their licenses.

We can no longer hide behind the misconception that birders are not consumers. The mere act of setting foot onto any natural landscape anywhere means you are consuming.

# Birdwatching from Your Vehicle

Most wild things, including most birds, do not recognize a motor vehicle as a threat until it moves. A parked vehicle, particularly with the motor off, becomes another part of the landscape to birds.

Because of this, a parked motor vehicle can make a wonderful blind, particularly if the vehicle can be maneuvered close to prime habitat. And on a hot and buggy day, a motor vehicle certainly offers extra amenities, such as shelter.

However, remember that a motor vehicle has windows. Tinted or not, windows allow views both out of and into the vehicle. Even inside a vehicle, it's best to keep movement to a minimum.

In addition, vehicles are not completely sound-proof. Noise from inside the car will travel to the outside, muted to some extent but still loud enough to be heard outside and to possibly alert the birds there. Even with the windows rolled up tightly, the radio should be off.

Of course, most of us will not want the windows rolled up tightly. The calls and songs of the birds and their environment are an integral part of the birdwatching experience. That increases the importance of keeping movement and noise to a minimum.

# Raptors: Andean Condor (*Vultur gryphus*)

WITH A WINGSPAN of more than 9' (2.7 m), the Andean condor is the largest and heaviest raptor in the Western Hemisphere. This majestic bird formerly commanded the skies in its native range in the Andes Mountains of South America. The bird's population has reached historic lows, but a breeding program has successfully raised new individuals. The San Diego Zoo (in California) coordinates the captive breeding of the raptor, to ensure consistency across all breeding locations and increase the likelihood of successful releases back into the wild, of which there have been sixty-five since 1990.

**PHYSICAL CHARACTERISTICS**: This immense raptor is unmistakable for any other bird. Other than its sheer size, diagnostic features include the plumage patterns of white wings against a black body, white collar of fine feathers at the base of the neck, unfeathered purple-red head, and, on the males, a large comb on the top of the head. Females lack the comb and are smaller than the males, a characteristic atypical of raptors.

**RANGE**: Confined to South America, the Andean condor's historic range included the Andean Mountains from Venezuela south to the Tierra del Fuego.

**HABITAT**: Cliffs serve as roosting and nesting sites for the Andean condor, and the open country above the tree line and, in some places, down to the coast, serves as hunting grounds. This open country is necessary for a bird of this size to be able to soar. Its large wings enable it to effortlessly ride the plumes of hot air, called thermals, which rise off the desert and bare mountainsides.

As a vulture, this condor feeds primarily on carrion, such as dead cattle and guanacos; the raptor will also visit seabird colonies and prey upon the eggs and nestlings.

**SONGS AND CALLS**: Males utter a *tok-tok-tok* call with open mouth while displaying for the female during courtship.

**CONSERVATION STATUS**: Hitting historically low population levels by the 1990s due to persecution by humans (shooting, poisoning), the Andean condor is now part of an active breeding program at zoos in the United States and Colombia. Numbers in the wild are only about a few thousand birds, at most.

Andean condor (*Vultur gryphus*)

# North America: Chiricahua Mountains, Arizona, United States

JUST SAY THE WORDS *elegant trogon* to a birder and he or she will usually begin to salivate. This rare, colorful bird is just one of the many jewels to be found in Arizona's Chiricahua Mountains. Tucked into the southeastern corner of the state a few miles from the New Mexico border and about 35 miles (56 km) north of Mexico, the Chiricahuas are a mecca to many birders. This range in habitat zones, from desert plains to mountaintops more than 9,000' (2,750 m) in elevation, as well as the location of the mountains along a major migratory flyway, are what prompt such a diverse array of birds—as many as 300 species throughout the year. Although many species can be seen year-round, birders often come between July and September, when the annual rains cause a flush of greenery and flowers, prompting more activity.

The area is remote, but enough amenities are nearby to make it a comfortable trip, with a bit of driving (campsites are also available). In addition, the American Museum of Natural History maintains a research station that offers cabin lodging and meals on a limited basis as part of birding tour packages with experienced guides.

Birders often head straight for Cave Creek Canyon, a rugged, beautiful area rich in species. Don't be surprised if a hummingbird alights on your brightly colored backpack in the parking area. Thirteen species of these much-sought-after diminutive birds can be found in the area, including some usually seen only in Mexico, such as the magnificent hummingbird.

One of the more accessible sites in the region is the Chiricahua National Monument, a park with stunning, natural volcanic rock formations of pinnacles and spires. Visitors can drive the 8-mile (12.9 km) scenic road up to Massai Point or hike the many trails, some remote and rugged, that wind through the canyons and rock formations.

**BIRDS TO SEE**: Many birders flock to the Chiricahuas to see Mexican species not normally found in the United States, such as the Mexican chickadee. Some of the hummingbird species seen here include rufous, Anna's, black-chinned, broad-tailed, Lucifer, violet-crowned, Allen's, and calliope. Strickland's woodpecker, hepatic tanager, and Juniper titmouse can be found in canyon bottoms, while painted whitestart and whiskered screech owl can be found in the forests. In the higher elevation conifer forests, birders may find western scrub jay, northern pygmy owl, pygmy nuthatch, and band-tailed pigeon. Chiricahua National Monument, on the west side of the mountain range, is home to the zone-tailed hawk and golden eagle.

# A More Advanced Brush Pile Design

A BRUSH PILE seems like such a simple thing. Just toss all the shrub and tree trimmings from a backyard onto the same pile, and over time a brush pile will have formed.

Although that's true and may even result in a perfectly serviceable brush pile—from the perspective of the birds and other critters, anyway—a more planned approach will result in a brush pile capable of better serving a much wider range of wild things.

The planned brush pile begins with five or six logs, each at least 5' (1.5 m) long and 6" (15.2 cm) in diameter, placed parallel to one another at about 1' (30.5 cm) intervals across a spot of relatively flat ground in an out-of-the-way location in the backyard. (This often means a spot that won't pose an aesthetic problem for the neighbors.)

The next layer up, on top of the initial log layer, should comprise something such as fresh-cut evergreen boughs, thick and tangled vines, or dense weeds, piled at least 6" (15.2 cm) deep and topped with a second layer of logs, laid perpendicular to the first log layer. That same layering should be repeated for another two layers, and then the whole affair should be secured in place with ropes across the topmost layer, and pulled tightly down to stakes in the ground at the sides of the brush pile.

Building with such solidly constructed initial layers provides a foundation for a brush pile that will last and grow for many years. On top of and around those initial layers, the lawn and garden trimmings of many years to come can be added to considerable depths and the brush pile will remain solid, thanks to that initial foundation.

Beyond providing a rock-solid foundation, those initial layers of logs create and maintain over the long term ample spaces, tunnels, and escape routes for all sorts of birds at various levels of the brush pile.

# Mythical Birds: The Halcyon Bird

THE KINGFISHER IS AN odd duck, or rather, odd bird, with its long, heavy bill seemingly out of proportion to its smallish stout body. The various taxonomic families come in an array of colorful species, and most of these birds are known to nest in the ground, usually on slopes near waterways, their hunting territories.

But how the ancient Greeks chose this bird to be the symbol of calm weather in December is a mystery. The bird represented that time around the winter solstice—seven days before until seven days after—when calmer weather was believed to have occurred, otherwise known as *halcyon days*. (*Halcyon* is also the name of one genus of kingfishers.) The kingfisher may have served as the inspiration for the myth, but it has clearly been given attributes beyond its natural habits and abilities.

In the legend, Alcyone, daughter of Aeolus, god of winds, married Ceyx, the king of Thessaly. After his brother dies, the grief-stricken Ceyx undertakes an ocean voyage to visit an oracle for guidance. His ship is destroyed at sea and his body washes up on shore at Alcyone's feet. In despondence, Alcyone throws herself into the sea. Taking pity on her, the gods lift her and Ceyx into the air and transform them into birds.

The halcyon birds are said to mate each year at the beginning of winter and brood their eggs on a floating nest of fish bones on the sea. Aeolus calms the water for this period, the halcyon days, to keep his daughter safe.

# For Hummers, Match Their Natural Food

HUMMINGBIRDS CARRY as much interest for many birders as any avian species. The attraction of the tiny jewels of the air into the backyard is nearly a universal concern.

However, many hummer enthusiasts are surprised to learn that their arrays of nectar feeders do not meet the dietary requirements of the hummingbirds visiting those feeders.

Although it's true that the sugary portion of the tiny birds' diet is essential for any creature with such a high metabolism, it's equally true that hummingbirds include a great deal of insect life in their daily intake for the protein in the bugs.

That still allows for our hummingbird feeders to play an important part in the lives of these tiny birds.

## Recipe: Hummingbird Nectar

THE OPTIMUM FORMULA for hummingbird nectar is four parts water to one part sugar. That will closely approximate the nectar of wildflowers, the natural source of sugar for the birds, which is generally 20 percent to 24 percent sucrose.

You will need:
- Table sugar
- Water
- Saucepan
- Wooden spoon

Mix one part regular, white, table sugar with four parts water in a saucepan. Do not use honey, molasses, brown sugar, or any other sweetener. It must be white table sugar.

Bring the mixture slowly to a boil on a stovetop burner, stirring constantly. Remove it from the heat as soon as it reaches boiling and the sugar is dissolved.

Do not boil the mixture beyond that point, because continued boiling will bring more concentration to the mixture and move it beyond the optimum 20 to 24 percent sugar level.

Boiling removes chemicals, mold, and any other contaminants that might be in the water. (If the goal was to dissolve the sugar, that could be achieved by simply stirring the mixture aggressively.)

Allow the mixture to cool completely before using.

To save time and energy, prepare double, triple, or even larger amounts of hummingbird nectar at the same time and save the extra for future use. Empty, clean 2-liter soda bottles make excellent containers for the sugar water, which needs to be refrigerated if it's being stored for subsequent fillings of the feeders.

# Part of the Crowd

IN PRIME WILDLIFE watching areas, visitors soon learn to use other visitors as a key indicator of something worth watching. Anywhere one vehicle has pulled along the side of the road warrants a close look by the next vehicle, and then the next vehicle, until a traffic jam of rubberneckers has formed.

In many of the top wildlife viewing areas around the world, the crowds usually form around big, charismatic animals, such as bison, moose, or even bigger animals like rhinos and elephants.

In spots more noted for their birdwatching, such as many of the points explored on Wednesdays in this book, groups of visitors more likely indicate some great bird sightings. When you spot them, join in, but don't crowd too closely on the birdwatchers who originally made the find, and do go out of your way to avoid doing anything that would spook the birds that have attracted all the attention.

In the interest of fairness of all, keep any negative reactions to yourself when other birdwatchers seek to join in a sighting that was yours originally. There's usually plenty for everyone to see.

# Wading Birds: Wood Stork
## (*Mycteria americana*)

A SYMBOL OF THE Everglades (see page 62), the wood stork is truly one of North America's most unique birds.

**PHYSICAL CHARACTERISTICS**: Standing approximately 3' (1 m) tall and with a wingspan of about 5' (1.5 m), the wood stork is a wading bird with all-white feathers except for its black wings and tail. The bird is also distinguishable by its bare head and upper neck of dark gray to black skin with large black bill.

**RANGE**: Relegated to wetland habitats in Florida, Georgia, and South Carolina, these birds also breed along the Yucatan Peninsula of Mexico and Central America. The stork is also resident in large portions of South America east of the Andes, from the Amazon Basin south through Brazil along the Atlantic coast.

**HABITAT**: The wood stork exhibits its densest populations in the swamps of the Everglades, where freshwater and estuarine habitats and concentrations of fish and other aquatic creatures during the dry season allow for groups of the birds to feed together. Wood storks feed by feel, waving their bills in the water until they touch prey, usually fish.

Nests are made from sticks in trees, usually in or near enough to wetlands for the trees to be surrounded by water during peak levels, when breeding occurs; this provides an added layer of protection to the nest.

**SONGS AND CALLS**: Adults generally make no sounds, but the young may utter a nasal barking call.

**CONSERVATION STATUS**: The population of the wood stork has declined significantly due to draining of wetland habitats and alteration of aquatic systems in Florida, where historic breeding colonies have collapsed. The bird has become an indicator species of ecosystem health in the Everglades and other wetlands of Florida. Ecologists recommend restoration of water flows on a large scale in Florida, which is currently being worked out amid much political difficulties. The wood stork is currently listed as endangered in the United States.

*115*

Wood stork (*Mycteria americana*)

# North America: Southwestern Idaho, United States

BIRDWATCHERS ENTRANCED by raptors usually have to content themselves with spring and fall migration to see a variety of species in large numbers. Although hosting nowhere near that quantity of birds, the Morley Nelson Snake River Birds of Prey National Conservation Area, spread out over 600,000 acres (2,428 square km) in southwestern Idaho, boasts more species in a concentrated area than anywhere else in North America and perhaps the world. The habitat here is precisely what these birds need to raise young, evidenced by the sixteen species that breed here. Eight more species can be found during winter and migration time. The cliffs gouged out by glacial Lake Bonneville provide ideal nesting sites for the 800 nesting raptor pairs, and the abundance of prey (ground squirrels, jackrabbits, pocket gophers, mice, and kangaroo rats) in the grasslands and sagebrush on the plains offers excellent nourishment.

This stunning assemblage of birds of prey and the need for their protection prompted much research and ultimately federal protection for the area. Other facilities have also sprung up, namely, the Peregrine Fund's World Center for Birds of Prey in Boise, just north of the Conservation Area. This facility is the center of research and advocacy for the Peregrine Fund, founded in 1970 and dedicated to understanding and conserving birds of prey. The Velma Morrison Interpretive Center welcomes visitors with raptor demonstrations and captive animal display areas.

**BIRDS TO SEE**: The best time to visit the area is between mid-March and June, which is prime breeding time for most birds. North America's only endemic falcon, the prairie falcon, can be found here in its densest concentrations of nesting pairs, where it feeds on its preferred prey, the Piute ground squirrel. Also resident is the ferruginous hawk, a species of western grasslands and sagebrush whose populations are heavily dependent on the fluctuations of the populations of its prey. Other resident species include American kestrel, red-tailed hawk, Swainson's hawk, northern harrier, osprey, turkey vulture, golden eagle, and seven species of owls (barn, burrowing, great horned, northern saw-whet, short-eared, long-eared, and western screech). Wintering species include merlin, peregrine falcon, Cooper's hawk, sharp-shinned hawk, rough-legged hawk, gyrfalcon, northern goshawk, and bald eagle.

# Crash-Test Birdies

WHEN A BIRD CRASHES into a window, human witnesses to the incident often are more stunned than the bird. If it hasn't been injured, it likely will shake it off, sit still for a bit, and then go about its routine.

For those in-between cases in which the bird can't immediately recover its faculties, a helping hand is best applied by moving the bird to a sheltered spot, out of the elements, and then allowing the bird time to recover on its own. If the bird has not recovered in an hour, place a call to a local wildlife rehabilitator.

If the worst-case scenario plays out and the bird dies from the collision with the glass, the birdwatcher should be aware that it is illegal for him or her to possess any portion of a protected bird—all species of birds that are not hunted, are not house sparrows, and are not European starlings are protected. Not even a single feather of a protected bird may be possessed by anyone who does not hold a special permit.

Technically, it's illegal for a nonpermitted person to even move the dead bird into the garbage can. However, most of us simply move the bird to an out-of-the-way spot and allow it to become food for other wild things.

# Pioneers in Bird Conservation:
# Roger Tory Peterson

EVEN PEOPLE WHO know little of birds usually have heard of Roger Tory Peterson. Credited as the creator of the modern field guide, Peterson's interest in birds and art was the perfect combination for him to create the first truly portable guide, *A Field Guide to the Birds*, in 1934. Departing from the typical bird books, which focused on evolutionary relationships, Peterson's guide focused on the visual similarities, making birdwatching much more accessible to the general public. Although considered a risk by many publishers, the book sold out its first printing of 2,000 copies in a single week. After more than five editions, seven million copies sold, and seven decades in print, the book is still the number one go-to guide for birders.

Born in 1908, Roger Tory Peterson was turned on to birds by his seventh grade teacher. He began sketching the birds as an aid in identification, and this pointed him toward studies in art. He created richly detailed paintings of birds and began showing them alongside some of the greatest wildlife painters of the day, including Louis Agassiz Fuertes (see Day 271), Peterson's idol.

He began sharing his passion for birds as a teacher himself, and continued for the rest of his life, creating other field guides collected in the Peterson Field Guide series. Widely recognized as one of the most important figures in the history of conservation, Peterson went on to inspire millions of people with his art, field guides, and teaching. No single person has done more for natural history education.

# Objects in Window May Be More Solid Than They Appear

WINDOWS ARE A difficult concept for birds. Panes of glass appear to be either passage-ways to be flown through or, if they reflect the bird's image, a rival to be attacked and battled. Either way, it's not a formula for a happy ending. If it's lucky, after its encounter with a window a bird will be able to shake off the near concussion and fly off with minimal damage.

The first step to make your windows safer for birds is to gain the birds' perspective on those windows. That means looking at and through the windows from the outside into the home, from the area frequented by the birds. Any window through which another, opposite window can be seen could appear to be an open flyway to birds. Any window that shows you a reflection also is likely to reflect images to birds.

Possible solutions to bird-hazardous windows range from the very simple and easy to the relatively time- and labor-intensive.

- Draw a curtain to eliminate the through-house view that appears to be a passageway.

- Suspend strips of paper, ribbons, yarn, or similar strands in front of the window, on the outside.

- Attach a silhouette decal of a hawk in flight to the glass of the window.

- Relocate things such as feeders and bird baths that are attracting birds into the danger zone to take away the direct angle that is causing the birds to see the window as a passageway or an adversary.

- Plant a tree, shrub, or vine in a spot that will remove the appearance of the open window or the reflections of the birds in the window.

# Electronic Call of the Wild

Most birds have very little resistance to the calls of others of their own kind. They spend a great deal of their daily energies responding to those calls, even more during the mating season. The birds are genetically programmed to respond.

That's why bird calls are so effective in bringing birds into easy viewing distance. And electronic calls—today ranging from cassette tapes to MP3s, but not too long ago also including portable record players and 45s—generally produce a much more authentic call time after time than can a human using a manual call or his or her own vocal abilities.

The birds' readiness to respond to calls lies at the heart of an ongoing debate among birdwatchers. Some believe the calls are so powerful and distracting to the birds that they divert the birds' attention from the more critical tasks of their daily lives, particularly during the mating and nesting season. The birds do seem to respond to calls at a heightened level of excitement during times of the year when they are defending their territory.

Calls may distract birds so much that we may want to avoid calls during those already stressful periods. However, outside the breeding and nesting season, birds seem to respond more with inquisitiveness than in an excited challenge. Calls used at those times likely waste far less energy for the birds.

Some people rebel at even that use of calls, particularly the highly effective electronic calls. They argue that causing birds to divert even slightly from their normal routine can stress them and expose them to increased danger from predators.

Outside that period of mating and nesting, over which there is much agreement against the use of calls, it's a personal judgment call for every birdwatcher to make for him- or herself.

There's another instance in which electronic calls can prove useful to the birdwatcher. When we discontinue our backyard feeding programs, for reasons ranging from end of season to thwarting the spread of disease among the congregating birds, calls can reduce the amount of time it takes for the birds to begin using the feeders again when the feeding program is restarted. Blast a mix of common bird calls out across the feeders and that natural curiosity and call response will soon bring the most exploratory of birds to the feeders. And they soon will be followed by others. As the birds gather they will discover the seed-filled feeders, and the feeding area's reputation will be made.

# Cormorants: Double-Crested Cormorant (*Phalacrocorax auritus*)

MANY PEOPLE ARE likely familiar with the double-crested cormorant, if not by name then at least by sight. These birds form colonies, especially along the coast where they can be seen on rocks in bays. They swim low in the water, diving suddenly to snatch food.

**PHYSICAL CHARACTERISTICS**: The most prominent feature on this overall dark-colored bird is the bright orange *gular pouch*, a flap of skin at the base of the bill that can expand when filled with food. During breeding season, two white crests, one on either side of the head above the eyes, may be visible. A dull green or bronze gloss may be visible on the plumage.

**RANGE**: The double-crested cormorant has a widely distributed but somewhat dispersed population across North America. There are distinct populations in coastal Alaska, along the Pacific Coast, the interior of the United States and Canada, the Atlantic Coast from Newfoundland to the Mid-Atlantic States, and Florida and some of the Caribbean islands. The species winters in the southeast and along the Gulf Coast, with some resident along the California Coast.

**HABITAT**: This cormorant species is not too picky about its habitat; as long as there are fish to eat and perches to rest on, they're good to go. They will live near ponds, lakes, large rivers, reservoirs, and coastlines. They are never seen far from shore.

The large mouth and gular pouch of the double-crested cormorant allows it to eat fish up to 16" (40 cm) in length, but normally around 6" (15 cm). They hunt by diving and swimming after prey, aided by their webbed feet, and they will even hunt in flocks.

Nests are a motley collection of materials picked up as flotsam in the water or on land. Items include sticks, plastic, seaweed, rocks, rope, fishnets, and even parts of dead birds. These nests are constructed on the ground, on cliffs, in trees, or on platforms, abandoned docks, or electrical transmission towers.

**SONGS AND CALLS**: Not known for its voice, the double-crested cormorant's only call is a guttural grunt.

**CONSERVATION STATUS**: Populations of this bird have expanded considerably since its decline in the mid-twentieth century due to pesticides. The birds have also long run afoul of commercial fishermen, who believe the birds are competing with them for fish. Cormorants have been killed and nests destroyed because of this, but hard evidence that cormorants negatively impact commercial fish stocks has not been gathered. Expansion of aquaculture sites has provided the birds with more habitats, much to the fish-raising companies' dismay.

Double-crested cormorant (*Phalacrocorax auritus*)

# North America: Point Reyes National Seashore, California, United States

SEVENTY-THOUSAND acres (283 square km) of open space within sight of the Golden Gate Bridge await nature lovers and especially birders. With more than 450 species recorded there, Point Reyes National Seashore is a must-see location for birders, with a special draw being vagrants carried by ocean storms to the point. The mix of habitats (coastline, tidal and intertidal zones, grasslands, scrub, sea cliffs, and forest), as well as the Mediterranean climate and the shape of the land, with its point jutting out into the sea, are what fosters the rich diversity of birds. Visitors can stay in the nearby quaint town of Point Reyes Station. The Point Reyes Bird Observatory was founded to study this rich avifauna, and travelers can stop by its visitor center to learn about the local species, observe a mist-netting demonstration, or tour the center's nature trail.

**BIRDS TO SEE**: The seashore provides various habitats to see and trails to study them. Seabirds found along Lighthouse Rocks and nearby cliffs include common murres, pigeon guillemots, pelagic and Brandt's cormorants, black oystercatchers, surf scoters, and loons. Tufted puffins are occasionally seen in spring and summer. Abbots and Bolinas lagoons are good sites for winter ducks, cormorants, pelicans, kingfishers, and raptors, such as the black-shouldered kite. The western snowy plover, a threatened species, nests on the beaches. The forested trails of Bear Valley attract a wide variety of songbirds, including sparrows, warblers, wrens, hummingbirds, thrushes, kinglets, acorn and pileated woodpeckers, and owls. Ponds attract great blue heron, green-backed heron, great egret, ring-necked duck, hooded merganser, grebes, and loons.

Seagulls at Point Reyes, California

# Little Orphan Birdie?

ABANDONED BABY BIRDS are much rarer than most of us assume. If there's no dead adult of the same species, or parts of a dead adult of the same species (such as scattered feathers), nearby, a parent bird likely is nearby and waiting for the opportunity to return to its baby. If the baby bird is not cold or wet to the touch, or limp in its posture, it's in no immediate danger of dying.

Although it runs counter to our inclination to exhibit compassion for small, helpless things, the best approach to a foundling is generally to be hands-off, at least for starters. If the baby bird is under no immediate threat from predators or the elements, leave it where you found it and check on it every few minutes, from a discreet spot that will not spook any parent birds attempting to return to the baby. If the young bird's condition doesn't appear to deteriorate, you can continue this observation for several hours before any more active intervention is warranted.

However, if there is a threat from predators or the elements, or no parent bird surfaces after several hours, stage two may be justified. Stage two is an effort to locate the nest from which the baby bird fell. While someone maintains a protective surveillance over the baby, someone else searches nearby trees and shrubs for the nest. If the nest is found, the baby can be returned to it. Handling the young will not cause the parents to reject it.

Stage three comes into play after surveillance and efforts to locate the nest have both failed. Create a substitute nest from a small plastic container, such as a berry carton from the grocery store. Pack the carton with tissues and attach it securely to the highest crook of a tree that you can reach and that is under cover of an overhanging, higher branch that will shelter the "nest" from the sun, rain, and other elements. Wire it in place there and gently move the baby bird into it. An additional period of protective surveillance must follow until a parent bird is observed tending to the baby. The wait might go on throughout the rest of the day.

The final stage is protective custody, in which the baby is removed from the wild and cared for by human foster parents. Most of us should never assume this responsibility, which requires much more constant attention than most can manage. The local wildlife rehabilitator is the person equipped and licensed to care for such foundlings. The baby bird's chance of survival and successful return to the wild lies with such a trained professional.

> **> Tip**
>
> It's a myth that brief handling of the young by humans will cause the parent birds to reject them. Birds do not rely on their sense of smell like mammalian parents.

# The Survival of the Ivory-Billed Woodpecker

UNTIL LONE KAYAKER Gene Sparling thought he spotted one in 2004, the ivory-billed woodpecker was considered extinct since the early 1900s as the result of extensive logging of the rich bottomland hardwood forests that were the bird's home (in the southeastern United States). After seeing postings about the sighting online, two researchers interviewed Sparling and thought his account was convincing enough to ask him to take them back with him to the Cache River National Wildlife Refuge in Arkansas where he claimed to have seen the bird. On this trip, the group also spotted what they thought was an ivory-billed woodpecker.

These sightings prompted the Cornell Lab of Ornithology in Ithaca, New York, to launch a major search operation, kept quiet to the public until they had what they felt to be incontrovertible evidence of the ivory-billed woodpecker's presence.

The search resulted in several additional sightings, audio recordings made of the bird's drumming, and a four-second video taken of one sighting, all revealed in 2005. The video has spawned intense controversy as many people feel that the resolution is not great enough for definitive identification. Others have stated that the bird in the video is clearly a pileated woodpecker, another large North American species with similar markings. Currently, no true hard evidence, such as clear photographs, bird droppings, or a feather usable for DNA analysis, has been obtained.

A substantial reward has been offered to anyone who can lead Cornell's researchers to a confirmed sighting of the bird.

An 1829 engraving of the ivory-billed woodpecker, from *Birds of America* in the collection of the Victoria & Albert Museum, London, UK

 # Any Color Is Fine, So Long As It's Red

RED IS HUGELY ATTRACTIVE to hummingbirds. That's a fact. It's also why countless recipes for hummingbird nectar have included all sorts of red dyes in their formulae. Many commercial manufacturers of the nectars sold to the public include red dye as a matter of course.

However, it's a chemical that the tiny birds do not need in their systems. A hummingbird eats a lot of nectar in a day and can quickly build up in its body concentrations of any chemicals included in its nectar, as its supersonic metabolism churns through every nutrient brought into its system to maintain a body always on the edge of collapse.

That's also true for any natural substances that might produce a red coloring in the hummingbird nectar for a backyard feeder. Some people have tried red beet juice, for example. But even natural chemicals are additional chemicals when we're really looking for a simple blend of one part sugar to four parts water, which closely mimics the nectar available naturally to hummingbirds in wildflowers.

Add nothing to the nectar to make it red. Instead:

- Use red feeders.
- Tie red ribbons to the feeders and their supports.
- Plant red flowers around the feeders.

Ivory-billed Woodpecker.

PICUS PRINCIPALIS.

# Respect Your Elders

IMITATION IS THE sincerest form of flattery. Experience is the best teacher. We could go on, adding many more platitudes that most of us know from generations of hearing them. However, for our purposes today, those first two will fit nicely.

Put them together, blend with a bit of birding flavor, and you arrive at a pertinent bit of advice: Follow experienced birdwatchers afield, go out of your way to finagle an invitation to accompany them, and watch them in the field as much as you watch the birds.

Anyone who's been birding longer, in different locales and under different circumstances, likely has knowledge that we can add to our own repertoire. No two birders come at this pursuit from the same background or through the same route, and therein lies an impressive possibility for sharing, expanding, and growing.

Some of the most famous birdwatchers—people who have reported amazing sightings, written birdwatching books, or run impressive nature centers—offer tours for all comers, often in various parts of the world at different times of the year. A quick search on the Internet will reveal several such upcoming trips, which are prime opportunities to learn from the best.

Birdwatchers as a group tend to be very welcoming of those with less experience and less developed skills, and that includes many of the most experienced in our ranks. The know-it-all newbie generally comes out as a significant irritant, but the respectful beginner with lots of good questions, asked quietly at the right times, is usually accepted into the fold.

# Pelicans: American White Pelican (*Pelecanus erythrorhynchos*)

A LARGE BIRD almost unmistakable in flight or at rest, the American white pelican is confined to North America, where it breeds in colonies on islands of inland lakes and migrates to the southern coast for winter. This bird also migrates and hunts in groups.

**PHYSICAL CHARACTERISTICS**: Easily distinguished from the only other North American pelican species, the brown pelican, by its nearly all-white plumage, the American white pelican is also distinguished from its family member by its larger size (5' [1.5 m]), greater wing span (9' [2.75 m]), and the year-round orange color of its bright orange bill. The outer wing feathers (primaries and upper secondaries) are black, most notable in flight.

**RANGE**: During breeding season, the white pelican can be found on inland lakes in south central Canada (British Columbia to Ontario provinces), northern Minnesota, and the upper inland western states of the United States, as well as isolated sites in California, Oregon, and Nevada.

**HABITAT**: When raising their young, American white pelicans make their nests on islands in freshwater lakes, in some cases many miles from their foraging grounds. They migrate to the Gulf Coast of the United States and Mexico and to the Pacific Coast of California for winter.

These pelicans feed on fish by wading in shallow water and dipping their bills. They also feed communally, coordinating a herding effort of a school of fish, driving it into shallower water where the fish can be easily harvested.

Nests are shallow depressions scraped in bare ground in colonies on islands in freshwater lakes. Nearby nests tend to be on the same breeding cycles; birds arriving later at the breeding location establish their own groups.

**SONGS AND CALLS**: Adults are known to utter grunts only during mating or to drive away others. Young birds will squawk for food.

**CONSERVATION STATUS**: Derided by some commercial fisheries, it has been shown that American white pelicans actually tend to take fish species not normally consumed by humans. Nests are easily disturbed by people, and alteration of water levels can have an impact on nesting success.

*127*

American white pelican (*Pelecanus erythrorhynchos*)

# North America: Sian Ka'an Biosphere Reserve, Quintana Roo, Mexico

THE SIAN KA'AN BIOSPHERE Reserve was established in 1982 to protect significant natural and cultural resources of Mexico's Yucatán Peninsula and the Mayan culture. Major archaeological sites exist within this 1.3 million-acre (5,260 square km) reserve, alongside an amazing floral and faunal diversity. Appropriately enough from a birder's perspective, the name Sian Ka'an can be translated to "where the sky is born" or "gift from the sky" in the Mayan language. At least 350 species of birds have been recorded here. Situated along the Mayan Riviera, as the east coast of the peninsula is known, the landscape is mostly flat, but with lush forest, wetlands, and savanna habitats and a vast underground aquifer.

Many tour companies operate within the reserve, and most of the local economy is dependent on the tourist income the region generates.

The Centro Ecologico Sian Ka'an (CESiaK) is an NGO that provides ecotours and accommodations, the proceeds of which go toward its primary mission of advancing sustainable use of the region's natural resources and educating the community about the natural world and Sian Ka'an in particular.

**BIRDS TO SEE**: Many wetland species can be found in the reserve, including the rare jabiru stork, wood stork, flamingo, fifteen species of herons, and egrets. The coastal mangrove forests also attract these and other species, including roseate spoonbill and white pelican. Forest excursions may yield sightings of two species of tinamous, slaty-breasted and thicket, as well as singing quail, pheasant cuckoo, nine species of woodpeckers, warblers, tanagers, orioles, hummingbirds, flycatchers, toucans, motmots, and perhaps even the near-threatened ocellated turkey.

# Growing Our Own Birdhouses

THOSE QUASI-PEAR-SHAPED gourds that you see dried, varnished, and with entrance holes cut into them as nest boxes are called birdhouse gourds. The scientific name is *Lagenaria siceraria*, and they have been used as birdhouses for hundreds of years.

You can find the dried gourds in abundance at farmers' markets and craft shops. However, nearly anyone can grow a birdhouse gourd. Seeds can be found in nearly all of the popular gardening catalogs. Like most gourds, the birdhouse gourd is relatively easy to grow. It requires space for the vines to spread and a steady supply of water for the vines to pump into full-size gourds.

Most importantly, it needs nighttime pollinators. That can be an issue in gardens in which overuse of pesticides and herbicides has depleted insect populations, including moths. The solution for many gardeners is to go out in the garden on nights when the white birdhouse gourd flowers have opened, and use a small, soft-bristled paint brush to gently transfer pollen from inside one flower to inside another flower, one after another.

After the gourds have formed, in autumn, they should be hung to dry in a spot out of the weather but with good airflow on all sides. After several months of drying, when the seeds inside the gourd bounce around like a rattle, the gourd is ready to be made into a nest box.

Drill an entrance hole into one side of the gourd. Remove the seeds and other dried contents. Save the seeds for next year's planting by drying them completely and sealing them in an airtight freezer bag in the refrigerator.

Drill two holes into the sides of the top of the gourd for attaching a cord, leather, or wire hanger. Drill several small holes into the bottom of the gourd as drainage holes.

Apply several coats of clear varnish or an exterior paint of your choice of color, and your new gourd birdhouse made from a birdhouse gourd is ready for hanging.

Many people want to use birdhouse gourd nest boxes to attract purple martins and swallows, but the gourds also make serviceable and attractive nest boxes for other species. The key is to give the gourd the correctly sized entrance hole and place it the correct space above the floor of the nest box, as detailed on page 151.

An egret at Sian Ka'an Biosphere Reserve

# Extinction in Birds

EXTINCTION IS A fact of life. As conditions change in an environment, species may either adapt to this new state of affairs, or die out if the changes are too dramatic. Although islands are often hotspots of biodiversity, they are often also subject to large numbers of extinctions, as animals with limited populations have evolved with very specific habitats.

Humankind is one agent of change that causes extinctions, on par with some of the worst cataclysms. Many bird species have been affected due to hunting, habitat destruction, introduced predators, and even global climate change at a more rapid pace than has formerly occurred through time.

The dodo may be the most famous of all species extinctions caused by humans. Discovered in the late sixteenth century by Dutch sailors on the island of Mauritius in the Indian Ocean, this large-billed, 50-pound (22.7-kg) relative of the pigeon quickly succumbed to the pressures of the colonists and was extinct by 1681. Although many were hunted for food, the dodo's extinction was largely caused by the change in its habitat as the colonists destroyed the island's forest. The animals that the colonists brought with them, including rats, cats, and pigs, also contributed to the dying out of the dodo, as these new animals raided the dodos' nests and preyed on young birds.

**A dodo from an 1828 natural history book by Clere and Buffon**

# Gathering Free Insect Food

HAVE YOU EVER noticed that insects gather in considerable numbers at wounds in trees and other plants that are oozing sap and internal juices? Did you also notice the inordinate amount of interest that insect-eating birds take in those spots?

Every time you trim a tree or shrub in the backyard, you create a natural insect feeder for birds. Most of us, however, have a limited amount of pruning we need to do, or even can do, in our backyards each year.

We can create similar feeders without doing any damage to any of our backyard plants.

Any tree trunk, tree branch, rock, shrub, and many other common backyard surfaces can be made into instate insect feeders. Simply applying sugar water to those surfaces will soon attract the attention of many species of backyard birds. Nectar-eating insects will home in on the available food and insect-eating birds will soon follow them.

Mix the same sugar-water brew you would prepare for hummingbirds (see Days 118 +119). About four parts water to one part sugar is about right. Nectar from wildflowers, the insects' natural source of food, contains 20 percent to 24 percent sucrose. Mix the ingredients in a pot and slowly bring the blend to a rolling boil. Remove it from the heat as soon as it boils.

Let the sugar water cool completely and then apply it like paint on the outdoor surfaces where you would like to attract the insects, and subsequently the birds. You can apply it with a paintbrush, with your fingers, with a spray bottle, or in a multitude of other ways that will spread it about the targeted surfaces.

# Birding Friends, Real and Otherwise

REMEMBER THAT imaginary friend you had in your childhood? Sometimes in birdwatching it might be a good idea to bring him, her, or it out of retirement, at least temporarily. Taking that "friend" along into the field, when we're working on our bird-finding skills, can help us focus.

Quietly directing the gaze of another person, even an imaginary person, to the location of one specific bird can really hone our spotting and watching skills. Putting those directional cues into words focuses us to a much deeper extent than simply pointing or whispering, "Over there." For maximum benefit, the directions must be spoken, even to an imaginary companion. Hearing them out loud, however softly, will help you to pick up on any fuzziness in your directions, which can indicate weak spots in your abilities to locate birds and maintain focus on the birds you find.

Guiding the eyes of another, even imaginary eyes, forces us to more precisely zone in on the birds. Leading the gaze of another up the side of a tree to sight a small woodpecker about halfway up builds the leader's skills in finding that woodpecker and maybe relocating it.

Directing another birder, real or imaginary, to one specific bird among an entire flock helps you develop and refine that same skill, which becomes more important as you advance and want to begin detecting important things about individual birds rather than birds in general.

# Tube-Nosed Seabirds: European Storm-Petrel (*Hydrobates pelagicus*)

THE SMALLEST OF ALL storm-petrels, this seabird is known for nesting in burrows on islands.

**PHYSICAL CHARACTERISTICS**: The small size of the European storm-petrel is perhaps its most distinguishing characteristic. Most of the plumage is all dark black, with white feathers sometimes showing on the rump and upper tail. Also, in flight a white band can be seen running longitudinally along the wings.

**RANGE**: Breeding on islands and islets along the coasts of Ireland, England, Wales, and Scotland, as well as in the western Mediterranean, the European storm-petrel migrates to the seas off the coast of Namibia and South Africa.

**HABITAT**: Like other storm-petrels, the European species makes its nest colonially on islands in burrows on rocky beaches and in stone walls. It visits its nest only at night to prevent larger birds such as gulls from raiding the nest.

Considered mostly a pelagic species when not breeding, this storm-petrel feeds by fluttering over the water with its wings held in a V pattern, picking out plankton from near the surface, and it also follows fishing boats.

**SONGS AND CALLS**: The bird gives only a few calls, notably a variable purr ending in a hiccoughlike note. It also squawks.

**CONSERVATION STATUS**: The species is notably declining, but the population size is still large enough not to prompt conservation measures.

European storm-petrel (*Hydrobates pelagicus*)

# Central America: Tikal National Park, Guatemala

GUATEMALA IS USUALLY not high on the list of places most birders visit, but this is slowly changing with its now stable democracy. This means there is still a good chance to explore this remarkably diverse country before it becomes as popular and expensive as other Latin American countries. Guatemala boasts nineteen different ecosystems—from mangrove swamps and humid lowland jungles to desert thorn forests and cool, highland pine-oak woodlands—within this relatively small geographic area. Birders will be able to travel between habitats with relative ease to search out their preferred species.

The Guatemalan Birding Resource Center out of Quetzaltenango offers tours throughout three general physiographic regions: Western highlands, Pacific foothills, and Pacific lowlands. This gives birders the chance to bag a lot of species. For visitors looking to embark on their own, Tikal National Park is a good start. Located in the northern part of the country, this stunning park features ancient Mayan archaeological ruins set within lush lowland tropical rainforest. A park that truly backs its talk of protection by enforcing its ban on hunting, Tikal supports an amazing diversity of bird life within a truly stunning setting of historical culture and nature.

**BIRDS TO SEE**: Visitors to Tikal will delight in seeing the normally elusive ocellated turkey strutting around the site's ruins. This more flamboyantly colored and smaller version of North America's wild turkey sports a bright blue head with orange skin tags and bright red ring around the eye. Its variegated plumage strays from emerald green to navy blue, rust-orange, and yellow. Other colorful birds at Tikal and the surrounding area include the blue-crowned motmot, keel-billed toucan, collared aracari, pale-billed and chestnut-colored woodpeckers, and no fewer than sixty-five species of hummingbirds. Early mornings at Tikal bring flocks of parrots (Jamaican parakeets, white-crowned parrots, and mealy, red-lored, and white-fronted Amazons) traveling over the ruins to their forest feeding grounds. Often following these colorful tasty treats are orange-breasted falcons and bat falcons. Other raptors seen at Tikal include gray-headed and swallow-tailed kites and white hawks.

Keel-billed toucan at Tikal National Park

# Grassy Wonders

MANY SPECIES OF native grass are top providers of seed, as well as sources of cover and shelter for ground dwelling and ground nesting. Here are a few that are highly recommended because of their consistency in growth and seed production.

- **Big bluestem**, *Andropogon gerardii*, seeds in fall, grows to about 6' (1.8 m) in prime conditions, which include well-drained soil of average fertility in full sun

- **Sideoats grama**, *Bouteloua curtipendula*, seeds in late summer and fall, grows to about 2' (61 cm) in dry, well-drained soil of average fertility in full sun

- **Cyperus sedge**, *Carex pseudocyperus*, seeds in summer and fall, grows to about 3' (91 cm) in wet soil of high fertility in partial shade

- **Switchgrass**, *Panicum virgatum*, seeds in late summer and fall, grows as tall as 7' (2.1 m) in moist, well-drained soil in full sun

- **Little bluestem**, *Schizachyrium scoparium*, seeds in fall, grows to a height of 5' (1.5 m) in all types of soil in full sun

- **Indian grass**, *Sorghastrum nutans*, seeds in early fall, grows to a maximum of 5' (1.5 m) in dry, well-drained soil of average fertility in full sun

Optimal value of grasses is best achieved by allowing the grasses to stand until they are naturally felled by winter's snow and ice. That allows for full use of the seeds hanging from the stems and for maximum value as shelter and cover.

# Ancient Egyptians and Birds

BIRDS FIGURED PROMINENTLY in the cultural beliefs of the ancient Egyptians. Many birds were considered sacred. Rulers often kept falcons and hawks and were often buried with them. Many of their gods were depicted in their art as having human bodies but animal heads.

Horus was a falcon-headed deity known as the god of the sky, war, and protection. The species appears to be the peregrine falcon, with its distinctive mustache stripes. The cult of Horus erected one of the oldest known temples in Egypt at Nekhen, the seat of cultural and religious life at the time.

The ibis-headed Thoth was considered the god of wisdom and knowledge and served as the scribe to the gods. In one Egyptian myth, Horus did battle with his uncle Seth over the throne of Egypt. During the battle Seth tore Horus's eye out, but it was restored by Thoth.

As a result, this eye of Horus became a powerful symbol depicted on tombs and in jewelry.

Even vultures were considered sacred to the Egyptians, and the goddess Mut was often represented as either a vulture herself or just with the head of a vulture. Mut was the wife of Amun, the ruler of Thebes, at one time the seat of Egyptian government. Mut is associated with creation, and because of this, white vultures were thought to be only female, giving birth to their offspring via the wind.

The Egyptian version of the ubiquitous phoenix deity was a heron-like bird called the bennu. It is thought to have come into being from the burning of a holy tree. It became associated with events of rebirth and renewal, such as the rising of the sun, the swelling of the Nile's waters, and resurrection.

*135*

# A Backyard Whodunit

IT'S NOT UNCOMMON for a backyard bird feeder to go missing every now and then. Often the disappearances will be repeated several times before a cause is determined and curtailed. Additional clues to the cause usually can be located, such as tipped over trash cans or more pet food being eaten than is normal for the number of pets in the household.

These disappearances are more common in less urban environments, because the culprits are wild things that share those spaces. Although the ubiquitous squirrels can be the thieves, more often a completely missing feeder is the handiwork of something larger—large enough to reach a hanging feeder or bend over a support such as a shepherd's hook.

The likely thief could be a large raccoon. Although most of the masked bandits weigh no more than 25 pounds (11.3 kg), some exceptional specimens have tipped the scales at 40 pounds (18.1 kg). That amount of weight hanging on a shepherd's hook could be enough to bend it.

However, in areas frequented by bears, they also should be placed in the suspect lineup, particularly in early spring and late fall when the bruins are looking for quick energy after hibernation or to pack on as many calories as they can in preparation for the winter denning period. Residential sightings regularly increase at those times of year, particularly if wild nut and berry crops are below average.

For residents in bear territory, restrict bird feeding to the period of bear hibernation, which is primarily from late November through late March.

In addition, avoid foods that are particularly attractive to protein- and sweets-hungry mammals, such as sunflower seeds, hummingbird nectar mixes, and suet; bring feeders inside at night or suspend them from high cross wires; and temporarily remove feeders for two weeks if visited by something such as a bear or a raccoon.

# Private Property Rights and the Birdwatcher

THE SIREN CALL of a special bird has an allure that is hard to resist, even when giving in might be trespassing on someone else's property. It's a big meadow. There are no signs warning against trespass. What harm could it cause to make a quick jaunt down there, to check out that flock of birds?

Many landowners will grant permission for access to a low-impact activity such as bird-watching (you do keep it low impact, don't you?), unless there exists some extraordinary circumstance. However, permission comes only after it is requested.

The fact that other birders are already in the desired destination does not automatically extend that right of access to other, later-arriving birders, even if you know the other birders. Nothing causes a property to sprout "No Trespassing" signs like uninvited guests acting as though it's their right to traipse across it.

On the other hand, permission is often easy to come by, and often can be arranged for future visits as well as the immediate visit.

And remember that a landowner's permission is a very real and tangible asset. We might consider ourselves indebted by the granting of permission. Consider a small gift in return: special homemade food maybe, or a favorite field guide. If the landowner is a farmer, a bit of help around the farm often is welcome.

Unless explicit permission has been granted to announce a sighting found on someone else's private property, keep it to yourself. With the instant connectivity to the world afforded by the Internet, any announcement of a specific spot is any announcement to hundreds or thousands of others. Even a detailed mention to a close friend can result in unwanted visits to a prime spot.

# Grebes: Western Grebe (*Aechmophorus occidentalis*)

FORMERLY LUMPED WITH Clark's grebe, the Western grebe is a well-known species in the western United States. Its courtship rituals are considered to be among the most complex among birds. Of the various displays, "rushing" may be the most dramatic: Two birds sit side by side in the water, lunge forward at the same time, with wings partially spread, and then rush forward on their feet before diving into the water.

**PHYSICAL CHARACTERISTICS**: The Western grebe's stark black-and-white plumage, with black top of head and back of neck, charcoal gray back, and all-white undersides up to the bill, makes it easy to spot at a distance. The exceptionally long neck for a grebe, red eye, and long olive-yellow bill clinch the identification.

**RANGE**: When breeding, the Western grebe can be found from southwestern Canada through the western United States as far south as the central Mexican plateau. The winter range of the species includes the Pacific and Gulf of California coasts.

**HABITAT**: Found on freshwater lakes and marshes ringed with vegetation during the breeding season, the Western grebe prefers coastal bays, estuaries, and sheltered coasts for its winter habitat.

Western grebes hunt in open water. With their heads dipped below the surface, they scan for fish and then dive underwater to pursue them. They use their bills to grab their prey, thrusting their necks quickly like herons.

These grebes build their nests on mats of floating vegetation; they construct them in a shallow cup shape out of sticks and wet vegetation and algae, which binds the nest together.

**SONGS AND CALLS**: The most common call of the Western grebe is a *cree creet* call, but the birds emit a variety of other vocalizations during their elaborate courtship ritual, most notably a trilling by the males.

**CONSERVATION STATUS**: Populations of the Western grebe are currently stable. However, the species was nearly wiped out in a very short period around the turn of the twentieth century for their white plumes, used to make clothing.

Western grebe (*Aechmophorus occidentalis*)

# Central America: Monteverde Cloud Forest, Costa Rica

A RELATIVELY TINY country, Costa Rica is astounding because it holds about 5 percent of the world's biodiversity. With 25 percent of the country protected in reserves, there are ample opportunities to see the resplendent plants and animals that reside in the wide variety of habitats. A series of mountain ranges lines the narrow country, dividing drier western forest slopes from the moister eastern ones. Birders flock here to see the many tropical specialties, some endangered, as well as many other of the approximately 850 species recorded in the country.

One of the country's best known and most visited sites, the Monteverde Cloud Forest straddles the mountain range in the north, thus giving visitors a chance to see both types of tropical forest—dry and wet—in a relatively small area.

**BIRD TO SEE**: An amazing array of birds awaits travelers to Monteverde, including toucanets, barbets, trogons, tanagers, and guans. However, many visitors make the pilgrimage here to see the extravagant resplendent quetzal, with its bright green back, wings, and head, bright red breast, and incredibly long tail feathers, up to 26" (65 cm) long.

Not to be neglected in the rush to see Monteverde are the other varied habitats and reserves in the country. The Costa Rican Bird Route, within the San Juan–La Selva Biological Corridor, provides birders with the information to see these habitats and birds. Located in the northeastern part of the country, the route takes visitors through varied habitats. The nonprofit group that created the route provides four different itineraries that allow visitors to see the varied habitats while learning about the country's culture. The group hopes to increase awareness of the area and the need to protect it, since much of the unprotected areas of the country are under dire threat of devastating logging operations and other environmental problems. By working with landowners to promote ecotourism, the nonprofit is seeking to protect more land from these threats.

**BIRDS TO SEE**: The trips provide opportunities to see some of the last remaining habitat for the great green macaw. Other species encountered include sunbittern, white-fronted nunbird, and royal flycatcher. Birds seen on the Sarapiqui River trip include blue-crowned motmot, white-whiskered puffbird, black-faced antthrush, collared forest-falcon, and scale-crested pygmy-tyrant.

# Trumpet Is a Hummer's Favorite Shape

THE TINY, HOVERING, long-beaked hummingbird has evolved to take best advantage of particular flower designs. Although hummers will take nectar from other flowers and from hummingbird feeders with no semblance to their preferred flowers, that long beak, with an even longer tongue inside, has evolved to probe deeply into long, tubular flowers.

Additionally, the bird has evolved a hovering method of feeding. In a wild, natural setting, hummingbirds hover at the flowers from which they take nectar. That means flowers growing around the outside of their plants, where the birds can hover and feed without interference from stems and leaves, provide the most efficient source of nectar.

And generations of hummers have found red flowers to be reliable sources of nectar, and thus warrant close inspection and probing.

Combine all those flower characteristics into one description and a particular plant emerges as a prime hummingbird attractor: the trumpet vine, which also happens to bloom in mid- to late summer across much of the Northern Hemisphere (exactly the time that the hummingbirds inhabit that same bioregion).

# Bird Sayings, Part III: Chickens Get a Bad Rap

OUR LONG RELATIONSHIP with chickens has spawned a large number of idioms featuring the common fowl.

"Chicken out" and "chicken-livered" are used derisively to accuse people of being afraid. When someone acts frantically or unable to focus, he or she is said to be "running around like a chicken with its head cut off." This idiom refers to the habit of a chicken's body remaining animated by natural electrical impulses after its head is severed during slaughter. "Chicken feed" is used to refer to a very small sum of money.

"Counting one's chickens before they've hatched" has been around since the sixteenth century, and refers to when current actions are based on an event that has not yet come to pass. A "cock-and-bull story" refers to an unbelievable tale. Its origins are unknown, but it has been in use since the seventeenth century.

"No spring chicken" refers to someone no longer in his or her prime. Prior to modern chicken raising, which utilizes heated henhouses, it was often not feasible to rear chickens in winter. This meant chickens raised and sold in spring were eagerly anticipated. Farmers sometimes tried to pass off older birds among their spring sales. When they were caught out, the buyer would exclaim, "That's no spring chicken!"

Formerly attributed to birds in general, the phrase "chickens coming home to roost" didn't come into common usage until the nineteenth century. But the meaning has been clear throughout: A person's misdeeds will return to haunt him or her.

# Timing Your Nestbox Cleaning

MANY BIRDERS GET around to thinking about cleaning the nest boxes in their backyards about the time of year when temperatures are dropping. However, soon after the fledglings leave the box—a point much earlier in the year, in early spring—is when you should clean out old nesting materials.

Make certain the birds have vacated the box, wait a few days more, and then clean to your heart's content. Timing the cleaning in that way will encourage other birds, or the same nesting pair, to use the box again to produce another clutch of eggs in the same nesting season. If you clean it again after that bunch leaves the box, you might encourage yet a third nesting that same season.

When old nests are left in the boxes, they might discourage subsequent nestings and provide attractive habitats for blowflies, mites, and ants, all of which can harm birds trying who will reuse the box.

Cleaning boxes later in the year has its benefits as well. For species that use nest boxes to lay their eggs and launch their nestlings, the nest box is less than a memory as fall settles in. Cleaning can be done quite safely at that time of year.

1. Wearing latex gloves and covering your nose and mouth, remove the old nesting materials. Scrape the interior of the nest box with a wire brush or similar tool.

2. Wash the interior with a mild solution of chlorine bleach in water, and rinse with clean water.

3. Prop the box open and allow it to dry for several days. Then close the open side.

Do not take your nest boxes down for winter. Some birds will find refuge from the coldest, stormiest nights inside the boxes.

# Here, Little Birdie, Birdie...

PISHING IS A TECHNIQUE many birdwatchers use to encourage birds out of hiding and into close proximity. They verbally produce a sound best described as *psh-psh-psh* in areas likely for locating birds and then wait for the results. Some make the sound with air through their lips. Others produce it by pressing their lips against the inside of their fist and forcing air through any openings that remain.

The technique works best for songbirds, but also has been known to bring in other larger birds, such as hawks, owls, ducks, and a range of mammalian predators.

There are several theories on why pishing works. The most common is that the birds hear the sound as an alarm being sounded by some other bird announcing the presence of a predator and respond to help gang up on that predator.

Group mobbing is a common predator avoidance behavior in songbirds. It can either drive off the predator or distract it from making a kill by offering it an overwhelming number of potential targets. And *psh-psh-psh* sounds a lot like the sound many bird species use to gather and initiate the behavior.

# Loons: Yellow-Billed Loon (*Gavia adamsii*)

ALTHOUGH VERY SIMILAR in appearance to the common loon, the yellow-billed loon is distinguished by the feature it is named for.

**PHYSICAL CHARACTERISTICS:** The adult breeding plumage of the yellow-billed loon is distinct, with nearly all-white plumes below and mostly black above. A gridlike white pattern on the back and a similarly patterned "necklace" are prominent features. A bold red eye above the yellow bill on a black head is striking. The black feathers on the back of the neck may have a green gloss in the right light, while the feathers surrounding that on the sides of the chin, throat, and sides of the neck have a purple sheen.

**RANGE:** The tundra regions of far northern Canada and Alaska's North Slope comprise the yellow-billed loon's breeding range, while the coastal waters of western Alaska and Canada are regular wintering sites. It has irregularly been seen along the western continental U.S. coast as well.

**HABITAT:** This loon breeds in freshwater lakes in open tundra regions. Its nest is made from scrapes in the ground or from mounded peat and mud.

Like all loons, this species hunts its main prey, fish, by swimming underwater, propelled solely by its feet.

**SONGS AND CALLS:** Both sexes utter a variety of calls, the most commonly heard being the tremolo, which is very similar to that of the common loon. This is usually voiced when the birds are alarmed. Other calls include yodels, moans, and wails.

**CONSERVATION STATUS:** With a relatively small population and a slightly declining trend, the yellow-billed loon has been listed as a species of global concern, and has been petitioned to be listed as endangered.

Yellow-billed loon (*Gavia adamsii*)

# Islands: Hawaiian Islands

AN ARCHIPELAGO OF volcanic origin, the islands of Hawaii are notable for the number of truly unique, endemic bird species that currently exist there as well as the ones that have disappeared. Although various introduced threats have severely reduced the number of species and individuals over the past twenty-five years, visitors still have a chance to see some incredible birds, namely, the endemic honeycreepers, a highly specialized family of nectar- and insect-eating finches on the islands. Here are a few sites that give a representative slice of the islands' avifauna.

Hakalau Forest National Wildlife Refuge on Hawai'i was created to protect some of the finest remaining stands of montaine rainforest on the islands as well as eight endangered and six other endemic birds. The Kona Forest Unit within the refuge was established in 1997 to protect the habitat of the nearly extinct 'alalā, the Hawaiian crow. Other endangered species that benefit from this protection are three species of honeycreeper—Hawai'i 'akepa, Hawai'i creeper, and 'akiapōlā'au—and the 'io, the Hawaiian hawk.

Haleakala National Park on Maui holds more endangered species than most other national parks in the United States. This 30,000-acre (121 square km) park is home to and named for the dormant Haleakala volcano. Lush rainforest can be found on the windward side, while dry forest is dominant on the leeward side of the volcano. Species of honeycreeper can be found here ('apapane, i'iwi, and amakihi,) as well as the nene, or Hawaiian goose, another endangered species and Hawaii's state bird. The park also includes the beautiful, lush, coastal Kipahulu area, with its waterfalls, grasslands, and forests.

The nene can also be found at Kilauea Point National Wildlife Refuge on Kaua'i, one of the most species-rich islands in the chain. The refuge, with its steep sea cliffs above crashing waves, was established to protect nesting seabirds, of which this refuge has the densest concentration. The Pacific golden plover, red-footed booby, red-tailed and white-tailed tropicbird, Laysan albatross, wedge-tailed shearwater, and 'a'o, or Newell's shearwater, are just some of the species that nest here. Visitors may also be treated to sights of humpback whales, green turtles, Hawaiian monk seals, and Hawaiian spinner dolphins. The island also boasts the spectacular Alaka'i Wilderness Area in Koke'e National Park. Within this area reside no fewer than eight species of rare Hawaiian alpine birds, all of them honeycreepers.

'Apapane at Hakalau Forest National Wildlife Refuge

# But Not a Drop to Drink?

BIRDS DO NOT HAVE sweat glands, which can make life tough on the hottest of days. They can lose some of their excess body heat directly through their skin, but not nearly as much as a creature with sweat glands could and not nearly as much as needs to be eliminated on many hot days.

They avoid the sun by resting in shaded spots and they can turn the lightest-colored parts of their body toward the sun to reflect some of the heat.

However, birds lose most of their heat through breathing and the high rate of evaporation of internal liquid that accompanies it. Each breath spills warm air and warm moisture from the body and passes fresh, cooler area over internal tissues.

To increase their respiration rate, and its evaporative benefits, birds pant, like dogs. Most also flutter their throat area, which increases the loss of heat from mucus membranes in the throat.

Drinking, wading, and bathing in water also help them to reduce their internal temperatures. For that reason, adding a water source to your backyard will almost always draw birds and provide countless hours of birdwatching pleasure.

A water source can be made more attractive to birds by adding a water dripper, mist sprayer, or cascading trickle. Birds seem to home in on moving water and the sound of it, particularly when it's found or heard in an area where water is hard to come by.

# Evolution of Birds II: Terror Birds

It may sound like a horror movie script, but terror birds once walked the Earth. From sixty-five million to two million years ago, the Phorusrhacids, as they are known in scientific circles, filled the role of top predator in South America.

The terror birds ranged in size from 3' to 10' (1 to 3 m) tall, and they had powerful beaks for grabbing and crushing prey and strong legs for running. Some of these creatures were thought to be able to consume prey as large as a medium-size dog in one gulp. But their legs were likely also used to kick their prey, breaking the bones. Scientists propose that this was to gain access to bone marrow, but it may have also been useful for crushing the bones to make for easier swallowing.

They could run at speeds from 30 mph (48 kph) up to 60 mph (97 kph) for the smaller species. Equipped with just vestigial wings, none of the roughly twenty-five known species of terror birds were capable of flight, although they were feathered.

One of the largest of these birds, *Brontornis*, stood 10' (3 m) tall and weighed about 1,100 pounds (500 kg). The smallest, *Psilopterus*, stood only about 2.5' (76 cm) tall and weighed just 15 pounds (6.8 kg). The only living relative of the terror birds is South America's seriema, a bird with long legs that runs down its prey and stomps on it to disable it. This species is very similar to Africa's secretary bird, and both are relatives of raptors.

# Suet: Food of Champions

Suet is raw fat from around the kidneys and loins of a cow, but in the bird-feeding, it also comprises all processed (cooked) beef fat. And in the do-it-yourself end of the hobby, the term is used for fat from other butchered animals.

Many do-it-yourselfers keep their suet simple by placing raw, freshly butchered suet into a suet cage. However, as air temperatures approach 70°F (21°C), unprocessed animal fat can turn rancid and begin to melt.

*Rendering* is the process that thwarts that normal decomposition in raw suet, and *double rendering* is the process that commercial suet-cake manufacturers use to produce suet that can withstand even the heat of summer.

To render fat for a suet feeder: chop fat into fine bits and toss it into a pot on the stovetop, set to a low to medium heat setting. Heat the suet bits until they melt, stirring constantly. That's one rendering. Allow the suet to cool and then heat until it melts once again. Once cooled, this twice-rendered suet will cake properly and resist turning rancid.

The melted fat can be poured into molds (waxed paper cups, tin foil cupcake cups, empty plastic tubs, shaped aluminum foil, etc.) The partly cooled suet can be spread into predrilled holes in a log feeder or dipped onto pine cones. Twice-rendered suet will keep for months in the freezer.

# Shhhhhhhh!!!

IT MIGHT SEEM obvious, but the quieter you can be in the field, the more birds you will see.

One of the primary alarms for birds is what they hear. And although we can't see external evidence of it, their hearing is much better than ours. Even noises that seem relatively quiet to us can be remarkably loud and star-tling to birds. They will take those noises as clues to seek cover.

Practice moving more quietly and you will increase your chances of getting close to birds. It's nearly impossible for any modern human to truly sneak up on wild creatures, but you can minimize the disturbance you telegraph to birds in advance of your arrival.

And fight the urge to issue an exclamation of excitement when you spot a special bird. Your birding companions will have a better chance of seeing the same bird if you quietly and calmly call it to their attention.

Keep all your movements in the field slow, flu-id, and focused on specific tasks. Jerky move-ments, flailing hands, and fast-paced strides all will spread alarm to the ever-vigilant birds. Even a sudden lifting of the binoculars to your eyes can be enough to send birds scurrying.

In all of this, the closer to the birds you find yourself, the quieter and more hidden your every sound and movement must be.

# Ducks, Geese, and Swans: Hooded Merganser (*Lophodytes cucullatus*)

COMMON IN FORESTED wetlands, the hooded merganser flies with continuous wing beats; it glides only when landing. Males conduct elaborate courtship displays including raising their showy crests, bobbing their heads, and performing ritualized drinking movements and stretches.

**PHYSICAL CHARACTERISTICS**: The males are especially striking with their white, fan-shaped crest set against an all-black head and back and their chestnut-colored flanks above a white breast. At rest, the crest appears as a broad, white line extending back from the bright yellow eye. Females have a dark gray back, white undersides, and a loose, pale reddish-brown crest. Merganser bills differ from those of other ducks in that they are narrow and serrated.

**RANGE**: The hooded merganser is a common breeding species in southeastern Canada and the eastern United States, with denser numbers around the Great Lakes. Year-round populations occur in the eastern United States, except for Florida, which, along with Texas, California, and parts of the Pacific Northwest, comprise the wintering range.

**HABITAT**: Forested wetlands are the chief habitat for hooded mergansers; this includes ponds, rivers, marshes, and swamps. With exceptionally acute underwater vision, they hunt aquatic insects, fish, and crustaceans by diving and hunting.

Females clear nest sites in tree cavities, and they will also use nest boxes with wood shavings as a base layer.

**SONGS AND CALLS**: Males utter a frog-like *craa-crrooo* call, during courtship, while females give a *croo-croo-crook* to communicate with young.

**CONSERVATION STATUS**: Although the species is increasing slightly, its numbers are lower than those of most other North American duck species.

Hooded merganser (*Lophodytes cucullatus*)

# Islands: The Bahamas

ALTHOUGH THE BAHAMAS are usually considered a place for a pampered vacation or spring break beaches, the islands are home to more than 300 bird species. Their location is the perfect stopover for many North American migrants. Top that off with fine, white sand beaches, beautiful green oceans, and comfortable accommodations and you have a birder's heaven.

More than 700 islands and thousands of smaller cays make up the Bahamas, but some of the best birding is found on the Abacos—Great Abaco and Little Abaco—and their offshore cays. These smaller islets are accessed via ferry, and tourists can get around by renting bikes or even golf carts.

Grand Bahama Island is also home to many of the birds found on the islands, including eighteen of the twenty-eight resident species. Many of these can be seen in the 100 acres (0.4 square km) of protected habitat around the Rand Nature Center.

**BIRDS TO SEE**: Many common birds on the Abacos are seen rarely elsewhere, such as the bananaquit, loggerhead kingbird, Bahama mockingbird, Bahama woodstar, and Cuban emerald. The endangered Bahama parrot can be seen in flocks in Abaco National Park, at the south end of Great Abaco. Other birds encountered include the Antillean nighthawk, white-tailed tropicbird, Western spindalis, red-legged thrush, black-faced grassquit, thick-billed vireo, more than forty species of warblers, and West Indian flamingo.

# Too Big, Too Small, and Just Right

BIRDS THAT NEST inside cavities, and the cavity imitations that we call nest boxes or birdhouses, will use structures of a wide variety of sizes and shapes to hold their nests, eggs, and nestlings.

For many species, the most important criteria are the size of the entrance hole and the drop from the entrance hole to the bottom of the inside of the cavity.

Here are the suggested nest box dimensions for some common bird species.

| SPECIES | FLOOR DIMENSIONS | HEIGHT OF NEST BOX | PLACEMENT OF ENTRANCE ABOVE FLOOR | DIAMETER OF ENTRANCE | IDEAL HEIGHT ABOVE GROUND |
|---|---|---|---|---|---|
| American kestrel | 11" x 11" (28 x 28 cm) | 12" (30.4 cm) | 9–12" (23–30.4 cm) | 3" x 4" oblong (7.7 x 10.1 cm) | 20–30' (6.1–9.1 m) |
| Barn owl | 10" x 18" (25.4 x 46 cm) | 15–18" (38–46 cm) | 4" (10.1 cm) | 6" (15.2 cm) | 12–18' (3.7–5.4 m) |
| Black-capped chickadee | 4" x 4" (10.1 x 10.1 cm) | 8–10" (20.3–25.4 cm) | 6–8" (15.2–20.3 cm) | 1.125" (2.7 cm) | 6–15' (1.8–4.5 m) |
| Carolina wren | 4" x 4" (10.1 x 10.1 cm) | 6–8" (15.2–20.3 cm) | 1–6" (2.5–15.2 cm) | 1.5" (3.8 cm) | 6–10' (1.8–3 m) |
| Common flicker | 7" x 7" (18 x 18 cm) | 16–18" (41–46 cm) | 14–16" (36–41 cm) | 2.5" (6.4 cm) | 6–20' (1.8–6.1 m) |
| Crested flycatcher | 6" x 6" (15.2 x 15.2 cm) | 8" (20.3 cm) | 6" (15.2 cm) | 2" (5.1 cm) | 8–20' (2.4–6.1 m) |
| Downy woodpecker | 4" x 4" (10.1 x 10.1 cm) | 9–12" (23–30.4 cm) | 6–8" (15.2–20.3 cm) | 1.25" (3.2 cm) | 6–20' (1.8–6.1 m) |
| Eastern bluebird | 5" x 5" (13 x 13 cm) | 8" (20.3 cm) | 6" (15.2 cm) | 1.5" (3.8 cm) | 5' (1.5 m) |
| Eastern screech owl | 8" x 8" (20.3 x 20.3 cm) | 12–15" (30.4–38 cm) | 9–12" (23–30.4 cm) | 3" (7.7 cm) | 10–30' (3–9.1 m) |
| Hairy woodpecker | 6" x 6" (15.2 x 15.2 cm) | 12–15" (30.4–38 cm) | 9–12" (23–30.4 cm) | 1.5" (3.8 cm) | 12–20' (3.7–6.1 m) |
| House finch | 6" x 6" (15.2 x 15.2 cm) | 6" (15.2 cm) | 4" (10.1 cm) | 2" (5.1 cm) | 6–12' (1.8–3.7 m) |
| House wren | 4" x 4" (10.1 x 10.1 cm) | 8–10" (20.3–25.4 cm) | 1–6" (2.5–15.2 cm) | 1.25" (3.2 cm) | 6–10' (1.8–3 m) |
| Purple martin | 6" x 6" (15.2 x 15.2 cm) | 6" (15.2 cm) | 1" (2.5 cm) | 2.5" (6.4 cm) | 10–20' (3–6.1 m) |
| Red-headed woodpecker | 6" x 6" (15.2 x 15.2 cm) | 12" (30.4 cm) | 10" (25.4 cm) | 2" (5.1 cm) | 10–20' (3–6.1 m) |
| Tree swallow | 5" x 5" (13 x 13 cm) | 6–8" (15.2–20.3 cm) | 5–6" (13–15.2 cm) | 1.5" (3.8 cm) | 6–16' (1.8–4.9 m) |
| Tufted titmouse | 4" x 4" (10.1 x 10.1 cm) | 8–10" (20.3–25.4 cm) | 6–8" (15.2–20.3 cm) | 1.25" (3.2 cm) | 6–15' (1.8–4.6 m) |
| White-breasted nuthatch | 4" x 4" (10.1 x 10.1 cm) | 8–10" (20.3–25.4 cm) | 6–8" (15.2–20.3 cm) | 1.25" (3.2 cm) | 12–20' (3.7–6.1 m) |
| Wood duck | 10" x 18" (25 x 46 cm) | 10–24" (25.4–61 cm) | 12–16" (30.4–41 cm) | 4" (10.1 cm) | 10–20' (3–6.1 m) |

# The History of Bird Protection and Conservation III: *Silent Spring*

THE POST–WORLD WAR II years spawned a new age of technology, with large-scale farming becoming prevalent and replacing small family farms. This type of farming was made possible by the use of synthetic chemical pesticides and fertilizers to keep the huge monocultures growing and free of insects. However, by the 1950s, scientists were starting to notice that birds and mammals were dying in large numbers.

One scientist in particular, marine biologist Rachel Carson, began to note all this information and started researching the problem. After four years of exhaustive study, in 1962 she released her report in the form of the book *Silent Spring*. Now hailed as the touchstone for the modern environmental movement, at the time the book set off a firestorm of controversy, with many in the press and the chemical industry calling into question the information and even the character of Carson. Patient, thorough, and determined, Carson stood up to all the scrutiny, including a presidential commission.

Her credentials, encompassing a master's degree in zoology and fifteen years working in the field, no doubt helped her cause. But it was also her emphasis on the potential dangers that these synthetic chemicals could cause humans that made the public stand up and listen.

The effects of DDT on bird populations were insidious, as DDT largely caused a weakness in the shells of many bird species so that the brooding mothers crushed their own eggs. Some of the species most severely affected included the bald eagle; the peregrine falcon, formerly the most widespread raptor in the world; the osprey; and the brown pelican.

Carson's studies eventually led to the banning of DDT, one of the most widely used pesticides, as well as to much more public attention being paid to the health of the environment and to individual species as well.

# An Easy Craft Project for Birders

SUET PINE CONES are a tried-and-true craft project to make with younger members of the family. They also are much appreciated by birds, which can obtain body-heating, life-sustaining nutrients from the cones.

You will need to gather several pine cones; cones with scales that have opened fully are preferred. Twist one end of a 1' (30.4 cm)-long piece of wire to the point of each pine cone.

Buy a few large chunks of beef suet (generally available from the meat counter in the super-market). Place the suet in a pan and slowly melt it down over low heat. When the suet has melted, allow it to cool fully, and then melt it

a second time. After the second melting, allow the liquid suet to begin cooling again. After five minutes or so, stir in a handful or two of the seed mixture you use in your bird feeders. Allow the mixture to cool a few more minutes, and then slowly roll and dip your pine cones into it, coating as much of each cone's surface with the suet-seed mixture as possible.

Lay the cones on a sheet of waxed paper on a plate and place them in the refrigerator for several hours. After the suet-seed mixture has hardened, hang your new bird feeders by the loose ends of the wires from tree branches in your backyard.

# Birdwatching as "the Hunt"

A BIRD'S LIFE depends on careful assessment of every living thing that approaches it. And as much as you may love birds, to them you look a lot like an approaching predator.

You can reduce your image as predator in a few ways.

- **Avert your eyes.** Birds are familiar with the two-eyed stare of a predator hoping to make a meal of them, and they tend to move away from such stares. Change that visage and you lower the anxiety just a bit. Watch the bird from the corners of your eyes. Look in directions away from the bird and past the bird occasionally. Wear a hat with the brim pulled low to hide your eyes, and tip it to the side to break up the body symmetry that birds find threatening.

- **Consider your approach.** Your approach toward the bird can also break body symmetry. Walk sideways as much as possible during the stalk. Present your sides to the bird rather than your full frontal image. Follow a zigzag-ging or roundabout path in your approach. Crouch to lower and distort your outline.

- **Observe body language.** The closer you get to the bird, the more you can rely on its body language for clues about how well you're do-ing. Among the signs of irritation and alarm, birds will crane their necks for a better look at what seems to be threatening them, they will fluff up their crowns, their eyes will grow wider, and they will move about their perch more nervously. When you spot these warn-ing signals of the bird's impending escape, stop, avert your gaze, move back or to the side, alter your posture, and you may still have a chance to get closer.

# Ducks, Geese, and Swans:
# King Eider (*Somateria spectabilis*)

ONE OF THE MOST northerly breeding bird species, the king eider moves north in spring in numbers greater than 10,000 individuals; it may take hours for a given flock to pass over an area. Researchers once observed 360,000 birds flying over Point Barrow, Alaska, in a ten-hour period.

**PHYSICAL CHARACTERISTICS**: The adult male and female king eiders have distinctly different plumages. The very showy male's head feathers consist of a pearl blue head with a drooping black eyebrow that connects to a black ring surrounding a swollen orange-yellow frontal lobe above an orange bill and pale green cheeks. The breast is a pale buff color grading into the all-white neck and back. The rest of the male's body is black except for a large white mark on the upper wing with white wing linings below. Scapular feathers point upward at the top of the wing when at rest.

Female king eiders are reddish-brown overall during breeding season, with black narrow barring all along the underside and broader barring above.

**RANGE**: The king eider sticks close to the northern extremes of land from northern Canada, Greenland, across Scandinavia, and through Eurasia during breeding season. In winter, the species moves south into the Chukchi and Bering seas and along the coasts of southern Alaska and the Kamchatka Peninsula in the west of North America, and down into the waters off New England in the east.

**HABITAT**: Tundra habitats are the common breeding sites for king eiders, with most making their nests in dense marshy vegetation. The female scrapes a shallow bowl in the ground, then after the eggs are laid, picks vegetation and lays it around the eggs, along with her own downy feathers plucked from her breast. During breeding season, these birds feed on vegetation and insect larvae.

King eiders spend winters at sea at the edge of ice, feeding at the bottom on crustaceans, mollusks, algae, and other sea life.

**SONGS AND CALLS**: Vocalizations of the king eider include low growl-like sounds (*gogogogogo*) for the females and dovelike sounds (*urrr, broo rroo rrooo*) for the males.

**CONSERVATION STATUS**: Although king eider populations have been estimated in the hundreds of thousands, their numbers have declined significantly. The species is not considered threatened.

King eider (*Somateria spectabilis*)

# Islands: Galapagos National Park, Ecuador

LOCATED 620 MILES (1,000 km) off the Ecuadorean coast, but still owned and administered by that country, the Galapagos Islands have achieved great fame as the birthplace of the scientific concept of evolution, pioneered by Charles Darwin in the nineteenth century. His studies of *speciation*, or the development of physical and behavioral traits in concert with a species' environment, have made the finches and mockingbirds of this volcanic island chain justly famous. Each island features a member of these genera, specifically adapted to their food source. The number of species on the island is limited, with only fifty-seven resident birds, but twenty-five of these are endemic.

Another draw of the islands is the relative tameness of the animals here. Because of the near lack of predators, birds and other animals do not scare easily and allow easy approachability. That being said, the Ecuadorean government has strict rules for visitors to the island. Only registered tour operators can bring tourists here, and these visitors must be accompanied by a guide at all times. The animals cannot be touched or fed. Despite this control, many visitors count a trip to these islands as a major milestone in their lives.

**BIRDS TO SEE**: The islands support thirteen species of finches, including the sharp-beaked ground (which feeds on the blood of red-footed boobies), woodpecker, large cactus, olive warbler, and dusky warbler finches. Mockingbird species include Floreana, Galapagos, Española, and San Cristóbal mockingbirds. Red-footed and blue-footed boobies nest on these islands. Other specialties include Galapagos hawk, Galapagos martin, Galapagos dove, Galapagos penguin, and flightless cormorant. Birds that use the island but are not resident include the vermillion flycatcher, short-eared owl, whimbrel, and magnificent and great frigatebird.

# Not Too Deep

ALTHOUGH A WATER source may enhance any bird-feeding area, acting like a magnet for birdlife throughout the surrounding area, it's also an area of habitat development where you can have too much of a good thing. Most songbirds do not want to wade into water any deeper than their knees. For most common species that means only 2" to 3" (5.1 to 7.6 cm) of water.

They also prefer to wade gradually into water, either from much shallower water of less than ½" (1.3 cm) or from a dry edge.

Most birdbaths incorporate those considerations into their designs, with gradually sloping sides leading to a center depth of no more than 3" (7.6 cm). Some, however, are designed more for human aesthetics than for bird utility and may even incorporate too steep sides and a surface that is too slippery.

All of these design miscalculations can be corrected with the addition of some flat, rough-surfaced stones across the base of the birdbath. Any interesting feature that also solves those design shortcomings can be added by leaning a small tree branch into the birdbath, from edge to center or across the entire water area.

Galapagos National Park's breeding center in Puerto Ayora,
Santa Cruz Island, Galapagos

# Mythical Birds: Turul, the Progenitor of Hungary

A MYTH FROM ninth-century Hungary tells of the origins of the royal line, beginning with a falcon that went on to rule the nation for several centuries. The legend tells of Emeshe, wife of Ügyek, who in a vision was said to have been impregnated by the Turul, a giant falcon and representative of their one god. In the vision, from her womb came a great torrent of water that became a river that rushed over the mountains and filled the plains below. A great tree of gold sprouted from the waters.

The couple's son, Álmos, went on to be a great leader of Scythia. Many bands of seven different tribes came to live under his banner. Álmos had a dream in which the Turul saved the tribes' horses from a band of eagles.

To Álmos, this symbolized that they must leave their land and find a new one. There was much crowding where they were with all the tribes living together, so moving to find a new land that could accommodate them all made sense. This new home was named Pannonia. It was founded on the land that was once the site of the ancient kingdom of Attila the Hun (Álmos's ancestor), and it became the future site of Hungary.

The Turul became a symbol of power, strength, and nobility, and it is still used today on the coat of arms of the Hungarian Army and the Office of National Security. One Turul statue built in Hungary on a mountain near Tatabánya is apparently the largest bird statue in Europe, with a wingspan of 49' (15 m).

**Statue of Turul at entrance to the Royal Palace in Budapest, Hungary**

# A Bucket List for Wrens

WRENS HAVE A REAL affinity for nooks and crannies, particularly during the nesting season.

They have made their "homes" in a wider array of unusual places than nearly any other bird species. Those spots have included everything from old boots to hats to mailboxes to aprons to buckets under shelter, such as hanging to the side of a shed under an overhang or on the inside wall of an open horse stall.

The key to attracting the attention of the birds is shelter. The wrens seem to live with a never-ending itch to place themselves in confined spaces. Those spaces must offer a quick escape route, but otherwise they will wiggle themselves into incredibly tight spots.

Their penchant for tight roosts continues beyond the nesting season, particularly in milder winters when the birds tend to extend their range to the north. Small buckets stuffed to half capacity with bone-dry grass and hung where they are protected from the elements can become favored nighttime roosts for wrens.

The birds often share their winter roosts with partners, adding to the insulating value offered by the dry grass with their shared body heat, and generally show no reluctance to use suitable night roosts in close proximity to other small groups of their species.

Wrens are insect eaters, so the attraction of a good nighttime roost can be enhanced with a good, hearty breakfast of fresh mealworms and suet at nearby backyard feeders.

# Listen for the Tattletale

DURING THE COLDER, leaner months of the year, small seed-eating birds, including chickadees, small woodpeckers, towhees, sparrows, titmice, nuthatches, and others, will band together into small, wandering winter flocks to forage the landscape.

They gather for the greater safety and food-finding capability that many pairs of eyes can bring to the group. And because remaining undetected is crucial to the security of the flock, most of the birds will remain relatively quiet most of the time.

However, there are usually a couple of birds in any group that just cannot keep their mouths shut. If you hear them, follow their calls and they'll likely lead you to the whole flock somewhere in the undergrowth.

You can enlist the same method to find flocks of warblers in fall, ducks on secluded ponds or coves, flocks of turkeys, family groups of bobwhite quail and ruffed grouse, and others.

Put yourself in close proximity for the preferred habitat of the species you're searching for at the right time of the year, put your sense of hearing into play, and wait for the signals that are sure to come.

# Ducks, Geese, and Swans:
## Snow Goose (*Chen caerulescens*)

THE SNOW GOOSE bucks the trend of many other bird species in that it has been increasing its populations dramatically. Recent estimates have placed the overall population at nearly seven million, this from a low of a couple thousand birds in the early twentieth century.

**PHYSICAL CHARACTERISTICS**: Two distinct color phases, or morphs, occur regularly in snow geese: The white morph is an all-white bird, except for black primary feathers (along the leading edge of the wing) and gray primary coverts (along the forward edge of the wing next to the primaries). The bird also sports an orange bill with a black lining along the upper and lower mandibles, resulting in the look of an odd smile.

The dark or blue morph displays a mostly gray-brown body with white head and neck. Upper and underwing covert feathers (nearest the leading edge) are gray.

**RANGE**: Snow geese breed in three distinct populations (Western, Mid-Continent, and Eastern) from northern Alaska east to Baffin Island and northern Greenland. These three populations move south into the United States during winter. The Western population spreads out along the coast from southern British Columbia into Washington, Oregon, and California, and inland into Arizona and Mexico.

The Mid-Continent snow geese winter along major rivers of the Midwest, in Nebraska, Kansas, Kentucky, Missouri, Texas, and Louisiana. The Eastern population can be found along the East Coast from New Jersey to North Carolina.

**HABITAT**: You can find colonies of snow geese nesting in open tundra habitat near waterways within vegetation. They prefer slightly raised ground, as on hummocks or small rises, but they dig a scrape in bare ground and then line it with plant matter and downy feathers.

During migration, these geese stop in various ponds, flooded farm fields, and slow-moving rivers in great numbers, affording those birders not near their breeding or wintering grounds a look at these beautiful birds.

**SONGS AND CALLS**: Snow geese are considered one of the noisiest waterfowl species, uttering their loud *whouk* at all times of the day.

**CONSERVATION STATUS**: With increasing numbers, the species is in no danger. Current hunting, although considerable, does not even come close to the reproduction rate of this species.

Snow goose (*Chen caerulescens*)

# Islands: Trinidad

THE ISLAND OF TRINIDAD, just off Venezuela's northeastern coast, offers birders the chance to see a wide variety of more than 400 species of birds, including tropical residents, North American migrants, and South American migrants, depending on the time of year. The island is small yet diverse enough that many different habitats—mountains, savannas, wetlands—can be explored with relative ease. The best time to visit is between January and May, during the dry season, although interesting birds can be seen any time of the year. Tour companies offer packages including room, meals, and birding tours.

Nowhere on the island is better for relaxed birding than the Asa Wright Nature Center, in the lushly forested Northern Range. Visitors to the Nature Center (which was formerly a coffee, cocoa, and citrus plantation) can sit on the veranda of the main house and continually add birds to their life lists. The grounds of the Nature Center, comprising 1,500 acres (6 square km), consist of mostly secondary forest grown back after the property was converted, and they are surrounded by tropical rainforest. Visitors can visit the center during the day, or they can stay overnight in comfortable accommodations. If you want to see the center's famous oilbird colony, you must be booked into a multinight tour package.

**BIRDS TO SEE:** Birds seen at and around the center's feeders include squirrel cuckoo, blue-crowned motmot, bananaquit, silver-beaked tanagers, woodcreepers, peppershrikes, and several species of honeycreepers and hummingbirds (tufted coquette and white-necked Jacobin, for example). Toucans, parrots, and parakeets call from the surrounding forest, and walks can yield sightings of them and other species such as oropendolas (species of blackbirds), antshrikes, antwrens, chestnut woodpeckers, golden-headed and white-bearded manakins, and bearded bellbirds. Raptors in the area of the center include ornate hawk-eagles, zone-tailed hawks, and double-toothed kites. The oilbirds of the center's Dunston Cave are nocturnal, fruit-eating birds, completely unique in the bird world.

# Trees, Shrubs, and Vines for Birds

HERE IS A GREAT LIST of some ideas for top trees, shrubs, and vines for attracting birds. Any tree or shrub with the "spp." species name implies that any species in the family will work.

## Large trees:

- **Birch**, *Betula* spp., good provider of food, especially in late winter, but not as valuable for cover or shelter

- **Hackberry**, *Celtis occidentalis*, top provider of food, especially in winter, but only fair provider of cover or shelter

- **Spruce**, *Picea* spp., fair source of winter food and top provider of cover and shelter

- **Pine**, *Pinus* spp., fair source of winter food and excellent provider of cover and shelter

- **Cherry (various species)**, *Prunus* spp., great source of food late summer through fall, but only fair provider of cover or shelter

- **Oak**, *Quercus* spp., strong but irregular source of food fall through winter, but only fair provider of cover and shelter

- **Hemlock**, *Tsuga canadensis*, good source of winter food and even better provider of cover and shelter

## Low trees or tall shrubs:

- **Serviceberry**, *Amelanchier* spp., and dogwood, *Cornus* spp., great sources of food from late summer through fall and good providers of cover and shelter

- **Eastern red cedar**, *Juniperus virginiana*, excellent source of food in winter and excellent provider of cover and shelter year-round

- **Crab apple**, *Malus* spp., good source of food late fall through winter and average provider of cover and shelter

- **Chokecherry**, *Prunus* spp., top source of food in summer, but only fair provider of cover and shelter

- **Sumac**, *Rhus* spp., good source of food, but poor provider of cover and shelter

- **Elder**, *Sambucus* spp., good source of food in later summer, but only fair provider of cover and shelter

- **Mountain ash**, *Sorbus* spp., excellent source of food fall through winter, but only fair provider of cover and shelter

- **Arborvitae**, *Thuja occidentalis*, fair source of food, but top provider of cover and shelter

- **Viburnum**, *Viburnum* spp., good source of food fall through winter and good provider of cover and shelter

## Medium and small shrubs:

- **Chokeberry**, *Aronia* spp., good source of food and fair provider of cover and shelter

- **Hazelnut**, *Corylus* spp., good source of food and good provider of cover and shelter

- **Juniper**, *Juniperus* spp., good source of food through winter and good provider of cover and shelter year-round

- **Wild rose**, *Rosa rugosa*, excellent source of food and good provider of cover and shelter

- **Blackberry, raspberry, etc.**, *Rubus* spp., excellent source of food and good provider of cover and shelter

## Vines:

- **Trumpet vine**, *Campsis radicans*, good source of food summer through fall, particularly nectar for hummingbirds, but poor provider of cover and shelter

- **Virginia creeper**, *Parthenocissus quinquefolia*, excellent source of food fall through winter, but only fair provider of cover and shelter

- **Wild grape**, *Vitis* spp., excellent source of food in fall, but only fair provider of cover and shelter

# Doves, the Birds of Peace

DOVES HAVE A LONG history as symbols, mostly favorable ones, in human cultures. They are thought to have a quiet and loving nature, as they are often seen in pairs, cooing to each other. This spawned the term *lovey-dovey*.

It is as a symbol of love that doves have their longest association with mankind. The earliest known association is with the Mesopotamian earth goddess Ashtoroth, whose incarnations in other cultures carried this connection with doves with them, including Atagartis (Phoenicia), Astarte (ancient Syria), and the most well known, Aphrodite (ancient Greece). One story even tells how Aphrodite was born from a dove's egg.

Many Islamic cultures also revere the dove. Legend has it that after Imam Shakir Padshah, a great Muslim leader, died in battle, two doves burst forth from his heart.

All of the doves that still fly around the Imam's shrine in Khotan, what is now part of China, are said to be descended from these birds.

The dove's role as a symbol of peace can be traced to the Old Testament story of Noah's ark. After many days at sea after the great flood, Noah sent a dove to search for signs of land. Noah was rewarded when the dove returned with an olive branch in its beak, indicating that it had found land. Both the dove and the olive branch thereafter became symbols connected with peace, the dove directly and the olive branch as a sign of truce or good intentions. Many Christian paintings depict the dove as a symbol of the Holy Spirit, and several kings and popes over the centuries have taken the image of a dove landing on their shoulders or head as a sign from god that they were meant to rule. In medieval times, it was believed that the dove was the one form the devil could not assume while on Earth.

# Speak into the Microphone

WITH MIND-NUMBING advances in electronics pervading our world with an almost daily cycle of new products, our ability to record the natural world has jumped light years ahead in just the past few years. Anyone who doesn't subscribe to at least one of the army of new technology blogs or e-newsletters likely has already missed a few hundred advances.

Much is awry in our frenetic, digital world. However, that same electronic landscape can bring so much to our pursuit of bird-watching. Recording the sounds of birds is one such niche.

Some of the newer cell phones and related portable devices are now capable of capturing perfectly serviceable recordings of bird song.

Tiny digital recorders, some even smaller than cell phones, can save exact replicas of the sounds of nature. Even the built-in microphones of digital video recorders are making near-miraculous advances.

All of them, however, will perform better if paired with an auxiliary microphone, which can be either corded or remote. Such microphones, which may be substantially larger than the recording device itself into which they feed the sound, are designed to better focus on one sound at a time and to reach out to grab more of the nuances of that sound.

Many digital devices no longer offer auxiliary plugs to accommodate extra devices such as microphones, but a few manufacturers have recognized the specialized market for that capability and kept at least a few models in their digital lines.

# The "Ideal" Birdwatching Plan

ON THE MORNING OF A birdwatching outing, avid birders rise well before sunrise. They've sorted and packed their gear, checking it at least twice, the night before. They eat a quick breakfast—something that takes little time to prepare, but nevertheless fills the belly—a filling of the thermal bottle with a starter beverage for the day, and a hasty launch of the day.

They know birds rise early and disturbances by humans during the first hour or so of daylight will have the most devastating effect on the success of the coming day. Opportunities are easily lost in the faint light of the rising sun.

The beginning site for the day's outing was decided last night, at the latest. The route has been set. At least some of the "target" species for the day are already in mind. Some questions of natural history related to those target species and perhaps the spot planned for the outing have come to mind, and maybe they've been discussed with birding partners for the day. A Plan B has been settled, maybe even a Plan C, just in case something interferes with the primary hopes of the day. Having the alternative plans agreed upon in advance makes for easy shifting of gears in response to circumstances and will quickly salvage a day that might otherwise be lost.

# Ducks, Geese, and Swans: Mute Swan (*Cygnus olor*)

ALTHOUGH A NATIVE resident of Eurasia, the mute swan was introduced more than 100 years ago into other countries, where it has escaped domestication and is expanding its range. As a habitat generalist, it can thrive in a variety of aquatic systems. Ecologists are concerned about the swan's effects on native waterfowl and ecosystems.

**PHYSICAL CHARACTERISTICS**: Adult mute swans are large, all-white birds with a bright orange bill and black knob at the base of the bill. The neck is much longer and more S-shaped than that of other swan species.

**RANGE**: A resident of Western and Eastern Europe, North Central Asia, and parts of the Far East, the mute swan has also been introduced into other countries, namely, Australia, New Zealand, South Africa, and the eastern United States.

**HABITAT**: You can find the mute swan in a variety of aquatic habitats, from brackish to freshwater, where it feeds almost exclusively on plants that it pulls up from shallow shorelines.

The birds' large nests (5' [1.5 m]) are on the ground near open water, but not close enough to be flooded. They make their nests from various nearby plant materials.

**SONGS AND CALLS**: Giving the lie to its name, the mute swan does in fact have several distinguishable calls, from snorts and grunts to whistles and bugling.

**CONSERVATION STATUS**: The population of mute swans is considered stable and increasing, and the species is moving into new territories.

Mute swan (*Cygnus olor*)

# Islands: Tiritiri Matangi Island, New Zealand

ONE HUNDRED YEARS AGO, Tiritiri Matangi Island, located just 20 miles (30 km) northeast of Auckland, was probably not much to speak about as far as birding was concerned. The island has seen 120 years of intensive farming, during which time 95 percent of the vegetation had been cut down and replaced with agricultural crops. However, thanks to an amazing effort by dedicated volunteers, the 568-acre (2 square km) island has been replanted with up to 280,000 trees, resulting in 60 percent of the island now being covered by forest. The rest has been left as grassland habitat. This, along with the reintroduction of some of the region's most endangered birds and the eradication of introduced predators and farm animals, has made the island, now called Tiritiri Matangi Scientific Reserve and managed by the New Zealand Department of Conservation, one of the most exciting birding spots in this island nation. This is a must-see site. There is no admission fee, but you must take a ferry to access the island.

**BIRDS TO SEE**: Eleven species of birds have been reintroduced to Tiritiri Matangi, including little spotted kiwi, brown teal, takahe, red-crowned parakeet, whitehead, North Island robin, North Island kokako, North Island saddleback, fernbird, North Island tomtit, and stitchbird. Other birds to be seen are the New Zealand dotterel, long-tailed cuckoo, bellbird, Eastern rosella, Barbary dove, reef heron, kookaburra, morepork, paradise shelduck, pied shag, silvereye, Arctic skua, and yellowhammer.

Tiritiri Matangi Island bird sanctuary, New Zealand

# Up Close and Personal

A window box feeder will bring some of your backyard birds right up to your window for close-up, intimate viewing. And it's easier to make one than you may assume.

Begin by cutting a 3/4" (1.9 cm) board into the following:

one 11³/₄ x 22" (28 x 56 cm) tray piece

two 11³/₄ x 12" (28 x 30.4 cm) walls

two 11³/₄ x 10" (28 x 25.4 cm) tray supports

one 2 x 23¹/₂" (5.1 x 60 cm) back support

Cut a piece of ¹/₈" (about 3 mm) acrylic sheeting into one 9" x 22" (23 x 56 cm) roof panel and one 11.25" x 20.25" (29 x 51.4 cm) back. Cut acrylic by scoring it deeply using a sharp utility knife. Use a rigid straightedge as a guide for the cuts. After scoring, clamp the acrylic between two pieces of wood, with the score line aligned at the wood edge, then apply pressure on the scored side to snap it.

Along the 22" (56 cm)-long back of the tray piece, ¹/₂" (1.3 cm) in from the edge, cut a groove that is ¹/₈" (about 3 mm) deep and ¹/₈" (about 3 mm) wide along the entire length of the tray piece. Use either a ¹/₈" straight router bit, or a circular or table saw with a ¹/₈" kerf.

Cut each wall with angled cuts that will allow the top of the wall to remain 11" (28 cm) wide while reducing the bottom of the wall to a width of 9" (23 cm).

Make additional cuts to the top of each wall at the corner opposite the 11³/₄" (28 cm) width of the angled cut to remove a rectangle measuring ³/₄ x 2" (1.9 x 5 cm).

Along the top edge and rear (the non-angled side) of each wall piece, cut a groove that is ¹/₈" (about 3 mm) deep and ¹/₈" (about 3 mm) wide, ¹/₂" in from the edge.

From each tray support, remove a 4 x 4" (10.1 x 10.1 cm) square from the same corner, resulting in an L-shape.

Cut a groove ¹/₈" (about 3 mm) deep and ¹/₈" (about 3 mm) wide along the entire 22" (56 cm) of the ³/₄" (1.9 cm) side of the back support and a groove measuring ¹/₈" (about 3 mm) deep and ¹/₈" (about 3 mm) wide along the entire 22" (56 cm) of the opposite 2" (5 cm) -wide side, ¹/₂" (1.3 cm) in from the edge.

Using waterproof wood glue and two deck screws for each wall, attach the walls to the tray, with the outsides of the walls (the sides without the grooves) flush with the outside of the sides of the tray and the short bottoms on top of the tray. The grooves along the back of each wall must align with the groove along the back of the tray.

Apply silicone glue in the grooves along the tops and backs of the walls and the groove along the rear of the tray. Slide the acrylic roof panel into the grooves along the tops of the walls and the acrylic back panel into the grooves along the backs of the walls and the acrylic back down along the grooves along the backs of the walls and into the groove along the rear of the tray. Clean away any excess glue.

Next, apply silicone glue into the grooves of the back support piece and wood glue along the edges of the small rectangular areas previously cut from the walls. Slide the back support into the rectangular areas, with its grooves sliding over the top of the acrylic back panel and the acrylic roof panel. Clean away any excess glue. At the back of the feeder, which is the point where the two acrylic pieces come together in the back support, drive a deck screw down through the back support into the wall pieces.

Attach the two tray supports to the underside of the tray, each with two deck screws driven down through the tray into the supports. The supports should be spaced evenly under the tray with the L-shape that each of them forms facing the back of the feeder.

Place your finished feeder on the outside ledge of a window, with the backs of the supports against the side of the house, affix it with wood screws, and fill it with a good seed mixture.

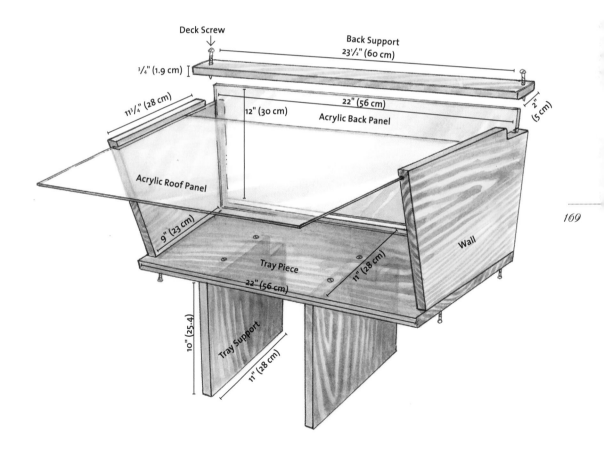

# The Eagle and the Turkey

THE CHOICE OF THE bald eagle as the national symbol for the Great Seal of the United States was not completely cut-and-dried. It actually took the Continental Congress three committees and six years to make a decision. During that time, various ideas were floated, including several birds such as a dove, a rooster, a two-headed eagle, and a phoenix in flames.

Charles Thomson, the secretary of the Continental Congress, was then tasked to come up with a design. He used concepts from all three committees, and drew a sketch of his idea. The front of the seal featured an eagle with outspread wings, a shield on its breast, an olive branch clutched in one foot and a bundle of arrows in the other, and a banner reading *E Plurbius Unum*, meaning "Out of Many, One," in the bird's beak. The Congress voted to adopt the seal on June 20, 1782, the same day Thomson submitted the design.

Not everyone was happy with the design, however. Benjamin Franklin complained of the choice in a letter to his daughter, calling the bald eagle a "Bird of bad moral Character." Franklin cites the bald eagle's habit of pirating food from the osprey, scaring the smaller bird away until it drops its just-caught fish. He also calls the bird a "rank Coward: The little *King Bird* not bigger than a Sparrow attacks him boldly and drives him out of the District."

Franklin instead suggests that the eagle on the seal looks more like a turkey, and that this bird would have been a better choice as a symbol:

> For in Truth the Turkey is in Comparison a much more respectable Bird, and withal a true original Native of America . . . He is besides, though a little vain & silly, a Bird of Courage, and would not hesitate to attack a Grenadier of the British Guards who should presume to invade his Farm Yard with a red Coat on.

**A nineteenth-century illustration of a wild turkey in America**

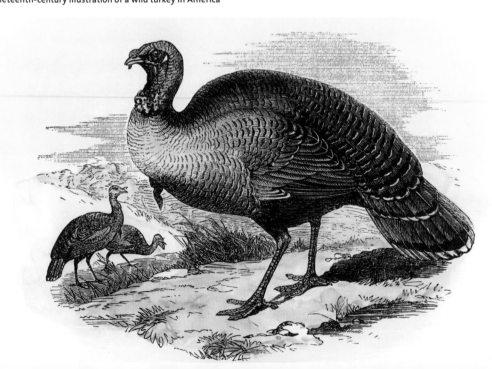

# Better Birdhouses

THE SELECTION IN nest boxes (or birdhouses) has never been greater. Never have more designs and plans for nest boxes been available. It's a confusing jungle out there whenever we set out to add a new nest box to our backyard, whether through purchase or do-it-yourself construction, because so many of the commercially available products and suggested building plans incorporate features that are downright harmful to birds.

Here are a few of the most egregious violations. Avoid nest boxes that make these mistakes. You must make good decisions here on behalf of the birds, because the ongoing shortage of suitable nesting cavities—the natural element that nest boxes seek to substitute for—often leads birds to accepting poor choices.

Although a perch might give a nest box that traditional, homey look, it also will make the nest box available to exotic, invasive bird species (such as the house sparrow or European starling).

A painted interior of a nest box is a constant source of baking, smoldering chemicals. Even the new, natural paints carry loads of toxins that baby birds don't need in their daily exposure. Interior paint also interferes with the natural heating and cooling capacity of the wood.

Metal is never a good construction material for a nest box. It provides no insulation and can become an oven if set in full sun during the intense hours of the afternoon. It's no place to raise a family of nestlings.

A solid-on-all-sides nest box, with no hinged side, will prevent the regular cleaning of the nest box, limiting its life span and creating unsafe parasitic conditions for subsequent users of the artificial cavity.

# Don't Overlook the Common Places

MANY BIRDWATCHERS may prefer to bird in special places, away from the hustle and bustle of our daily lives. But many species of birds do not share our biases against the more common, less appealing places. This is often true of the rare, extralimital birds, who visit spots well away from their normal ranges.

Although these spots may not encourage day trips or extensive travel, they are often found along the routes of our daily lives:

- Small community parks with interesting hedgerows, tree lines, groves of trees, ponds, streams, and the like
- Cemeteries
- Water and sewage treatment facilities

- Shopping centers with undeveloped areas or waste areas not intended for development
- The edges of school or college campuses
- Dumps
- Median strips and edges along highways
- Abandoned sites and vacant lots
- Inactive and future construction sites
- Church campuses
- Roadside rest stops and picnic areas
- Edges of amusement parks, zoos, and the like
- Golf courses

Add some of your own spots to the list.

# Shorebirds and Relatives: Marbled Murrelet (*Brachyramphus marmoratus*)

UNFORTUNATELY FOR THE marbled murrelet, because of its habitat and feeding preferences it has found itself up against major industries for its very existence. Its declining numbers have spawned threatened designation and, consequently, a backlash from the logging, oil, and fishing industries, all of which impact the bird's habitat and are impacted by its protection.

**PHYSICAL CHARACTERISTICS**: The breeding plumage of the marbled murrelet seemingly makes the bird less distinctive, with its brown-and-black feathered back and brown mottled undersides and a black crown on the head. The winter plumage is stark black above and white below, with dark wings except for some white flecking underneath.

**RANGE**: The marbled murrelet breeds from the Alaskan Aleutian island chain down along the Pacific Coast of North America to southern California. It doesn't move far in winter, mostly offshore, but again, little is known about its movements.

These birds can most commonly be seen at sea, feeding on fish and other sea life.

Although far northern populations nest on the ground or on cliffs, most marbled murrelets nest in trees, specifically in coastal old-growth forests. This species doesn't construct nests, but relies on natural depressions on limbs in large trees where needles and lichen collect as sites to lay their eggs.

**HABITAT**: Unknown until recently, the marbled murrelet is now known to nest in trees, as opposed to the ground burrow nesting of its nearest relatives. This, along with their secretive nature (going to their nests only at dusk), makes them a difficult bird to study.

**SONGS AND CALLS**: This murrelet is quite vocal, emitting a series of *keeer* calls in flight near its nest or at sea.

**CONSERVATION STATUS**: The species is considered in decline and is listed as threatened in several U.S. states, where its old-growth habitat is disappearing to logging, it becomes ensnared in gill-fishing nets, and it does not survive oil spills well. Avian predators, such as ravens, Steller's jays, and sharp-shinned hawks, severely limit nesting success.

Marbled murrelet (*Brachyramphus marmoratus*)

# Islands: Papua New Guinea

PERHAPS NO OTHER group of birds is more sought after, more mysterious, or more regal-looking than the birds of paradise. It's hard to believe that these birds aren't some bizarre creation of a fantasy artist. But they are real, and they can only be found on the island of New Guinea, in the Pacific Ocean north of Australia. One site in particular, the Tari Valley in Papua New Guinea (on the western side of the island), with its rich montane forests, supports the most species of all. Searching out these birds requires some work, so be prepared for quiet walks. Yet how can anyone complain about a quiet walk in a Papua New Guinea forest?

**BIRDS TO SEE**: The island of New Guinea as a whole contains some 400 endemic bird species, while Papua New Guinea has twenty-five. The species that can be found in the Tari Valley include Princess Stephanie's and ribbon-tailed astrapias, black and brown sicklebills, Lawes's parotia, and blue, crested, superb, Raggiana, and King of Saxony birds of paradise. The major groups of birds found here include honeyeaters, Australasian warblers and fantails, monarchs, bowerbirds, Australasian robins, kingfishers, owlet-nightjars, parrots, and pigeons.

# Killer Cats

DOMESTIC CATS ARE responsible for more bird deaths than any other predator, estimated to be in the millions every year.

These killer cats comprise not only barn cats and feral cats, but also free-roaming pets, including those kept mostly outdoors, those left out daily by their owners, and those that slip out occasionally. As much as some cat owners may want to deny it, cats are predators. They arrived in their form today from thousands of generations of predatory felines.

They kill to eat, but they also kill as part of their pouncing play and they kill just because they can. Dead birds deposited on owners' doorsteps bear mute testimony that not all of the birds being killed by cats are eaten by those same cats.

Research evidence suggests that cats do not have a significant impact on populations of widespread, common bird species. However, when cat/bird interaction takes places in an isolated, contained setting, such as an island, the devastation can be more complete, particularly on isolated species or populations of birds. And of course, when a cat meets an endangered or threatened bird species, the impact can have new significance.

Keeping a cat indoors at all times is the surest means of guaranteeing that cat kills no birds. The next best means of protecting birds from a cat is to attach a warning bell to the cat's collar to give birds an escape advantage. The third most effective means of preventing successful cat attacks on birds, particularly at feeding areas in our backyards, is to plant thorny plants or plants that produce strong scents around those areas as natural fencing.

# Storks as Baby Bringers

THERE IS NOT A LOT OF clear evidence as to the origin of the belief that storks bring babies to homes and deliver them via chimneys, but it is clear that storks have a long association with humans, which has spawned many myths.

One theory for storks' child-delivery service is that they return to Europe after their long migration back from Africa in early spring, about nine months after the commonly held summer solstice celebrations on June 21, a time of great revelry. In addition, storks were often seen nesting on or near human dwellings. Some farmers even encouraged the birds to nest on their barns by mounting a wagon wheel on the roof, as it was thought the birds brought good luck.

The habit of young storks staying with their parents as a family group for a relatively long period (common among larger birds) spawned an early belief that the young cared for the parents. A law in ancient Rome called Lex Ciconia, or stork law, mandated that Romans care for their elderly relatives. Ancient Greece had a similar law, called the Pelargonia, after *pelargos*, meaning "stork".

Sculpture of a stork holding a baby at a Bavaria, Germany children's clothing shop

# Photographing Personality

WE'VE ALL BEEN THERE. While on a birdwatching excursion we saw a wondrous bird of incredible coloring. We carefully raised our camera, maybe even already had it mounted on a rock-steady monopod or tripod, composed the shot and coaxed the focus into the exact spot, and clicked off a series of shots that we just know would be frameworthy. Back home, the photo has all the color and it's tack-sharp, but it's not the image we thought we had captured. We can't put our finger on it, but something we saw out there, when we pressed the shutter-release button, did not show up in our photo.

The subject or subjects of the photo may lack a sense of character or personality that first amazed you in the field. The character of the subject is often the quality lacking in our photos. Most of us have developed our photography skills taking not-so-candid photos of our friends and families. Capturing personality or character is not a consideration, when the subject is posing for the camera.

However, in our nature photography, we expect more. We want to capture the feel and texture of the experience, and to bring that back for others to share. We want them to feel, see, and think what we felt, saw, and thought when we shot the photo.

A few simple techniques will allow more of your photos to capture the character and personality apparent in the field:

Get in close, but not in a way that endangers or frightens off your subject.

Position your camera at eye level of the main subject of your photo. If that's not possible, take a second to think about an angle that might add something to the image or highlight some aspect of the image. More often than not, a camera held up to your eye while you're in a standing position will not produce the most interesting image.

Zoom in, enough to almost fill the frame with that main subject, but not enough to exclude the setting and the environment of the shot.

Take a few quick shots to make sure you leave with something to show for your effort. But then wait for the main subject of your photo to make what looks like eye contact directly into the lens. The subject might even provide some fascinating facial expression or body language. Digital photography is inexpensive and it is easy to shoot lots of images whenever you have the opportunity.

After getting the images of the main subject that you want, zoom back a bit to see if there might be even more interesting images waiting to be shot, showing the relationship of the main subject to other elements of the setting.

# Where Did She Hide Her Eggs?

LOCATING A BIRD'S NEST, particularly of a less-than-common species that prefers a highly secretive location for its eggs and nestlings, takes time and effort, but both will be rewarded many times over in subsequent visits to snatch new glances of the developing babies.

Watch the female closely during the period of the year her species is generally on the nest. Note any spot where she spends considerable time, and pay even closer attention to any spot where she hangs out just before disappearing into the trees or underbrush. Try to observe the path she takes when she disappears and, as much as possible, her apparent destination.

If she gives you the slip, stop and closely observe the last spot you saw her. Maybe you can catch a new glimpse of her.

Failing a new sighting, move a bit and look at that last spot you saw her from a different perspective.

Still nothing? Listen for her call, or maybe the call of her mate. Scan the entire area for any movement.

If all of that fails, note the spot carefully and return later to repeat the process. Or if you happen to spot her again, start the process again right there.

Patience is key in this process, as she may only be scouting for possible nest locations rather than actually tending a clutch of eggs or a nest of nestlings. Of course, spotting her when she is carrying some bit of nesting material will help to better pinpoint the stage of mating and nesting at which she currently finds herself.

**Northern cardinal in her nest**

# Songbirds: Cactus Wren
## (*Campylorhynchus brunneicapillus*)

THIS ATTRACTIVE AND talkative bird can be seen year-round in its habitat.

**PHYSICAL CHARACTERISTICS**: This largest of all wrens is unmistakable for any other species. Although its general shape is wren-like (downward-curved bill), the bird is more thrush-size. A chestnut cap sits atop a broad white eyebrow. The brown back and upper wings are streaked with white; white underside streaked or spotted brown; with a pale chestnut lower breast.

**RANGE**: The cactus wren is found from southern California east through Arizona, New Mexico, and into central Texas; south through most of southern Texas, central and Western Mexico, and Baja California.

**HABITAT**: Commonly inhabiting all southwestern desert habitats, the cactus wren can be seen both in deep wilderness and in and near towns. It prefers dense and/or thorny growth, such as saguaro cacti, creosote bushes, mesquite, cholla, acacia, and others, for building its beautiful, globe-shaped nests from grasses, shredded woody plants, and downy feathers.

This wren hops on the desert floor, turning over rocks, leaves, and sticks to find insects, its main prey.

**SONGS AND CALLS**: Not as lyrical as other wren species, the cactus wren does have a wide variety of calls, the most common of which may be the simple *krrr krrr krrr krrr*.

**CONSERVATION STATUS**: The population is considered stable.

THE BIRDWATCHERS' DAILY COMPANION

# Islands: New Caledonia

THE SOUTH PACIFIC ISLANDS are known for species richness due to their isolation, tropical climate, and varied geology and soils. Even with much of its original vegetation altered, New Caledonia, a group of islands about 750 miles (1,200 km) east of Australia, can still boast some of the most unique flora and fauna in the region. Of its many plant species, 74 percent are endemic. A mountain range runs the length of long, narrow Grande Terre, the largest island, and divides it ecologically—the eastern side contains moist tropical forests, while the western holds dry forest and *maquis*, a fire-prone scrub community.

One site rich in biodiversity is Rivière Bleue Provincial Park on the main island, Grande Terre. This 22,240-acre (90 square km) park features patches of virgin forest as well as secondary growth. The dry season, from April to November, is the best time to visit.

**BIRDS TO SEE**: The star of the show here is the kagu, a truly unique bird that has no close living relatives. Somewhat similar in appearance to rails and herons but nearly flightless, this white and ash-gray bird roots around in the soil for insects. There are more than twenty endemic bird species, such as the New Caledonia imperial pigeon, cloven feathered dove, and New Caledonian owlet-nightjar.

Cactus wren (*Campylorhynchus brunneicapillus*)

# Kitchen Scraps for Birds

NONMEAT AND NONDAIRY scraps from the kitchen, even fruit that you're about to toss into the trash, can be offered to birds as supplemental food and potential variety in their diet. Most vegetables hold very little interest for birds.

The key is to remember that most backyard bird species prefer their food in relatively small pieces. Crumble the old cookies and stale bread. Dice the old apples or grapes or oranges.

If rodents are a concern in your backyard, string the old produce on a wire and hang it below one of your feeders. Offering all kitchen scraps on a raised platform feeder also has been known to limit rodent response.

Kitchen scraps may not attract rare birds, although some new fruit eaters might visit. And scattering the scraps on the ground will most likely attract common blackbirds, such as starlings and grackles. Large scraps visible from the sky often will draw in crows, which many backyard feeder arrays normally do not attract.

# Bird Artists: John James Audubon

STARTING LIFE inauspiciously in 1785 as the bastard son of a French plantation owner in Haiti, John James Audubon went on to make both a name for himself and incredibly significant, groundbreaking contributions to ornithology and wildlife art.

His early interests in the natural world, and birds in particular, were encouraged by his father during his early years in France. After immigrating to the United States, Audubon spent several years on the family farm near Philadelphia where he passed his days hunting and drawing. This is where he hatched his idea to embark on a project to paint the birds of the New World more lifelike than had ever been done before.

Audubon became an expert taxidermist. Instead of stuffing and mounting birds in stiff poses for rendering as his predecessors had done, Audubon mounted them with wire in lifelike action poses based on his detailed studies of bird behavior. His conviction to render the birds life size made for cramped pages when illustrating larger species. The artist used a variety of media—first watercolor,

then pastel and chalk for feather texture, and sometimes gouache. He was constantly seeking improvement, sometimes destroying his earlier paintings to prompt himself to do better.

After a failed business venture on the U.S. frontier, in 1820 Audubon embarked on his greatest journey: traveling throughout the United States to observe, document, and render the birds of the country. When attempts to publish his work in the United States failed for lack of interest, Audubon took his work to England, where he was received like a celebrity. The work was published through subscriptions raised by the artist himself in the 1830s. (Even King George IV was a subscriber.) The first edition was rendered in aquatint with hand-coloring, then later printed via lithography.

Audubon returned to the United States with the proceeds and settled in to continue his work, publishing an expanded edition of *The Birds of America* in 1842. He also worked on other projects, including paintings of the mammals of North America, posthumously published by his sons.

# Giving Your Backyard Birds the Test

A BIRD SEED preference test platform is a simple do-it-yourself project requiring just a couple hours of work.

Cut an 8' (2.4 m) one-by-twelve board into two 4' (1.2 m) -long sections.

Use one of the two cut boards as the base/platform; from the other one, rip four 2" (5 cm) -wide, 4' (1.2 m) -long strips. Cut five 10" (25 cm) -long strips from two of those strips.

Align the two 4' (1.2 m) -long strips upright along the edges of the long sides of the base/platform. Attach each strip to the base with four evenly spaced nails or screws. These two strips are now the sides of the seed preference test platform.

Attach two of the 10" (25 cm) -long strips as the ends between the two sides. Attach the other three 10" (25 cm) -long strips, evenly spaced, between the two sides to create four equal sections of the base/platform. With all five of these strips, attach them with the 2" (5 cm) -wide sides upright. Use two nails or screws through the base/platform into the strip and one nail or screw through each side into the strip to attach each of the five strips. Drill five $\frac{1}{16}$" (1.6 mm) drainage holes in each section.

Your seed preference test platform is now ready for placement atop a pole, legs, saw horses, cinder blocks, or large rocks.

Fill each of the four 2" (5 cm) -deep sections of the test platform with a different type of seed. Keep track of which type of seed is in each section.

Find a concealed location from which to observe the test platform (indoors, if desired).

Observe the platform for fifteen seconds every hour throughout the daylight hours for several days, keeping the sections filled with the same types of seeds throughout the test, and recording each bird you see and the section in which it is feeding.

Next, remove all seeds from the sections and then refill them, each with a different type of seed. Rotating the location of the different seed types ensures that your observations on seed preferences are not being influenced by location on the test platform. Repeat the observation period again over the same number of days, with the seeds in their new locations.

Repeat the process with the seeds moved twice more to different sections of the platform so each type of seed has been tried in all four sections. Compare the results from each of the four trial periods, watching for trends in seed preferences demonstrated by the different bird species.

# Birds of the Shore

Exposed rocks along the seashore, along with all the small edibles the churning ocean deposits in the nooks and crannies among the rocks, attract a wide range of birds looking for a bite to eat.

Gulls, terns, oystercatchers, plovers, and pipits are among the predominant bird species in this particular ecosystem. As if from thin air, the birds seem to materialize as soon as the ocean begins to pull back from the rocks, often even between waves. They disappear as the water covers the rocks once more.

Change the rocks for a sandy beach and the mix of birdlife scurrying before the wash changes just a bit.

Although many of those species will be dashing about, grabbing small crustaceans and organic debris from among the seaweed and flotsam, they'll be joined by other species such as sandpipers and sometimes even pigeons.

Beaches of all sorts are incredibly rich ecosystems, but they also are extremely exposed. Any bird foraging there feels exposed and vulnerable. A direct approach, the type of stroll you might follow on a shell-gathering foray, generally will drive the birds ahead of you, usually out of optimal viewing range, and keep them in constant motion. A much better vantage can be had from dunes or rises overlooking the rocks or beach, with binoculars or spotting scope deployed.

# Songbirds: Northern Mockingbird
## (*Minus polyglottos*)

Renowned in its home range for its incessant calling and adaptable nature, the northern mockingbird readily makes its home around human habitations.

**PHYSICAL CHARACTERISTICS**: This robin-size, long-tailed bird with a long tail is pale gray-brown above with a slate gray upper tail, and very pale gray below. Slaty wings are accented with white edges to the primary feathers. A slim dark line connects the eye to the bill.

**RANGE**: The entire continental United States and most of Mexico are home to the northern mockingbird.

**HABITAT**: The northern mockingbird is unique in that it seems to prefer cultivated and managed landscapes, such as parks, suburban lawns, and agricultural fields, over natural ones. Even when it does occur outside towns and cities, it

is often at forest edges or in previously cleared forests. These birds feed on insects found in open areas, such as bees, beetles, ants, and grasshoppers. They pounce on their prey while on the ground, and sometimes take them from the air. They also feed on fruits.

**SONGS AND CALLS**: North America's most accomplished mimic, the northern mockingbird copies the calls of many other birds, as well as the sounds of modern technology, such as cell phones and car alarms. The species may be able to acquire as many as 150 songs. Unmated male birds will sing at night, often vexing their human neighbors.

**CONSERVATION STATUS**: The widespread northern mockingbird has expanded its range northward into Canada.

Northern mockingbird (*Minus polyglottos*)

# Islands: Sulawesi, Indonesia

THE ISLANDS OF INDONESIA lie geographically between Asia and Australasia, and the animal life there reflects the blending of the two zones. Birders will be excited that they can see representatives of both faunas here, and especially on the island of Sulawesi. The island's long period of geographic isolation (it formed from pieces of other land masses starting forty million years ago) has fostered a very rich and unique biota, and many endemics are present, including about 100 bird species out of a rough total of 330.

Several national parks offer birders the opportunity to see much of this avifauna. Tangkoko-Batuangas Dua Saudara National Park and Bogani Nani Wartabone National Park are in the northeast area of the island, and Lore Lindu National Park lies toward the center, near the city of Palau.

**BIRDS TO SEE**: At any of these sites, one of the main attractions is the maleo, a megapode. This is a fowl-like group of birds known for burying their eggs in the ground to incubate them, using the heat of the geothermal activity below ground, in the maleo's case, or the heat of mounds of decaying vegetation piled on top, in other megapodes.

Kingfishers are well represented at Bogani, with species including Sulawesi dwarf, green-backed, great-billed, and lilac. Other exceptional species include ivory-backed wood-swallow, grosbeak starling, Sulawesi masked owl, yellow-breasted racket-tail, and purple needletail.

At Lore Lindu, visitors can see red-knobbed hornbill, speckled boobook, yellow-breasted and golden-mantled racquet-tails, green imperial pigeon, gray-headed imperial pigeon, Sulawesi hanging parrot, pygmy and ashy woodpeckers, purple-bearded bee-eater, white-necked myna, red-bellied pitta, Sulawesi woodcock, and Heinrich's nightjar.

# An Attempt at Squirrel Proofing

PEOPLE WHO TRY to keep squirrels away from their bird feeders should be aware that they face some formidable adversaries. Squirrels can jump as much as 5' (1.5 m) straight up and more than 10' (3 m) laterally. They can climb nearly any surface, from trees to sides of houses to bird-feeder poles. Using their tails for support and balance, they can hang from their back feet to reach and grasp with their front paws. They have two sets of sharp incisors for gnawing through their primary food of nuts, but those choppers also can do incredible damage to feeders and nest boxes. They have a superior sense of smell that enables them to locate a source of food at a considerable distance. Apart from finding a mate and remaining safe from predators, squirrels focus nearly all their time and energy on finding and consuming food. They will eat more than their own body weight every week, and still hoard as much additional stores for future use as they can.

Against that arsenal, we have come up with a nearly endless array of squirrel-proof bird feeders; squirrel-proofing retrofits and add-ons such as baffles; and squirrel-proof bird foods or food additives.

Over time, squirrels have defeated nearly all those devices and techniques. And we often assist them by poor deployment of our squirrel-proofing weapons. Regardless of the gizmos and gimmicks we might buy, position—beyond the squirrel's leaping range—is always our first line of defense.

The most effective squirrel deterrent is a mesh-wire excluder that fits over existing feeders to prevent squirrels, but not birds, from reaching the seed in the bird feeder.

Commercially produced versions exist, both installed on new feeders and as retrofits for existing feeders, but it's an easy do-it-yourself project. A variation is a wire cage erected around the feeder, incorporating wire spacing that will allow small birds to pass through, but will keep out the squirrels.

Baffles can be effective in thwarting squirrels, and can be made even more so through various creative adaptations. Hanging feeders and their overhanging baffles from thin but strong wires doubles the level of difficulty for the rodents. Adding a second baffle also can bump up the obstacle level facing the squirrels.

Offering only safflower seed in the feeders will encourage the squirrels to lose interest and seek their seeds elsewhere. They show a distinct lack of preference for safflower. Unfortunately, so do many, many bird species, including a majority of the common backyard feeder birds.

Various capsaicin (hot pepper)-based products have been shown to be effective in causing squirrels to avoid bird seed. They are available in premixed seed blends and as additives. They also can be homemade with ground cayenne pepper.

Capsaicin is effective because mammals, including squirrels, can taste the heat, but birds cannot. However, the fiery spice still gets into their systems with the seed, which raises questions about its impact on birds.

# Mythical Birds: Stymphalian Birds

IN GREEK MYTHOLOGY, the son of Zeus, Heracles (known as Hercules in Roman mythology), after being driven mad by Hera, slew his own children. As penance, he was assigned the Twelve Labors. One of these tasks was to destroy the feared Stymphalian Birds who had taken over a deeply forested region of Arcadia around Lake Stymphalia, where they destroyed crops and fruit trees. One version of the myth states that the birds had migrated to the region after being driven out of their former home by a pack of wolves.

In any case, these birds were fearsome creatures, with metal feathers that they could shoot like arrows and kill men with.

After arriving at the lake, Heracles realized his task would not be as easy as he thought, as the forest was too dense and dark to fight in and the muck around the perimeter of the lake was too deep to move through. Two gods friendly to Heracles appeared to assist him: Athena, the goddess of invention, and Hephaestus, the god of blacksmiths and metallurgy. Together, they crafted a set of immense clappers, or cymbals, which Heracles smacked together from an adjacent mountain. This sent the Stymphalian Birds up from the trees and into the sky, from where Heracles was able to shoot them down with his bow and arrows. Some birds escaped the barrage, but they left the region, never to return.

# Recycled Mini Ponds

IN THE THROWAWAY society that we occupy, an incredible numbers of bathtubs and sinks find their way into our landfills as we remodel and upgrade our homes. Usually those tubs and sinks are not structurally flawed. They just don't fit the new decor.

With a bit of permanent plastic sealant for the drainage holes and some admittedly strenuous labor, we can repurpose those tubs and sinks into perfectly serviceable mini ponds for our backyards.

The most difficult part of the process lies in digging a hole that is large enough to bury the tub or sink where you want to have your new mini pond. It's hard enough work to pain the back, but it's probably not a large enough job to justify hiring or renting heavy digging equipment.

Although some people will want to allow a bit of the tub or sink to remain above ground and exposed, to showcase their creative abilities, most prefer to sink all evidence of the tub's or sink's former life, to achieve a more natural appearance with the new mini pond. That's really a personal choice that will not interfere with avian use of the final product.

Moving the tub or sink into the hole you dig is another back-straining part of this job. Remember that many hands make for lighter work.

With the tub or sink submerged in its new home, and the drainage holes sealed, add rocks and stones to create various depths—including an edge depth of no more than 2" to 3" (5 to 7.6 cm) for wading by the birds. Position a mini pond pump and filter to meet your personal aesthetics, and fill your new mini pond with water. You can add water plants in commercially available planting baskets.

Albrecht Dürer's 1600 painting (oil on panel)
*Hercules and the Stymphalian Birds*

# Fall Flocks

LATE SUMMER THROUGH early winter, birds of all sorts gather into their fall and winter flocks.

"Black birds," the collective name for various species including grackles, red-winged blackbirds, starlings, and others, are the first to flock together.

Mourning doves are among the next species to build larger and larger flocks, as birds already moving south from regions to the north.

Canada geese soon collect in groups larger than the family subflocks in which they've spent the summer. The impending migration to warmer, more food-rich environments—as signaled by decreasing amounts of daylight and slowly declining food supplies—is the big motivator.

During migration the birds will need to constantly find new food, roosting sites, and safe zones and stay on course, tasks made easier when the senses of many birds are tuned into it and when some of the group may have experience along the route from previous years.

To many species of birds, notably many duck species, the presence of others of their kind increases the appeal of a site. This phenomenon is called *local enhancement*.

For large, formation-flying birds such as geese, migrating in flocks also has added aerodynamic benefits. When they fly in a V formation, the whole flock increases the distance it can cover. As each bird flaps its wings, it creates a vortex in the air that provides an uplift for the bird following it. Lead birds regularly tire and fall back into the flock, with another of the group taking their place for a period.

Flocking also provides defense against predators that could make short work of any of the birds on their own. In a flock of birds, many sets of eyes are always scanning the environment in many different directions for the first hint of any danger. When one bird spots an approaching predator and takes flight, others can take their clue to do the same.

And when a flock of similarly colored birds takes flight, a predator has difficulty focusing on just one target and may become confused. It may even hesitate in entering the rolling, changing, swirling mass of birds.

Some bird species also gather in flocks for social and reproductive reasons.

# Songbirds: Bicknell's Thrush
## (*Catharus bicknelli*)

ALTHOUGH BICKNELL'S THRUSH was first discovered in the late 1800s, it wasn't designated a distinct species until 1995. Formerly, it was considered a subspecies of the gray-cheeked thrush. Now that its presence is confirmed, ecologists are racing to find out as much as they can about this secretive bird before its small numbers diminish even further.

**PHYSICAL CHARACTERISTICS**: This handsome bird sports a brown to olive-brown back with chestnut-colored edge feathers on its tail and wings. The head is a similar color with a white eye ring. The bird's undersides are white, with the upper breast covered with broad spots of dark brown over a pale yellowish color. One characteristic that separates this bird from the gray-cheeked thrush is the yellow color of the Bicknell's lower bill.

**RANGE**: From southern Quebec east to Nova Scotia and south through the mountains of northern New England in the United States, to as far south as New York's Catskill Mountains, is where the Bicknell's thrush makes its breeding home. The bird winters in the Caribbean islands of the Dominican Republic, as well as in Jamaica, Puerto Rico, and Cuba.

**HABITAT**: The Bicknell's thrush breeds in dense balsam fir forests at greater than 3,600' (1,100 m) in elevation. The species prefers recently disturbed habitats, such as the dense plant growth that occurs after wind, snow, or ice damage to trees; it also uses forests adjacent to ski slopes and road cuts. This thrush also utilizes high-elevation forests in its wintering range.

Insects are its primary food, and it gleans these by hopping around the forest floor. The birds build cup-shaped nests out of twigs and moss primarily in young balsam fir trees.

**SONGS AND CALLS**: Like other thrushes, the Bicknell's thrush's song is complex, melodious, and flutelike. Peterson's field guide describes it as *whee-toolee-wee*. Another researcher described it in more detail as *chook-chook, wee-o, wee-o, wee-o-ti-t-ter-ee*. The most common call note can be described as a whistling, modulated *beer* note.

**CONSERVATION STATUS**: Reliable census numbers are difficult to gather, due to the bird's secretive nature. Researchers suspect that habitat changes in the species' wintering range may be responsible for the decline.

Bicknell's thrush (*Catharus bicknelli*)

# Islands: Spiny Forest, Madagascar

THE NUMBER AND TYPES of bird species on Madagascar are truly unique—nothing of its kind can be seen anywhere else in the world. Many areas of the country are home to great birding, but the Spiny Forest offers birders the chance to see some of the most unique habitats and birds on the island.

Located in the southwest corner of Madagascar in the rain shadow of the eastern highlands, the Spiny Forest is best known for its unique family of cactuslike plants, the Didiereaceae, which only exist on Madagascar. They thrive in the subarid conditions of this region and, along with the unique baobab trees and other endemic plant species, play host to some very unusual birds. One of the most notable is the subdesert mesite, a ground-dwelling bird possibly related to rails and similar in appearance to the roadrunner. The mesite's long, curved bill is used for picking insects and seeds off the dry ground. They do not have well-developed flight and will often climb up to their nests in trees rather than fly.

**BIRDS TO SEE**: Species found here include red-shouldered vanga and Madagascar hoopoe. The mesite and the elusive long-tailed ground roller are found only in the small sliver of coastal strip in the northwestern corner of this ecoregion.

Couas are also endemic to Madagascar, and five of the ten species (crested, Verreaux's, red-capped, giant, and running) occur in the Spiny Forest. Related to cuckoos, couas of the Spiny Forest are both ground-dwelling and tree-dwelling. Their name comes from their calls—*koa-koa*—and the birds are known for their colorful skin patches behind their eyes.

# Winter Roosting Box

SOME SPECIES OF backyard birds seek interior spaces to escape the coldest nights of winter. They may use regular nest boxes left in place year-round, but a specially made winter roosting box can make them even more comfortable.

A winter roosting box has its entrance hole moved down to be level with the floor with a small landing perch outside the hole, like a front porch with a welcome mat. You can alter a basic nest box into a winter roosting box by adding dowel-rod roosting perches inside the box. Drill holes into both sides of the box, offsetting and alternating placement. Insert dowels cut to half the width of the box. Use wood glue to secure the rods in place.

The perches should be alternated front to back, so birds are not perching directly above other birds on lower perches.

The birds will snuggle tight against one another inside the box, sharing body heat and feathery insulation. The alternating perches allow the birds to achieve that goal.

Hinged access for cleaning a winter roosting box should be through the top. The walls and floors should be intact with minimal leaks to protect the birds from cold winds, snow, and sleet.

For added shelter, place the box on the side of a tree, post, or wall with the entrance hole facing away from the direction that most winter winds blow.

# The Owl's Many Faces

PERHAPS MORE THAN any other group of birds, the owl has been the source of many myths and much folklore through the ages. This is probably due to the bird's mysterious nocturnal habits, as well as its unusual, haunting calls. From the ancient Egyptians to today's Harry Potter stories, owls have been assigned all sorts of powers and have been held responsible for deeds both good and evil.

The ancient Greeks saw the owl as a positive force, with their goddess of wisdom and war, Athene, often accompanied by an owl. An earlier form of the goddess was aligned with the power of lightning and storms. This may account for later European practices of nailing a dead owl to a barn to ward off lightning strikes. The goddess's later association with war led to the view of owls as a good omen on the battlefield. The expression "There goes an owl" was used when success or victory was assured.

The owl also became associated with Minerva, the Roman goddess of prophetic wisdom. This led to the owl becoming a symbol of this quality, a belief that still lingers in popular culture today. The use of owl parts in witchcraft no doubt arose from these beliefs. Owls' powers of prophecy evolved into the bird becoming linked with death, so that in many cultures the sight of an owl is considered a bad omen. During later periods of the Roman Empire the birds became despised by some, and were thought to have caused the deaths of three emperors. The Roman goddess of the underworld, Hecate, had an owl as her companion. The Christian Church also assigned evil qualities to the owl, likely as a way to combat paganism but also likely out of fear of the owl's nocturnal habits.

Various other beliefs have grown up around owls, including the assigning of gender to a baby (France, Germany, Jewish folklore), choosing whether a child would live or die (Berbers of North Africa), eating owl eggs as a cure for drunkenness (ancient Greeks) and improving night vision (India), and using the heart and legs as a truth serum (nineteenth-century Amish folklore), among many other myths.

Owls are also used commonly as symbols or featured as characters in literature and popular culture, including in works by Shakespeare (*Hamlet, Henry VI*), J. K. Rowling (*Harry Potter*), T. H. White (*The Once and Future King* and *The Book of Merlyn*), and Farley Mowat (*Owls in the Family*). Some well-known owl characters in comics include Nite Owl from *The Watchmen* and Howland Owl from the classic *Pogo* comic strip, to name just a few.

# Trailcams: Eyes on the Ground, Other Than Your Own

USE A TRAIL CAMERA, or trail cam, to track birds and other wildlife in your backyard when you can't be there to enjoy the show in person.

Trail cams are motion-triggered cameras inside weatherproof housings mounted to trees along game trails or other spots where unmanned surveillance is wanted, and are left there to record images of whatever happens to pass. Models are available in styles from bare-bones basic to ultra-slick, ultra-fast, nothing-gets-by-me, full-color infrared devices.

Although there are plenty of high-tech add-ons that are not necessary for enhancing the outdoor experience, trail cams really are a great investment, whatever level of investment fits the budget.

The low-end camera models many birders use may not produce great photography, but they sure are great fun. With them, you can know what birds are at your feeder any time of the day, regardless of where you happen to be. (For more on trail cams, see Days 223+224.)

# Understanding Your Binoculars

MANY SPECIES OF birds aren't interested in venturing close enough to humans to give us the detailed views we hope to experience, but a good set of binoculars will extend our vision into the bird's personal space without alarming the bird in any way.

Although good binoculars range in price from the affordable to nearly unimaginable luxury prices, the basic mechanics are similar across them all and must be understood by those aiming to make a smart buying decision.

The *power* of the binoculars, or *magnification*, is expressed by a number followed by the letter X. The number is amount that the binoculars will magnify an image. For example, binoculars with a power of 7X magnify the image seven times. Binoculars of 7X or 8X are useful for most backyard and casual birders.

The number after the X reveals the size of the binocular lens (such as 30 or 35). The larger it is the more light-gathering capability the binoculars will offer. And the better the light-gathering capability of the binoculars, the better the images viewed through them will be, especially under low-light conditions.

A third number indicates the field of view for images viewed through the binoculars. This third number might be in degrees or in feet, and it notes the width of the image being viewed when seen through the binoculars from 1,000' (305 m) away. As this third number grows larger, the binoculars' field of view grows wider. A wider field of view makes binoculars easier to focus and find targets through the lens, while a narrower field of view offers fewer extraneous details but a higher level of difficulty in focusing.

# Songbirds: Red-Breasted Nuthatch (*Sitta canadensis*)

LIKE OTHER NUTHATCH species, the red-breasted nuthatch feeds by climbing downward on a tree trunk, probing the bark for insects. Many species prefer different habitats within their ranges, but may be seen at birdfeeders together.

**PHYSICAL CHARACTERISTICS:** The dynamic plumage of the red-breasted nuthatch includes a black cap with bright white line below and another dark line through the eye from the bill to the back of the head. A white throat grades into a rusty-colored belly in males and pale orange in females. This color contrasts nicely with the blue-gray back.

Like other nuthatches and like woodpeckers, this bird's flight is undulating, a helpful identification feature.

**RANGE:** This species can be found year-round from the edge of the tree line in Alaska and Canada south through the inland and coastal western United States, and in New England and south along the Appalachian Mountain chain down to Georgia.

In years when there is a poor conifer seed crop, populations will irrupt, or move south out of their normal range in search of food. This can extend as far south as the rest of the United States to the Mexico border.

**HABITAT:** Spruce-fir forests in the boreal region are the preferred habitat of the red-breasted nuthatch. The bird feeds on insects in the breeding season and on conifer seeds in winter.

These small birds excavate their own cavities in trees to make their nests. They line the cavities with grasses, pine needles, fur, feathers, and other plant material, and sometimes coat the entrance with tree sap, perhaps to make the hole smaller to deter predators.

**SONGS AND CALLS:** The common call of the red-breasted nuthatch is a nasal *yank yank*, similar to but more nasal than that of the white-breasted nuthatch, whose range overlaps with it.

**CONSERVATION STATUS:** Populations of the red-breasted nuthatch are healthy and increasing.

Red-breasted nuthatch (*Sitta canadensis*)

# Islands: Andasibe-Mantadida National Park, Madagascar

LOCATED ON THE eastern escarpment of Madagascar, Andasibe-Mantadida National Park is a prime birding site to visit on the Malagasy island. Subject to the southeastern trade winds coming off the Indian Ocean, this part of the island comprises mostly rainforest habitat, so the plant and animal species are very different from the Spiny Forest.

Only about a three-hour drive from the capital, Antananarivo, Analamazoatra Reserve, one of the two components of the park, is a good first stop on a birding trip. Mantadida is farther and requires a guide. Several hotels are located near the park entrance.

**BIRDS TO SEE**: Fully seventy species of birds can be found in this park, including several species of vangas, a genera of birds endemic to Madagascar. Other rainforest species seen in the park include the common sunbird-asity and the velvety asity. Malagasy bulbill, Madagascar wagtail, Souimanga sunbird, Malagasy paradise flycatcher, Henst's goshawk, Madagascar sparrowhawk, Malagasy scops owl, and Madagascar pygmy kingfisher.

# Knitting Nests

MANY SPECIES OF BIRDS are not very picky about the materials they incorporate into their nests. Grass, sticks, lichen, mud, and the like, of course, are the basics for a great many species. But plastic bread bags, old discarded twine, balloon shreds, and a thousand other cast-offs from everyday human life are also acceptable to many nest builders.

You can play into that in your backyard by offering appropriate but colorful materials to your backyard birds. Brightly colored yarn is a good choice, but must be cut into short lengths before being offered to the birds to avoid potentially deadly entanglements.

Simply cut the yarn and drape it atop shrubs, feeding platforms, benches, and similar surfaces around the backyard. Then watch for birds coming to that new source of nesting materials. And a few weeks later, see how many nests you can locate in your backyard and neighborhood that have incorporated your yarn.

Another great nesting material for many species of birds is human or pet hair, which can be gathered from the shower drain, from a vacuum cleaner bag, or after a haircut.

# The Birdman Cult of Rapa-Nui

A FASCINATING RELIGIOUS cult that developed on Easter Island in the Polynesian region of the Pacific Ocean was centered on a ritual involving the theft of bird eggs from nests.

Emerging sometime in the eighteenth century, the *Tangata manu*, or birdman, cult of the Rapa Nui people revered a once minor deity in the previous religious pantheon of the island's people (which spawned the creation of the moai, the Easter Island statues for which the island is world famous). In this new cult, Make-make became the chief god (among four) and therefore was the creator of humanity and the god of fertility.

A ceremonial, springtime ritual aided the Rapa Nui in determining the next ruler of the island's people. Seers of the tribe saw the contestants in dreams. Each of these chosen contestants then picked their *hopu* to be the participant in the competition.

Just offshore from the village of Orongo at the southwest corner of the island lies Moto Nui, a small islet which served as the nesting ground for the sooty tern. The hopu needed to scramble down a steep rock face, dive into the ocean, and swim across to the islet, avoiding hungry sharks along the way. Many hopu were killed in the trying. Once there, the hopu needed to snatch an egg from a tern nest (while likely being attacked by the protective parents), secure it on their person, and swim back to the island.

Once back, the successful hopu presented the egg to the winning contestant, who then became the leader—Tangata manu—of all the Rap Nui people, although he spent most of his reign in seclusion. But his clan was given the distinction of having sole right to harvest the eggs from Moto Nui.

# Personal Narrative: Trail Cameras at Home

INSTALLING A TRAIL CAM in your backyard will give you a wonderful glimpse into the private lives of some of the wildlife that calls your property home. Think of all the places you could watch the local visitors: the brush pile of felled tree branches, along the stream, out by the bird-feeder array, by the trash cans, in the garden, at the base of the ancient oak, and beyond.

One of the trail cams I placed last winter along one of the primary game trails crossing my property clicked away at critter after critter until the batteries died.

Minutes after I left the scene, a gray squirrel darted into range and hopped to the side of a tree trunk. He posed again a few minutes later, on his way in the opposite direction.

A few days later, a red fox in its prime winter coat skulked by at the edge of the cam's range.

Later, the same squirrel made its appearance, leaping onto that same spot on that same tree.

Days later, an enormous raccoon stopped on the trail to scratch behind its ear. He was back three mornings later, and again the next predawn morning, in the early evening two days later, and again about eight hours later.

These motion-activated cameras will capture anything that flits, crawls, hops, or skulks past it.

# Getting the Bird-Finding Edge

THERE'S A LOT OF technique and technology behind those wonderfully unique photos in our favorite birding and nature magazines. The professional photographers behind those photos do much more than simply stroll along a trail or drive slowly along some rural roadway, pointing their cameras and snapping the shutter.

Long lenses, photo blinds, and time are principal tools in their arsenal, and give the pros the advantage over the hobby shooters, though all are available to hobby birdwatchers.

Telephoto and tourists. The first of these, telephoto lenses, ideally of at least 300 mm, carry hefty price tags, but are a long-term investment that has been made more affordable by the rise of digital technology and generally will pay dividends of satisfaction many times over.

Photo blinds are more attainable, even more so by the proliferation of deer-hunting blinds, but can still veer into the very expensive range for top of the line models. They can be replicated in the field with branches, twigs, and leaves, although that requires significant labor and can disturb a site much more than the quick erection of a commercially produced, portable blind. Another alternative is the homemade blind, as explained on page 206.

The third is simply a matter of taking the time to be present in the field at prime locations for long enough periods at critical times of day and season to get the desired photos.

THE BIRDWATCHER'S DAILY COMPANION

# Songbirds: Great Tit (*Parus major*)

A COMMON BIRD OF Europe and Asia, the great tit is often seen at feeders and is considered an aggressive bird. Researchers in Hungary have demonstrated that a population of these birds is killing and feeding on pipistrelles, a species of bat one-third the bird's size.

**PHYSICAL CHARACTERISTICS**: Sporting the dark cap and throat common to other tits and chickadees, the great tit also has a bright yellow underside and prominent white cheek (as the dark cap and throat color also encircles this patch). The black throat narrows into a line that extends down the chest. An olive green back and gray wings are broken up by a white wing bar. The bird also has a relatively long tail.

**RANGE**: The great tit has a wide distribution from Europe south to North Africa in the west through Siberia and into East Asia south to Southeast Asia in the east.

**HABITAT**: In addition to its woodland habitat, this species has adapted to a wide variety of urban and rural human habitats, such as hedgerows, gardens, and parks.

Like other tits and chickadees, the great tit feeds primarily on insects, but will also eat seeds, nuts, and fruits; it is a common visitor to feeders.

In woodlands, great tits nest in tree cavities, while near towns and cities they will utilize holes in walls and nest boxes.

**SONGS AND CALLS**: This is a very active caller. The most common sounds being uttered are those likened to *teacher teacher*.

**CONSERVATION STATUS**: With a wide distribution and increasingly large numbers, the great tit population is considered more than stable.

Great tit (*Parus major*)

# Europe: Falsterbo, Sweden

GEOGRAPHY PLAYS A huge part in the where and when of birding, especially where migration is concerned Coastal edges of narrow north-south oriented land masses often see a "funneling" of species as they make their way along flyways between their breeding and nonbreeding ranges. Falsterbo, a small town on a peninsula at the extreme southwestern tip of Sweden, is one of the best spots in Europe to see this phenomenon.

Millions of birds pass this way on their journey south in autumn. Most notable are the great skeins of raptors, which number in the thousands and sometimes tens of thousands. Visitors can stay in Falsterbo at hotels and campsites, or limited accommodations are available at the Falsterbo Bird Observatory. Planning ahead is recommended, as during peak migration it is often difficult to find space.

The reef farther south along the peninsula near the town of Nabben features some of the best swimming and sunning in Sweden.

**BIRDS TO SEE**: As many as thirty species of raptors have been spotted making their homes over this spit of land; up to 14,000 individuals in one day. The most numerous are Eurasian sparrowhawk and Eurasian buzzard, with lesser totals for rough-legged hawk, western marsh harrier, red kite, Eurasian kestrel, osprey, hen harrier, and merlin, among others. Many other species of birds pass through as well, including warblers, flycatchers, starlings, chaffinches, pigeons, pipits, bramblings, and finches. Tens of thousands, and in some cases more than 100,000 individuals of some species, have been recorded during one season.

# Acorns Aplenty

OAK TREES FOLLOW a multiyear cycle of boom and bust that varies by species. Most of them produce a bumper crop of acorns every two to four years, followed by a year or two of little or no production. During those flush years, we can gather excess acorns and store them for future dispensing to the birds in our backyards.

Gather as many of the acorns as you want in baskets or sacks. Hang them in containers that allow substantial airflow, such as mesh onion bags, in a protected location for several weeks to let them dry.

Check the acorns after a few weeks and remove any that have small holes in their shells.

Those have insect eggs and grubs inside them, and their inside meats will be eaten by those insects. Store the insect-bearing acorns in separate containers, such as glass jars, with wire mesh secured around the mouths instead of a lid.

During the winter feeding season, dole out your acorns, both the insect-infected and the "clean" ones. The "clean" ones can be served whole in your feeders or feeding platforms, just as you would do with in-shell peanuts. Crack open the insect-infected acorns and serve them in the same feeders or feeding platforms, both the remaining nut meats and the grubs.

# Rubber Duckies in the World's Bathtub

THE RUBBER DUCKY, that ubiquitous companion of childhood and adult bath times, was probably first made in the late 1800s, when rubber manufacturing became common. Originally made of the much harder rubber normally utilized at the time, it is made today of a softer type of rubber or plastic, no doubt to suit its role as tub friend. The rubber ducky also became much more widely known and collected after being featured on the television show *Sesame Street* as a favorite toy and friend of the character Ernie. Many charities run rubber ducky races to raise money.

Ironically, this mass-produced plastic toy has achieved another kind of fame as a monitor of global ocean currents. Some well-publicized cargo spills of lightweight, floatable toys and other goods from Chinese freighters in the Pacific Ocean in the 1990s unintentionally gave ocean researchers the tools they needed to keep track of ocean currents and sea ice.

The primary research scientist who monitored their movements was Curtis Ebbesmeyer from the University of Washington School of Oceanography.

One of the best flotsam for the task turned out to be the plastic bath toys, including duckies, beavers, turtles, and frogs. Using satellite tracking and an established network of beachcombers, Ebbesmeyer was able to track the toys as they moved around the Pacific. Some of them even made their way out of the Pacific gyre, the main ocean current moving in a counterclockwise direction around the Pacific Rim, through the Bering Strait, and were caught up in the sea ice for months. But eventually some of them made it over the top of the world into the North Atlantic.

This information gave climate scientists a finer level of information about the movement of wind and ocean currents than ever before achieved.

# Apples as Bird Food

APPLES THAT HAVE passed their prime can be a welcome treat to many birds, including blue jays, bluebirds, chickadees, mockingbirds, robins, thrashers, titmice, and wrens.

**An apple sliced in half** and jammed onto the end of a broken tree branch on a trunk will soon attract small, clinging feeders such as bluebirds, titmice, and wrens.

**Apples cut into small chunks** and tossed into a thicket or hedge, or under an evergreen shrub or tree, will have the same effect on ground feeders such as robins and thrashers.

You do not need to core the apples before you put them out for the birds. The birds will peck away the pulp of the apple and then continue right into the core, eating nearly everything, *particularly* the seeds.

Apples may also be a big hit with less desirable or invasive species, such as the European starling in North America or the Canada goose in England. Many birders prefer not to attract exotic invaders, but the starling's exuberance for apple chunks can be real entertainment.

# Finding Raptor Migration

A SYSTEM OF HAWKWATCH sites has developed that track many of the best spots to sight raptors on the move during migration seasons. Many of these hawkwatch sites welcome the public during their prime hawk-counting seasons, as well as at other times of the year. Some offer programs about hawk migration, with knowledgeable staff members on-site.

To find hawkwatch sites and detailed information closest to home, or in places where you will be traveling, are places such as the Hawk Migration Association of North America (HMANA).

HMANA maintains a thorough and active website, with listings for most of the hawkwatch sites, and links to the sites' individual websites. (See Resources, page 310.)

Many of the hawkwatch websites also offer some specific hints on the best times for visiting when certain species of raptors are a visitor's goal, including time of year, even weather forecasts, and making recommendations for the best times to spot particular birds.

Harris's hawk (*Parabuteo unicinctus*)

# Songbirds: Northern Shrike
## (*Lanius excubitor*)

THE "BUTCHER WATCHMAN," as its Latin name is translated into English, is an unusual songbird in that it is predatory on a wide range of animals, including small mammals and other birds, which it scans for as it sits atop fence posts and in treetops. This species is also known as the great gray shrike in Europe.

**PHYSICAL CHARACTERISTICS**: The northern shrike is a handsome bird, with a soft gray back and cap, black wings (with white patch), pale gray undersides, long black tail edged in white, and striking black mask across the eyes to the bill, also black.

**RANGE**: The Eurasian population of the northern shrike breeds across Eurasia and into northern Africa, with northerly populations moving south to the southern edge of the breeding range for winter.

The North American population breeds along timberline in northern Canada, migrating to southern Canada and the northern United States, penetrating farther south along the Rocky Mountains.

**HABITAT**: The northern shrike has very specific habitat requirements, namely, shrubs or trees near open habitat, where it can hunt and build nests. In the north, this translates into the taiga, or boreal forest edge, where the bird prefers stands of young willow trees. In the winter range, the shrike frequents wetlands, estuaries, and forest edge habitat.

Feeding habits of this species are much more complex than most songbirds; shrikes hunt and feed more like raptors. Northern shrikes employ several different hunting styles, including perching and dropping onto prey, hovering to flush prey, and hopping around on the ground to stir up prey. They eat everything from insects to small mammals and birds up to the size of robins. The northern shrike often takes larger prey back to a known spot, such as a tree, wooden fence, or barbed wire fence, to secure it before tearing it apart with its bill.

**SONGS AND CALLS**: Most of the songs uttered by shrikes are very variable, unstructured, and complex, with whistles, warbles, and gargles punctuated by chatters and screeches; they have been compared to the songs of thrashers. Calls are sharp, harsh, and nasal.

**CONSERVATION STATUS**: The Eurasian population is seemingly stable, but there is evidence of some decline in the North American population.

Northern shrike (*Lanius excubitor*)

# Europe: Wadden Sea—The Netherlands, Germany, and Denmark

STRETCHING FOR 250 miles (400 km) and comprising an area of 3,900 square miles (10,000 square km) along the North Sea coast of Holland and Germany is the Wadden Sea, a vast intertidal zone which serves as feeding grounds for millions of shorebirds and waterfowl. Declared a World Heritage Site in 2009, the Wadden Sea consists of mud flats and salt marshes where birds feed on bountiful shellfish, and barrier islands and beaches where they roost and breed. Nowhere else in the world do such large concentrations of birds exist in such close proximity to large human population centers.

This World Heritage Site encompasses the several Dutch and German protected areas of the Wadden Sea. Three German national parks and one conservation area in Holland provide access to the area for birding.

**BIRDS TO SEE**: Birds that use the Wadden Sea include hundreds of thousands of shorebirds: dunlin, red knots, bar-tailed godwits, and Eurasian oystercatchers, as well as tens of thousands of waterfowl including common eiders; common scoters; northern pintails; common shelduck; and pink-footed, barnacle, and brent geese. Other species occur in lesser but no less impressive numbers; these include pied avocets, gray and European golden plovers, curlew sandpipers, and terns. Barrier islands support populations of Eurasian spoonbill, long-eared owl, hawfinch, and black-tailed godwit, while salt marsh and dune habitats house, harrier, rough-legged hawks, and white-tailed eagles. The list is endless, meaning explorations will be, too.

# How Important Are We?

SOMEWHERE IN THE history of backyard bird feeding the myth arose that birds become dependent on the seed we pack into our feeders, that they will be unable to survive without the free handouts we supply.

Although that may be true for some individual birds, particularly those that are old, injured, or sick, it does not hold across whole populations of birds, not even across all the birds that frequent a single backyard. Sure, they'll take advantage of a steady source of food, and will even spend long hours at a particularly good source of food.

If a food source suddenly disappears, nearly all of the birds will simply shift their daily routine to incorporate more time at other nearby sources. It may seem that they've been spending all their time at your feeder, but they actually visit many sources of food throughout the day, even when one source—such as your feeder—offers food in abundance. Generations of life in the wild have created a natural penchant for constantly finding and exploiting new food sources, replacing those that are not quite as abundant with better sources again and again.

# Bird-People in Greek Mythology

MYTHS FROM MANY different cultures highlight characters that join the features and qualities of birds and humans—and understandably so, as the mystery of bird flight is a persisting human occupation.

The ancient Greeks had a plethora of deities and other mythological characters that possessed, among other things, the wings of birds. Nike, the female goddess of strength, speed, and victory, flew around battlefields bestowing glory upon the victors. Eros, the Greek god of love and sexuality, is usually portrayed with wings, as is the Roman version, Cupid, still seen on Valentine's Day cards.

The Greek gods of the four winds, the Anemoi, were depicted as winged men. Boreas, the north wind, was an elderly man with long hair and beard. As befitting mankind's view of winter, Boreas was described as of ill temper, subject to outbursts. The south wind, personified as Notus, was also to be feared, as he brought drying winds and strong summer storms, damaging to crops. Eurus, the east wind, brought warmth and rain in autumn and as a god, dwelt in the East near the sun god Helios. The gentlest of all winds, Zephyrus was the god of the west wind, the bringer of spring.

The original depiction of the Sirens of Greek myth, who lured mariners with their enchanting songs to crash on the rocky shores of the island where they lived in a flowery meadow, were that of winged women, not the mermaid-like creatures from later Greek myth. Harpies were sometimes confused with Sirens and came to be portrayed as ugly human-headed birds of nasty, thieving dispositions, although originally they were just winged spirits. The fearsome Gorgon, usually depicted with hair of snakes, whose stare caused men to tun to stone, were also sometimes shown with golden wings.

# Bacon Fat as Suet

ALTHOUGH WE NORMALLY think of beef fat when we think of suet, any meat fat will be welcomed by birds. The fat that cooks off meats we prepare at home is ready-made for birds. After we finish the frying or the roasting, that fat is in liquid form, and you can easily pour it into a mold.

Bacon grease, steak or roast drippings—all those leftover products from cooking can be poured into empty, cleaned tuna or cat food cans, muffin tins, or similar metal frames.

You do not need to filter out bits of meat, onions, mushrooms, and the like from the fat before putting it to this use. Place the forms in the freezer for a day or so to harden.

After the fat has solidified, it can be used like any other suet, in cages or bags, whatever is available. You can punch a small hole into tuna or cat food can molds (or some similarly disposable container) and fit the molds with wire so that you can hang them on a hook or nail.

# Making Your Own Blind

ALTHOUGH THE RECENT proliferation of commercially produced blinds, primarily targeted at deer hunters, has driven down the prices of those essential pieces of birdwatching gear, blinds remain a nice do-it-yourself project.

Begin with four 6' (1.8 m ) -long, 1" (2.5 cm) -diameter poles. Sharpen one end of each pole into enough of a point for easy shoving into the soil, but not so sharp as to pose a risk of injury.

With the pointed ends of all four poles pointing in the same direction, attach one end of a 16' (4.9 m) length of camouflage-printed fabric to one pole, with the top of the fabric aligned with the nonsharpened ends of the poles. Attach a second pole about 12' (3.7 m) from the first. Space the other two poles evenly between the first two and attach them to the fabric, also with the top of the fabric aligned with the nonsharpened ends of the poles. Use staples to attach the fabric to the poles.

Repeat the process with a separate 16' (4.9 m) length of camouflage-printed fabric on the open half of the poles. Use a few safety pins along the line where the two lengths of fabric meet, to hold them together.

At various eye-level points along the fabric—eye level when standing and when seated on a folding chair or stool—cut rectangular flaps, large enough to allow the lenses of cameras, spotting scopes, and binoculars to extend through the blind. Cut only three sides of each rectangle into the fabric,

maintaining the connection to the rest of the fabric across the top of the rectangle. That will allow the flaps to hang closed whenever a lens is not sticking through them.

Connect two additional 5' (1.5 m) lengths of camouflage-printed fabric, along their 5' (1.5 m) sides, with a series of safety pins. This will be the roof to the blind when it's set up in the field.

Choose your site for birdwatching. Push the pointed ends of the poles into the earth to form a square. Toss the 5' (1.5 m) roof over the top of the blind, holding it in place with a few safety pins. Arrange your gear inside the square of the blind and close the last side behind you by pinning the loose end of the fabric to the other end of the fabric already stapled to the pole.

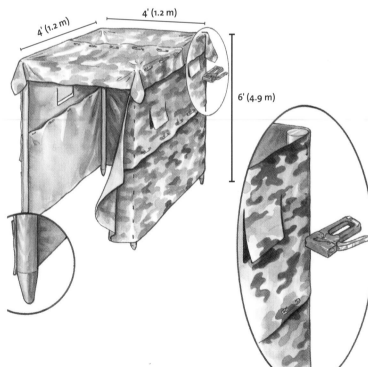

# Songbirds: 'Alalä, or Hawaiian Crow (*Corvus hawaiiensis*)

ON A LONG LIST OF endangered Hawaiian wildlife the 'Alalä ranked highly. By the 1990s, only two 'Alalä were left in the wild, and they were not breeding successfully after 1996. They disappeared in 2002, meaning the bird is now extinct in the wild. Fortunately, a captive breeding program was initiated before this occurred, but efforts to reintroduce the 'Alalä to the wild have been unsuccessful.

**PHYSICAL CHARACTERISTICS**: Very similar in appearance to other crow species the 'Alalä is all black with a stout bill and squared-off tail.

**RANGE**: The 'Alalä is known to have occurred only on the western and southwestern sides of the big island of Hawai'i.

**HABITAT**: The dry to seasonally wet forests on the slopes of the Hualälai and Mauna Loa volcanoes are this bird's habitat. Most of these forests have been logged and replaced with grazing land.

The 'Alalä feeds mainly on fruits, nuts, and seeds but will also feed on insects as well as eggs and nestlings of other birds. They make their nests of sticks, which they line with mosses, grasses, and other material.

**SONGS AND CALLS**: A very vocal crow, the 'Alalä has been documented to utter thirty-four different calls. Shrieks, yells, and howls are used to communicate over great distances, while growls and mutterings are used for nearby communications.

**CONSERVATION STATUS**: The 'Alalä has had a hard time ever since the Hawaiian Islands were colonized by Europeans. Efforts are still underway to reintroduce the 'Alalä to the wild; these involve habitat restoration and reduction of threats.

Hawaiian crow (*Corvus hawaiiensis*)

# Europe: Doñana National Park, Andalusia, Spain

BECAUSE OF ITS geographic location, Spain has much to offer the birding traveler. It sits along the flyway between Africa and Europe, so many migrating species stop here. In addition, the climate and geology work to create rich habitats. Two sites in particular will give you a taste of the country (see page 214 for the second location), although there are many other areas to be explored.

Doñana National Park, located in Andalusia along the Guadalquivir River where it enters the Golfo de Cádiz, provides the birder with thousands of acres of rich wetland habitat, dunes, and scrub woodland to explore. The area's long history as a hunting reserve for royalty has left it largely intact for hundreds of years. Now a UNESCO World Heritage Site, the park and surrounding wetlands support hundreds of thousands of migrating waterfowl and wading birds.

**BIRDS TO SEE**: Nearly 400 species of birds have been recorded at Doñana. Waterfowl are abundant, with such species as red-crested pochard, white-headed duck, marbled duck, Eurasian teal, and greylag geese. Wading birds are also well represented, including Squacco heron, purple heron, black-crowned night heron, little and great white egrets, spoonbill, glossy ibis, white and black storks, and the greater flamingo. The varied birds, mammals, and reptiles provide food for various species of raptors, including short-toed, booted, and spotted eagles, black and red kites, osprey, and griffon and Egyptian vultures. This is also one of the few sites that the Spanish Imperial eagle can be found, although there are only a few pairs. And the lesser kestrel, a globally threatened species, also hunts here. The songbird family can also be seen in great numbers, including crested and short-toed larks, hoopoe, red-rumped swallow, several species of Old World warblers, penduline tit, southern gray shrike, and azure-winged magpie.

# Bird Cookies

FOR THOSE WHO would like to go further than keeping their feeders filled with seeds, the kitchen offers a wide range of possibilities. Here are a few recipes for homemade bird treats. Each can be used as a starting point for developing your own special blends.

**FRUITY TREATS**
Ingredients:

3 large egg whites

3 tablespoon (45 ml) vegetable oil

1 cup (240 ml) apple juice

2 cups (256 g) flour

1½ cups (192 g) instant oats

3 cups (384 g) assorted dried fruit, diced into small bits

1 teaspoon (4.7 g) baking soda

Beat the egg whites with the vegetable oil until frothy. Blend in the apple juice.

Mix in the flour, instant oats, fruit, and baking soda. Blend well.

Drop spoonfuls of the batter onto a cookie sheet, and bake at 350°F (177°C) for 10 minutes.

**NUT BARS**
Ingredients:

3 large egg whites

3 tablespoon (45 ml) vegetable oil

1 cup (240 ml) apple juice

2 cups (256 g) flour

1½ cups (192 g) instant oats

3 cups (384 g) assorted nut meats, diced and cracked into small bits

1 teaspoon (4.7 g) baking soda

Beat the egg whites with the vegetable oil until frothy. Blend in the apple juice.

Mix in flour, instant oats, nut meats, and baking soda. Blend well.

Roll bars, about 1" (2.5 cm) in diameter and 3" (7.6 cm) long, from the batter, and place them on a cookie sheet. Bake at 350°F (177°C) for 10 minutes.

**SEED BISCUITS**
Ingredients:

3 large egg whites

3 tablespoon (45 ml) vegetable oil

1 cup (240 ml) apple juice

2 cups (256 g) flour

1½ cups (192 g) instant oats

3 cups (384 g) assorted bird seed, including black-oil sunflower, safflower, and niger

1 teaspoon (4.7 g) baking soda

Beat the egg whites with the vegetable oil until frothy. Blend in the apple juice.

Mix in the flour, instant oats, seeds, and baking soda. Blend well.

Drop spoonfuls of the batter onto a cookie sheet, and bake at 350°F (177°C) for 10 minutes.

# Bird Sayings, Part II: Goose Lore

GEESE ARE YET another example of a domestic fowl that has inspired many idioms. These sayings run the gamut in meaning and focus.

Someone awaiting punishment for a misdeed may be said that his or her "goose is cooked." Although there is no agreement on the source of this idiom, another one regarding mistakes has clear origins in Aesop's Fables. To "kill the goose that lays the golden eggs" means to get rid of or to destroy the best part of something, thereby spiting yourself. The fable tells of a countryman who found a golden egg each day he visited a particular goose. In his greed, he killed the goose and cut it open to get all the eggs at once, but found nothing inside.

Equality is at the heart of the meaning of the centuries-old saying, "What's good for the goose is good for the gander." The original phrase was "What's good sauce for the goose is good sauce for the gander." The phrase is often associated with gender.

The origin of the idiom "wild-goose chase" is less obvious than expected. The phrase means to be led on a fruitless search. However, it arose in connection with a sixteenth-century horse race, in which riders had to follow a leader on whatever course he chose, thereby mimicking the flying formation of geese. Another allusion to the alleged erratic behavior of geese is the phrase "as silly as a goose," the origins of which are unclear, but the meaning of which isn't. Geese were for some reason considered silly animals.

Although the effect can happen to any bird, the English version of a reaction to fear or cold is called "goose bumps." Other cultures use different fowl for the same idiomatic meaning. This is simply an equation of the raised bumps on a fowl's skin after it is plucked to the pilo-erection of the human epidermis that occurs during cold or fright, apparently a reaction of adrenaline, which causes raised bumps on the surface of the skin at the base of body hairs.

**A small flock of Canada geese**

# Walking on Eggshells

EGGSHELLS SHOULD NEVER find their way into the trash. For those without tomato plants in the garden that can use the calcium boost, anyone with a backyard bird-feeding program can offer the shells to birds.

The shells of chicken eggs are about 94 to 97 percent calcium carbonate. The rest of the shell is about 0.3 percent phosphorous and 0.3 percent magnesium, with traces of copper, iron, manganese, potassium, sodium, and zinc, plus a small amount of organic material that forms the matrix into which the calcium and other minerals are bound.

Particularly during the egg-laying season, but also year-round, birds can use the extra source of calcium, which can be hard to come by in the wild.

To prepare the eggshells:

Bake the eggshells for 10 minutes at 200°F (93°C) to dry out all remaining albumen.

Crush them between two sheets of waxed paper and spread the particles on a feeding platform, flat rock, or open area of ground.

You will find that the birds quickly take advantage of this new source of calcium every time you offer it.

# Rookeries for Mass Sightings

A ROOKERY IS AN exciting place to be in the middle of summer, when the chicks from dozens of nests have hatched from their eggs, are not yet ready to leave the nests, and focus all their energy on issuing constant demands for more and more food to their parents, who shuttle back and forth between the nearest sources of food and the nests.

Although other terms are scientifically more accurate for the nesting colonies of many species of birds, such as *heronry* when the gathered birds are herons and egrets, *rookery* is a generic term for any breeding or nesting place for birds or mammals that gather in colonies.

However, *rookery* started as a word with its own much more precise meaning centuries ago in England, when it meant a colony of rooks, which are a species of small European crow.

Several theories explain why some birds nest in colonies while so many more nest alone.

For instance, cliff swallows returning to the colony after an unsuccessful hunt for food (mainly flying insects) appear to follow other, more successful members of the colony back to prime hunting spots. Seabirds nesting in colonies forage for fish together, again pointing to the benefits of group hunting. However, herons and egrets generally nest together but forage for food alone. For them, the colony probably is less valuable as a source of information on the best hunting spots.

Another theory suggests that young birds in a colony learn essential things about being a heron and surviving as a heron from older members of the gathering.

And a third theory sees the colony as being a safer place to nest, more guarded from predators, by the many pairs of eyes constantly on watch.

# Songbirds: Bohemian Waxwing
## (*Bombycilla garrulus*)

BECAUSE OF THE abundance and short season for the fruits that are the bohemian waxwing's main food source, the birds are not territorial and travel in flocks, especially in winter and during migration. These fruits also provide the waxwings with the bright colors that ornament their wings and tails.

**PHYSICAL CHARACTERISTICS**: Bohemian waxwings are mostly varying subtle shades of brownish gray, including the crest. A black mask and throat are separated by a thin white line, with a cinnamon-colored forehead above. This color is even deeper on the undertail feathers. Dark, nearly black primary feathers are accented with a white wing bar and bright yellow on primary tips and red tips on secondary flight feathers. A bright yellow band also appears at the edge of the tail. These accent colors apparently get larger with age.

**RANGE**: During breeding season, the North American population of bohemian waxwings makes its home in Alaska and northwestern Canada, while during winter, the birds move south into southern Canada and the northern United States. The species also has a wide range in Eurasia, across the entire northern part of the continent.

**HABITAT**: In breeding season, bohemian waxwings are commonly found at the edges of the taiga, or boreal forest, where coniferous and mixed woodlands are somewhat open and full of fruiting plants. Nests are usually in trees close to water, and they construct these out of twigs, then building up gradually finer plant material.

Sweet fruits are the preferred food for waxwings, including apples, cherries, rosehips, strawberries, serviceberries, and others. They also feed on insects, often alighting from their perch in trees to pick them out of the air.

**SONGS AND CALLS**: Because of their lack of territoriality, waxwings do not have songs. But they do utter a variety of calls, most based on a whistle or trill, similar to a rattle.

**CONSERVATION STATUS**: The bohemian waxwing is most abundant in southwest Canada and the northwest United States, and the overall population of the species is stable and even increasing.

Bohemian waxwing (*Bombycilla garrulus*)

# Europe: Monfragüe Natural Park, Extremadura, Spain

As a counterpoint to Doñana National Park in nearby Andalusia (see Day 241), the Extremadura region in east-central Spain offers a much different habitat of steppe, or dry grassland, scrub, and Mediterranean woodland. This is a region well known for its rich biological diversity, and Monfragüe Natural Park, a UNESCO World Biosphere Reserve, is considered a prime example of what the region has to offer. Along with terrestrial habitats, Monfragüe also offers small peaks with exposed cliffs and lakes and rivers. The village of Villarreal de San Carlos serves as the gateway to the park, with a visitor's center and nature center; usually in February, the village hosts a yearly festival, the Extremadura Birdwatching Fair. The rural towns and villages in the area also offer pleasant diversions.

**BIRDS TO SEE**: Considered one of the best places to see raptors in Spain, Monfragüe provides breeding grounds to sixteen raptor species, including the largest populations of two endangered birds of prey: the Spanish imperial eagle and the monk vulture. Other raptors include black and black-winged kites; peregrine falcon; osprey; Bonelli's, booted, golden, and short-toed eagles; black, Egyptian, and griffon vultures; and Eurasian eagle owl. Large numbers of white stork and a small population of black stork can also be found in and near the aquatic habitats.

# Beautiful Brambles

Blackberries, raspberries, wineberries, and their many close relatives are collectively known as *brambles*. The fruits and thorn-covered canes and branches bear a striking family resemblance to one another.

If you are looking for a beautiful and productive plant to spruce up your backyard bird habitat, consider planting brambles. Grown in clusters across significant areas, brambles produce not only an abundance of fruit in season, but also a lot of cover and protection for a wide range of birds and other critters.

Brambles are easy to grow in any area of reasonably good-quality, moderately moist soil that receives at least partial sun throughout the day. A location in full sun is even better.

Berries are produced only on second-year canes, but a mix of older canes, fruit-bearing canes, and new, first-year canes will provide the most density of cover and shelter. To achieve that mix requires judicious pruning each winter to remove just the right amount of older canes, while leaving plenty of the second-year, fruit-bearing canes for the coming fruiting season. The new canes, which will be next year's second-year canes, will take care of themselves, sprouting from the crowns in spring.

Planted in a staggered pattern along the edge of a property, bramble canes will produce an informal but thick hedge that also will be a magnet for birds.

# Evolution of Birds III: Elephant Birds

ALTHOUGH THE ELEPHANT birds of Madagascar are some of the most recent prehistoric birds to go extinct, scientists are still in disagreement about their origin, when exactly they went extinct, and how they became flightless.

The largest of these, *Aeproynis maximus*, stood 10' (3 m) tall and weighed up to 1,000 pounds (454 kg), similar in size to the largest terror birds (see Day 159). However, unlike these vicious predators, elephant birds are thought to have been wholly vegetarian. It is suspected that these birds, alive in the Pleistocene, went extinct recently enough to have spawned the myth of the roc (see Day 103), the immense raptor "documented" by Marco Polo and in *The Arabian Nights*. The eggs of *Aeproynis maximus* were 3' (1 m) across and weighed up to 20 pounds (9 kg), the equivalent of about 183 chicken eggs and seven ostrich eggs.

This last comparison is relevant because the elephant birds are members of the ratite family of birds, one of the most ancient families still in existence. Ostriches, rheas, cassowaries, and kiwis are all members of the ratite family, and it is believed that they and the elephant birds all evolved from a common ancestor.

All of these ratites are flightless like the elephant birds. Some researchers believe that this trait evolved in elephant birds when they became isolated on Madagascar. Without predators, their need for flight decreased to the point of nonexistence. Others theorize that the birds were always flightless, and their size is what protected them from predators. However, there were much smaller species of elephant bird as well.

Researchers suspect that elephant birds were driven to extinction about 1,000 years ago by humans who hunted them and collected their eggs. Fortunately, they still live on in the fossil record and in our collective imaginations.

Ostritch (*Struthio camelus*)

# Making a Feeder Tray

A FEEDER TRAY provides a large space for seed and a large feeding area to accommodate the many birds that often will gather on it.

Feeder trays are available premade from commercial sources. However, they are among the easiest of feeders to build.

1. From two 6' (1.8 m) two-by-fours, cut the following: two sections, each 36" (91.4 cm) long; and three sections, each 24" (61 cm) long.

2. Form a rectangle with the two 36" (91.4 cm) sections and two of the 24" (61 cm) sections, with the ends of the 24" (61 cm) sections butting against the inside of the 36" (91.4 cm) sections.

3. Lay the third 24" (61 cm) section of two-by-four across the rectangular box, parallel to and centered between the other two 24" (61 cm) sections. Attach it there with two 2.5" (6.4 cm) deck screws at each end.

4. Lay a 36 x 26" (91.4 x 66 cm) piece of screening and then a 36 x 26" (91.4 x 66 cm) piece of hardware cloth across the rectangle. Tack or staple them to what is now the top of a rectangular box, but will eventually be the bottom.

5. Flip over the rectangular box and place it between some large rocks or affix it to the top of a post, attaching that center 24" (61 cm) section to the post. Fill it with your favorite seed mixture, and it's ready to begin serving the birds.

> › Tip
>
> The screening and hardware-cloth bottom will allow the tray to drain quickly after rain or snow, which will mean less spoilage and waste in the seed.

# Call of the Owls

Owls are very vocal about the best way to find and watch them. As a matter of fact, it's the owls' calls that are key to finding the nocturnal birds.

The action begins around sunset, as the owls begin calling from the roosts they have occupied throughout the day. The calling intensifies and grows more frequent as the night takes hold.

And winter is generally the most vocal season of the owl year.

By starting in the early evening, listening carefully, and moving slowly in response to the calls that are heard, birdwatchers can follow the calls to the owls. Maybe it will be the accomplishment of a single night.

However, finding the bird may require effort across several nights. Return in the late afternoon or early evening to the spot closest to the owl achieved the previous night, make yourself comfortable, and wait for the calling to begin. Repeat the process, getting closer and closer to the bird, over as many nights as necessary. That process is possible because the owls will return to good daytime roosts again and again.

Each species of owl has its own distinctive call. Among the most common North American owls, the barn owl produces a series of hisses, clicks, screams, and grunts; the great horned owl is the source of the hoot we all associate with owls, *whoo, who-who, whoo, whoo*; and the screech owl is named for its call, which starts high and descends over the course of the call.

# Songbirds: Say's Phoebe (*Sayornis saya*)

SAY'S PHOEBE DARTS from its perch to scoop up insects. It repeats this motion countless times and is a delight to watch, which is easy to do because the bird often nests near houses in seldom-used buildings.

**PHYSICAL CHARACTERISTICS**: The head and back of the Say's phoebe are brownish-gray, and the relatively long tail is a darker brown. The breast is a pale gray grading into a cinnamon color down to the tail.

**RANGE**: The range of Say's phoebe extends all the way from the Arctic to southern Mexico. Breeding populations occur in Alaska and northwest Canada and in the western inland United States. Year-round populations can be found in the southwest United States and northern Mexico, while solely wintering populations extend as far as southern Mexico.

**HABITAT**: Canyon, desert, ranch, and plains country is the preference for Say's phoebe. The main habitat requirement is perches from which to scan for insect prey.

Like other phoebes, the Say's phoebe perches and waits for flying or crawling insects to come by, then darts out, grabs the insect, and returns to the same perch. This can be repeated seemingly endlessly. The Say's phoebe's preference is for perches lower to the ground than that of the Eastern phoebe.

This species makes its nests on ledges, in rock holes, or in caves where there is a flat ledge. A variety of construction materials are used, including rocks, sticks, grasses, mosses, and spider webs, and nests are lined with wool, hair, and other fine materials.

**SONGS AND CALLS**: The Say's phoebe utters a song consisting of two phrases: a low whistle similar to *pidiweew pidireep*. The calls are single noted whistles, *phee-eur*.

**CONSERVATION STATUS**: This widespread phoebe's populations fluctuate regularly, but it seems numerous enough to consider the species stable.

Say's phoebe (*Sayornis saya*)

# Europe: Danube Delta, Romania and Ukraine

NESTLED AT THE northwest corner of the Black Sea, the Danube Delta splits the Danube River into three channels: the Chilia, Sulina, and Sfantu Gheorghe rivers. Vast amounts of alluvium have been deposited over centuries, created a vast expanse (2,200 square miles [5,700 square km]) of wetlands and reedbeds that thousands of birds in more than 300 species have chosen to call home, for at least part of the year. This World Biosphere Reserve contains the largest expanse of reedbeds in the world, as well as various aquatic habitats, forest, grasslands, and sand dunes. Eighteen protected areas make up the reserve. Small fishing and agricultural communities populate the area.

The best birding is done by boat, and visitors can rent canoes (after obtaining a permit to enter the reserve) or take advantage of the many tour boats that ply the waters. Visitors can take a tour boat from Tulcea, the area's largest city near the start of the three channels, to Sulina at the other end of the channel. However, many birds can be seen from land in the region's lakes and ponds. Many islands, created by years of accumulated dead reeds, serve as nesting sites for many birds.

**BIRDS TO SEE**: Some of the rarer species encountered in the Danube Delta include the white-tailed eagle, red-footed falcon, and Dalmatian pelican, whose population has dipped to around fifty pairs. More common species include great white pelican, glossy ibis, little egret, purple heron, common moorhen, water rail, little and spotted crakes, little bittern, marsh sandpiper, and Temminck's stint, which are just some of the wading bird and shorebird species seen in spring and summer. Breeding season raptors include marsh harrier and Eurasian hobby. Wintertime features tens of thousands of duck species, including lesser white-fronted and red-breasted geese, northern shoveler, common and red-crested pochard, and ferruginous duck.

# Storing Seed

BUYING SEED IN 50- or 100-pound (22.7 or 45.3 kg) sacks brings enormous savings over bags of 5 (2.3 kg), 10 (4.5 kg), or even 25 (11.3 kg) pounds. However, having that much seed on hand and gradually doling it out to the birds creates a new set of storage problems.

The seed must be protected from rain, snow, humidity, and rodents, all of which will quickly damage the supply and lead to enough waste to more than offset the savings of buying in bulk.

Large metal trash cans with tight-fitting lids are the first line of defense against all those destroyers of seed. Plastic trash cans are vulnerable to the sharp, gnawing teeth of rodents.

1. Position the metal trash cans in your planned storage area. By placing them under a roof cover, protection from precipitation will be doubled.

2. Fill the bottom of each trash can with 2" to 3" (5.1 to 7.6 cm) of large gravel or pebbles.

3. Line the inside of the trash can with a double layer of industrial-strength garbage bags, with their bottoms atop the layer of gravel or pebbles.

4. Do not fold the open edge of the bags around the outside of the trash can, as you would do with a can intended to actually hold trash. Instead, dump your bulk seed into the innermost trash bag and seal it with a metal twist-tie. Drop a large plastic scoop inside the outer trash bag, atop the sealed top of the inner trash bag, and then seal the outer bag with a twist-tie.

5. Press the lid of the garbage can firmly in place, and you've securely stored your bulk seed.

You won't want to drag those heavy, seed-filled garbage cans around your yard, so find some smaller plastic buckets for transporting the seed from cans to feeders.

# Mythical Birds: Caladrius

SEVERAL ANCIENT TEXTS, including the Greek *Physiologus* (second century C. E.) and the medieval English *Aberdeen Bestiary* (twelfth century C. E.), discuss the caladrius, a mythical bird that attends kings' houses. They are kept for their remarkable abilities to both detect mortality in people and disperse sickness.

A caladrius is placed with a sick person. If the bird holds the patient's gaze, this means the person will not die. The bird can then draw the illness into itself and fly up into the sky, where it will disperse the sickness. However, if the caladrius looks away and refuses to hold the gaze of the sick man or woman, the legend says that the person is fated to die.

Most researchers have equated the bird with Jesus Christ, who is usually depicted wearing all white and who can heal sick people who are repentant, and ultimately takes all the sins of people into himself when he dies on the cross.

It has never been stated which species of bird the caladrius is based on, but birds such as the wagtail, heron, and dove have been suggested.

# Hanging Branch Feeder

THE HANGING BRANCH feeder is a unique but decorative feeder that offers the birds treats. It's also a simple do-it-yourself project that utilizes basic, readily available materials.

1. Start with a board 1" (2.5 cm) thick by 12" (30.4 cm) wide and 18" (46 cm) long. Consider the 12" (30.4 cm) edges to be the top and bottom of this flat feeding device.

2. At the corners of the top, about ¾" (1.9 cm) in from the edges, drill two ¼" (0.6 cm) holes through the board.

3. About 2" (5 cm) below those first holes, centered from side to side on the board, drill a small starter hole, about ¼" (0.6 cm) in diameter, nearly through the board. Into this hole, turn a small screw eyelet until it is tight. The side of the board with the eyelet protruding is now the front of the feeder.

4. About 2" (5 cm) up from the bottom of the board, attach a small, hardwood tree branch, vertical with its ends protruding several inches (or centimeters) beyond the sides of the board. Twigs can be left attached to the branch for added aesthetic appeal. Attach the branch securely to the board with three or four deck screws through the branch and into the board.

5. Attach one end of heavy-gauge wire to one of the corner holes you drilled near the top of the board.

6. Select a support, such as a tree trunk, fence post, feeder pole, or side of a feeder, and lead the wire around that support—above some protrusion that will keep the feeder from sliding down the support; complete the attachment by twisting the loose end of the wire into the opposite hole near the top of the board.

You can hang various foods from the eyelet for birds perching on the branch to peck. These can include berry-laden twigs from brambles or junipers, bird doughnuts or cookies (see Days 83+84 and Day 242), suet bags, cranberry strands, and more.

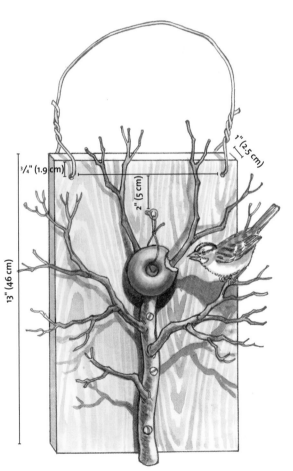

¾" (1.9 cm)

1" (2.5 cm)

2" (5 cm)

13" (46 cm)

12" (30.4 cm)

# Types of Bird Tracks

KNOWING ABOUT BIRD tracks can be a useful tool in finding birds. Most of those tracks fall into one of five types.

**Anisodactyl**: The stereotypical bird track that most of us would sketch from memory is in the anisodactyl category. It has one toe pointing to the rear and three toes pointing to the front. Most common birds leave aniso-dactyl tracks.

Game birds, such as pheasants, grouse, and turkey, produce a variation of the anisodac-tyl track. The rear-pointing toe is generally abbreviated, sometimes to the point of near disappearance.

**Palmate**: Geese, ducks, gulls, and the like have palmate, or webbed, feet. As in game bird feet, the rear-pointing toe is almost nonexistent, but the web between the other three toes shows very clearly in the tracks of these birds.

**Totipalmate**: Webs also appear in totipal-mate tracks, which are produced by a limited number of birds, including cormorants, gan-nets, and pelicans. The middle, front-pointing toe of a totipalmate track is noticeably longer than the other two toes.

**Zygodactyl**: Woodpeckers, owls, ospreys, cuckoos, and parrots have zygodactyl feet, with two toes pointing forward and two pointing to the rear. Owls, however, are able to rotate the rear-pointing toes and thus pro-duce tracks of wide variation. Often, one toe will be pointed to the side rather than to the front or the rear. There also are three-toed woodpeckers that produce zygodactyl tracks, but with two toes pointing to the front and only one pointing to the rear.

**Anisodactyl**

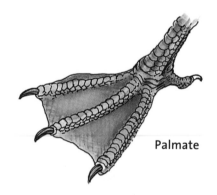

**Palmate**

**Zygodactyl**

# Songbirds: Bobolink (*Dolichonyx oryzivorus*)

THE BOBOLINK IS A champion migratory bird, traveling 12,600 miles (20,000 km) round-trip between North American and South America.

**PHYSICAL CHARACTERISTICS**: The male bobolink's black-and-white plumage and yellow head prompted the nickname of skunk blackbird. Most of the bird's underside is black, and the upper body is white with two wide dark bands running down it. The upper and lower sides of the wings and tail are also dark. A large yellow patch covers the back of the bird's head and neck.

The bobolink is *dimorphic*, meaning the male and female have different plumages. The female bird's feather coat recalls that of a sparrow, with its brown and buff streaked back, brown cap, gray face, dark eye stripe, and pinkish bill.

**RANGE**: The bobolink is a breeder in the northern tier of the United States, and it migrates the long distance to central South America.

**HABITAT**: The grassland habitat that the bobolink prefers has shifted in the past 150 years, with the original, native prairies having been converted to monoculture crops. Bobolinks shifted their ranges to adjust to these changes with a good number moving from the Midwest United States to the Northeast, where forests were cut to open up for hayfields. In time, these fields were abandoned as food production shifted, so their numbers there decreased. The pampas (grasslands) in the countries of Brazil, Paraguay, and Argentina serve as the species' winter home.

The bobolink's polygynous breeding habits ensure good reproduction of the species. The males mate with several females, and they often raise more than one brood. Females construct a cup-shaped nest with high walls out of dried and living grass on the ground at the base of a clump of vegetation.

**SONGS AND CALLS**: The extremely complex bubbling, warbling song uttered by the bobolink is the source of the bird's name. Its call note of *chuk* is similar to other blackbirds.

**CONSERVATION STATUS**: Considered a pest of cultivated rice fields in South America, the bobolink is often destroyed as a result. Although the species has large populations, numbers are thought to be in decline.

Bobolink (*Dolichonyx oryzivorus*)

# Africa: Caprivi Strip, Namibia

AN AMAZING AMOUNT of bird diversity can be found in an odd little belt of land in northeast Namibia known as the Caprivi Strip. This land, bordered by the Kwando, Linyanti, Chobe, and Zambezi rivers, was ceded to German South West Africa (Namibia's former name) by the British in 1890 to allow Germany access along the Zambezi River from its eastern African lands to its western holdings. Today the region is home to no fewer than six ethnic tribes.

One of the reasons the land was important politically is the same reason it's important ecologically: the rivers. These create an area of rich wetlands much needed by wildlife in an otherwise parched region. Four national parks dot the strip (Popa Falls, Mahango Game Reserve [part of Okavanga National Park], Mudumu National Park, and Mamili National Park), and more than 450 bird species can be found within them. Although it is the wet season, the best time to visit the area is between November and April, when the greatest number of bird species are in their breeding plumage.

Travelers can utilize primitive camping sites or stay in posh lodges, including two on Impalila Island, at the eastern end of the strip where the Zambezi and Chobe rivers meet. The Caprivi Strip also lies just north of the species-rich Okavanga Delta in Botswana, where travel is much more expensive.

**BIRDS TO SEE:** The various wetland and flood-plain habitats on Impalila Island make for excellent birding. Visitors here and elsewhere on the strip can see white-backed night heron, slaty egret, African finfoot, rock pratincole, brown firefinch, coppery sunbird, Luapula cisticola, redfaced cisticola, and coppery-tailed coucal. Pel's fishing owl is a special treat. This owl perches above streams and then drops down to snatch fish out of the water.

In the woodlands throughout the strip, birders can often see a wide variety of raptors feeding on termites as they emerge from their mounds. Species include bateleur, African hawk eagle, African fish eagle, steppe eagle, lesser spotted eagle, dark chanting goshawk, black kite, and an amazing array of falcons—African Hobby, red-footed, lanner, and peregrine falcons, as well as lesser and Dickinson's kestrels. Storks (Abdim's, wooly-necked, and Marabou) and hornbills (Bradfield's, gray, red-bellied, and southern yellow-billed) can also be seen feasting on the insects.

Old World orioles, weaver birds, owls, nightjars, babblers, barbets, rollers, shrikes, barbuls, flycatchers, and many other birds abound throughout the strip, so take your time and enjoy the sights.

# A Citrus Feeder

THE RIND OF A large orange or grapefruit can be made into a small feeder for birds, if the fruit inside has been removed carefully.

1. Cut the orange or grapefruit in half. Scoop out the fruit, taking care not to remove any of the rind or to crack the rind at all.

2. With a large needle or other sharp implement, make four holes, equally spaced around the cut edge of the rind cup and about ¼" (0.6 cm) from the top of the edge.

3. Thread twine through each of the four holes, bringing the loose ends together at the center and tying them together, with enough slack to form a hanger for the feeder.

Pour a cooling suet-seed mixture (see Days 167+168) into the cup, filling it to the top edge. As an alternative, fill the cup with seeds. Or to make the rind cup into a feeder for fruit-eating birds, chop up the orange fruit that you previously scooped out of the rind.

Hang several of the rind feeders from the branches of a tree in the backyard for a particularly decorative look.

› Tip

Rind feeders usually can be used only once or twice before they deteriorate and fall apart.

# Carrier Pigeons

HUMANS HAVE MADE use of the natural instincts of birds for centuries via the practice of falconry (see Day 61), but another beneficial use is that of the carrier, or homing pigeon. Many birds have a natural instinct to return to the same roosting location after foraging each day. Much research has gone into determining how these birds accomplish this task. It is now believed that they use a combination of cues to detect their location, including the Earth's magnetic poles, olfactory clues, and even visual landmarks. When people discovered this trait, they realized these birds could be bred and trained to carry messages and other small items over long distances relatively quickly.

The first people to use carrier pigeons were the ancient Egyptians more than 3,000 years ago, but their use became widespread in subsequent millennia. Many forts and other remote outposts utilized carrier pigeons to send news of events back home—the outcomes of the Olympics, battles, and even stock prices. In the mid-nineteenth century, the founder of the Reuters Press Agency, Paul Reuters, had a flock of forty-five pigeons that he used to transport news between Brussels and Aachen, where the information was then relayed by telegraph to other locations. As late as the 1970s and 1980s, carrier pigeons were used to transport laboratory specimens between hospitals in both England and France.

The modern method is for messages to be written on small, thin pieces of paper, which are then rolled up and slid into small, unbreakable tubes and attached to one of the bird's legs. Information can be conveyed using carrier pigeons round-trip when they are "homing" between two known locations, but only one way when one of the locations is on the move. Such was the case during World War I and World War II, when pigeons traveled with soldiers and were used to send messages back to their headquarters. Much vital information was conveyed this way. Pigeons were even outfitted with small cameras that were used to take pictures of enemy locations.

Only recently, with the advent of wireless Internet communication, has the use of homing pigeons been discontinued in Orissa, India, where remote police outposts used them to convey information during natural disasters, when other modes of communication were rendered useless.

# A Nest Box from a Log

FOR A NATURAL-LOOKING nest box, create one from a log. Start with a fresh-cut log, rather than an old one that has already begun to rot. You'll need one that is at least 8" (20.3 cm) in diameter.

1. Cut an 18" (46 cm) section of the log, which will become your new nest box.

2. Saw a straight line across the log but only halfway through, 12" (30.4 cm) from the wider end of the log, which will be the bottom of the nest box.

3. Cut along the length of the log, through its middle, intersecting with the straight line you cut in step 2.

4. The two cuts will meet and remove a section of the log, leaving an inverted L-shaped cut in the log.

5. Using a wood chisel and a hammer or a Dremel-type tool, hollow out the inside of the larger part of the log, leaving about a 1" (2.5 cm) -thick shell of wood on both sides and the back, and about 2" (5.1 cm) of wood at the bottom. Hollow out the larger part of the log all the way up to the L-shaped cut.

6. Into the section of the log you hollowed out, drill a 1.5" (3.8 cm )-diameter hole completely through the wood, about 1" (2.5 cm) down from your previous cut and centered side to side.

7. Reposition the previously removed section back into the spot it previously held in the overall log. Drill four holes for deck screws— two at the top and two at the bottom— through the previously removed section and into the larger section of the log. Attach the two pieces by turning deck screws through the holes and into the back part of the log.

The log-based nest box is now ready for you to place and for the birds to use.

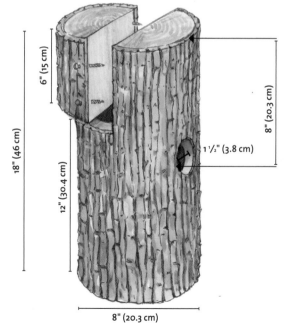

# Commuter Birding

WE TEND TO AFFIX mental blinders to ourselves as we make our way through the quotidian world of our daily lives. As we move from home to workplace, and vice versa, often very little breaks through our mental focus on getting to that workplace or back home. Our minds home in on the route we are taking, potential obstacles along that route, the time required to complete that route, and, if we have any brain capacity left, the goals and tasks awaiting us at the end of the route.

The natural elements of the world around us often are blotted out by the singlemindedness we apply to our day-to-day existence.

Enjoyment of nature is relegated to our leisure hours and open space better suited to that area of our lives.

Such a shame! Most of us pass through an assortment of habitats on our way to and from the workplace. Roadsides and median strips are wondrous wild spaces that we pass by daily without affording the time of day. They are attractive, too, and often packed with a full array of birdlife. And they're right there, on the other side of our vehicle's windows, often still ignored even when we're sitting in a traffic jam.

Add a few more minutes daily to your birding life. Look out through that side window when it's safe to do so. There's a world of birds you've been missing every morning and afternoon.

# Songbirds: Golden Oriole (*Oriolus oriolus*)

THIS SPECIES, also known as the Eurasian golden oriole, is a member of the Old World oriole family, Oriolidae, and is unrelated to the New World orioles of the family Icteridae. It is the only member of its family not to breed in the tropics.

**PHYSICAL CHARACTERISTICS**: The bright yellow plumage covering the head, back, and undersides of the male golden oriole is unmistakable, especially as it contrasts with the jet-black wings and tail. A small black streak between the eye and the deep red bill are also distinguishing features.

The female is olive green above and white below, edged in yellow along the flanks on up to the head. The primary feathers are black, and the top of the tail is yellow edged with black feathers.

**RANGE**: The golden oriole breeds in the forests of Europe and Central Asia, and it migrates for the winter to the tropical regions of India and Africa.

**HABITAT**: A forest-dwelling bird, golden orioles prefer dense forest but are adaptable to a wider range of conditions, including plantations and hedgerows. Like the New World orioles, the golden oriole prefers to feed high up in the canopy of trees, so it is more often heard than seen. Its cuplike nest is elaborate, shaped somewhat like a hammock between two branches.

**SONGS AND CALLS**: A loud, flutelike, three-note whistle is the song of the golden oriole.

**CONSERVATION STATUS**: This species of oriole is quite numerous, with a wide distribution.

*Golden oriole (Oriolus oriolus)*

# Africa: Kruger National Park, South Africa

LARGE GAME ROAMING endless open savanna and woodland, congregating at water holes: This is the stereotypical view of the African bush, but it is one that comes alive at Kruger National Park. One of the largest national parks in the world, Kruger NP in Limpopo and Mpumalanga Provinces in northeastern South Africa encompasses approximately 7,335 square miles (19,000 square km). Not only is the park large, but it also boasts some of the best birding in South Africa and even the entire continent. More than 500 species have been recorded in the park's wide variety of habitats.

Although quite wild and remote, the park's long history as a game reserve means there is good access and several choices of accommodations, from rest camps to private lodges. There is also a wide variety of safaris to choose from. Most travelers fly into Johannesburg.

**BIRDS TO SEE**: Birds of the open savanna include kori and black-bellied bustards; harlequin quail; Kurrichane buttonquail; red-crested korhaan; black coucal; chestnut-backed, flappet, and monotonous larks; and Coqui and Shelley's francolins. Montagu's and pallid harriers quarter low over the open ground, hunting small mammals and sometimes other birds.

The park's woodland and *bushveld* (the transition zone from savanna to woodland) habitats are particularly rich in species, including several species of cuckoos (such as African great-spotted and thick-billed), bee-eaters (blue-checked and southern carmine), rollers, hornbills, woodpeckers, swallows, cuckoo-shrikes, orioles, oxpeckers, weavers, starlings, and sunbirds, among many others.

On rivers through open country, many large wading birds can be seen. These include several species of stork (African openbill, black, Marabou, saddle-billed, yellow-billed, and wooly-necked), goliath heron, white-backed night-heron, and dwarf and least bitterns. Where rivers pass through woodlands, different species of songbirds—Narina trogon, green twinspot, blue-mantled crested flycatcher, and red-capped robin-chat, for example—and the raptors that hunt them, African goshawk and black sparrowhawk, can be spotted.

Birders especially interested in raptors will be in heaven, as there are many species here, hunting the open country for the profusion of prey: from eagles (martial, lesser spotted, African crowned, steppe, tawny, African fish, African hawk, brown snake, and black-chested snake) and falcons (black, little, and Ovambo sparrowhawks; Eurasian hobby; and Amur and Lanner falcons) to vultures (Cape, hooded, lappet-faced, white-backed, and white-headed).

Some camps offer night excursions, during which various species of owls and nightjars can be seen and heard. Lucky birders may see the unusual bat hawk, which hunts bats at dusk.

# Compost As Feeder

ANYONE WITH ANY type of backyard should have a compost bin or compost pile, if for no other reason than to handle the vegetable matter in kitchen scraps, the material that we all should be diverting from the waste stream.

All birdwatchers, of course, should heed that environmental call, but they have an added reason for creating and using a compost pile: That mixture of household trash and yard trimmings is rich in bird-feeding insect and worm life. It's probably one of the most diverse areas of animal life in any backyard or garden.

Birds will naturally scratch through the compost pile for the insects and earthworms as well as the kitchen scraps, if the top is open without any screen or wire over it. They will spend even more time in the compost if the top and at least one side are open.

Maintaining a compost pile is as simple as finding an out-of-the-way spot and getting into the habit of tossing your vegetable scraps from the kitchen and your trimmings from around the yard and garden onto that spot. The composting chemistry of the pile will be enhanced if you also occasionally add a layer of leaves, dried grass, or straw to the kitchen scraps.

# Bird Artists: Louis Agassiz Fuertes

THE INTENSITY WITH which he approached his subjects is one of the qualities most fondly remembered of Louis Agassiz Fuertes, the early twentieth century's most accomplished bird artist. Fascinated by birds from an early age (his parents discovered once that he had tied an owl to the leg of their kitchen table), his interest was encouraged and he began drawing the birds that he watched and studied.

His talents and focus were recognized while studying at Cornell University in his hometown of Ithaca, New York. The preeminent ornithologist Elliot Coues was an early supporter of Fuertes, became his mentor, and helped him make valuable connections, notably to members of the American Ornithologist's Union. From this came artistic commissions and eventually offers to travel on expeditions. His work from the Harriman expedition to Alaska in 1899 and other expeditions, such

as to Ethiopia, Jamaica, Mexico, and Canada, made him famous in ornithological circles, and he eventually became the artist of choice for many major publications on birds in the early twentieth century. Fuertes's work also appeared in children's books and even on a series of bird cards inserted into boxes of baking soda. He primarily drew and painted from dead specimens, as most bird artists of the day did, but he also did many quick sketches of birds in flight.

Fuertes worked with Frank Chapman at the American Museum of Natural History on various projects, including field work and pioneering museum bird displays where multiple taxidermied species were displayed in groups in their respective habitats. A species of oriole that Fuertes discovered while in Mexico with Chapman now bears his name, the Fuertes' oriole.

# Playing in the Mud

MANY SPECIES OF bird use mud to build their nests. There are times when natural mud is scarce within a short flight from a nesting site. Birds will be very resourceful with any mud puddle they find, both naturally occurring and man-made.

To provide a mud puddle for birds, select a flat area of your yard away from overhanging shrubs or dense herbaceous growth, in a spot that affords easy discovery, easy landing, and easy takeoff. Remove sod from the spot, in a rough circle about 2' (61 cm) in diameter. Remove soil or other material until the hole is at least 3" (7.6 cm) deep.

Soak the hole and the area around it with water, until it takes several minutes for the water to leach away. Fill the hole twice more.

After that second batch of water has soaked into the soil, leaving just a wet hole behind, use a clawed, garden hand tool to scratch up as much of the soil in the hole as you can. Scratch, beat, and agitate it until you have a sluice of finely textured mud.

Soak it a few more times and then "fluff" it up with the clawed tool. Your man-made mud puddle is ready for the birds to use.

Maintain the mud puddle throughout the nesting season by soaking it several times each week and "fluffing" it up as needed. The goal is to maintain a loose sluice of mud for the birds for the whole season.

# The Early Birder Gets the Sighting

EARLY EACH DAY of the breeding season, male birds set up a chorus of their species-specific song. It reaches its peak around dawn, hence the name of "dawn chorus." The early-rising birdwatcher will experience the greatest diversity of bird sound of nearly any time of the year. A few minutes' less sleep, a jacket or blanket to ward off the early morning chill, and wet feet from the morning dew are more than compensated for by the avian chorus.

Careful listening and observation will reveal that birds with larger eyes are the first to launch into the chorus, gradually joined by species with smaller eyes and poorer vision in dim light. In addition, the healthiest, strongest males generally will sing longer and louder.

As song is a partly learned behavior, older birds often will have more developed songs of greater length and complexity.

> › Tip
>
> For each singing male, song is primarily a means of attracting a mate and convincing her of her worthiness to breed. Song also is a means of defending a territory and demonstrating dominance among all males in a given area.

# Songbirds: Rose-Breasted Grosbeak
## (*Pheucticus ludovicianus*)

GROSBEAKS ARE KNOWN for their large, seed-cracking bills and dramatic plumage. The rose-breasted grosbeak is no exception, as the male displays a bright red splotch on its breast.

**PHYSICAL CHARACTERISTICS**: The male of this species is extremely distinctive—all-black above, including the head and except for the rump. The upper wings are patterned black and white. The underside is white with a bright rose-red triangle starting at the throat and grading down to the breast. This same red color is found on the underwing coverts (feathers closest to the body and the leading edge of the wing). In the females, this color is yellow.

The female of the species is similar in plumage to sparrows or other female finches, but the sheer size of this bird's body and bill prevents misidentification.

**RANGE**: The breeding range of the rose-breasted grosbeak comprises parts of inland western Canada and upper midwestern and northeastern United States. The species migrates to southern Mexico, Central America, and northern South American for winter.

**HABITAT**: This grosbeak species breeds in a wide variety of habitats, many of them at the edges of other habitats, but mostly in or near deciduous or mixed forests and often near waterways. It can usually be seen in the canopy gleaning insects from leaves and twigs. The species also feeds on fruits and seeds. Rose-breasted grosbeaks locate their nests of sticks, leaves, and grasses in the crotches of trees, shrubs, and vines.

**SONGS AND CALLS**: The song of the rose-breasted grosbeak has been likened to that of the robin, although more melodious, "as if a robin has taken voice lessons," according to Roger Tory Peterson.

**CONSERVATION STATUS**: Surveys have shown that the rose-breasted grosbeak has experienced a long-term decline in numbers in the last half of the twentieth century, probably due to changes in forest habitat.

Rose-breasted grosbeak (*Pheucticus ludovicianus*)

# Africa: Hottentots Holland Nature Reserve, Western Cape, South Africa

THE IMMENSE SIZE of South Africa almost automatically means the country plays host to a large variety of ecosystems and habitats. But nowhere is the diversity of the country more unique and more specialized than in the Cape Province of the southwestern part of the country. Excellent birding can be had along the coast and on sea tours. However, no visit to the Cape Province would be complete without an exploration of the fynbos. One of the most floristically diverse areas in the world, the Cape region is, in fact, one of just six floristically distinct "kingdoms" that make up all of the plant life in the world, as designated by botanists. Fynbos are the main ecosystem of the Cape. The word translates from Afrikaans as "fine bush," which refers to the slender needles of many fynbos plants. These leaves are also hard and resist evaporation in the harsh winds and heat.

The Hottentots Holland mountain range, about 55 miles (90 km) east of Cape Town, provides a good introduction to the fynbos landscape and the unique birds that it supports. The mountains are fairly rugged and difficult to access, so a good starting point are the trails leading from Sir Lowry's Pass, the main route over the mountains along the N2.

**BIRDS TO SEE**: Birders come to this area specifically to seek out Cape rockjumper, Victorin's warbler, and Cape sunbird. Other species seen here include Cape grassbird; gray-backed cisticola; orange-breasted, malachite, and southern double-collared sunbirds; Cape and sentinel rock thrushes; striped flufftail; Hottentot buttonquail; ground woodpecker; and white-necked raven. The rocky outcrops of the park are often hunted by various raptors, including peregrine falcon, rock kestrel, jackal buzzard, and Verreaux's eagle.

# Creating a Dust Bath

MANY BIRDS WILL take a refreshing bath in the dirt if they come across a nice dry spot of loose, fine soil or sand—not as many as will bathe in water, but still enough to warrant adding a dust bath to any feeding area. A dust bath is a simple bird-serving feature to add to your yard and to maintain.

Begin by removing a patch of grass 2 to 4' (61 to 122 cm) in diameter (or square) near your bird feeders, in a sunny spot. As with a water-based birdbath, you don't want any overhanging, low branches immediately adjacent to the dust bath area.

Make sure you get all the roots and rootlets, which will save maintenance time.

From a different spot in your yard, dig a pile of root-free soil. Lay out some newspaper on the ground and spread out the soil. Allow it to dry for a few days. Crumble the soil and mash it with a garden rake into fine particles. Spread the particulate soil across the dust bath hole.

As an alternative to digging soil from another location in your yard or garden, you can mix commercial potting soil, sand, and perlite, and spread that in the dust bath hole.

**Malachite sunbird feeding on a flower**

# Mythical Bird-People in Ancient Traditions

As in Greek mythology (see Day 236), the qualities of birds and humans were often mingled in ancient myths and legends of many cultures. Their allure is so great that it has persisted to this day in fiction and comic books. The most common use of these figures is angels, of course, which stem from Christian and Judaic traditions.

Egyptian gods were depicted with bird heads, notably Horus (falcon) and Thoth (ibis). The Chinese god, Lei Gong the Thunderer—similar to the Thunderbird, the bird-god from North and South American native mythology—is a man with wings. He is armed with a mace and a hammer to create thunder, and is believed to punish evildoers. Perhaps the most prevalent mythological creatures in Japanese culture are the tengu, bird-human creatures that are usually considered dangerous but not always malevolent spirits of forests and mountains. The Faravahar of Zoroastrian mythology was a winged human character, the origin and details of which are not well recorded. The figure was adopted in the early twentieth century as the symbol of Iran.

The Gardu of Hindu mythology is a giant birdlike creature with the body of a man and the beak and wings of a bird, usually an eagle. Considered a minor deity and often the mount of Vishnu, the supreme Hindu deity, Garuda is described as immense in size, with a wingspan that is miles long. He is often associated with the battlefield, as he is a violent god of swift vengeance. This figure also appears frequently in Buddhist mythology, but there are many garudas that dwell in their own cities, and they can take human form.

Bird-people are still commonly featured in popular fiction, including characters in the Flash Gordon, Tarzan, and Buck Rogers stories. Some well-known characters in other fiction and comics include the Veela of the Harry Potter series, Howard the Duck and Angel of Marvel Comics, and Hawkman and Hawkgirl of DC Comics.

# Slugging It Out

SLUGS, THE SCOURGE of millions of vegetable gardens worldwide, happen to be on the menu for many species of insect-eating birds (such as robins and thrushes). They are always happy to help us with our slug problems in the garden. And we can help them by offering better access to the vegetable-destroying slugs.

Lay a board or two flat on the ground (any size board will do), particularly in places you want to reduce the slug population, such as in the vegetable patch. Twice each day, late morning and midafternoon, for example, turn the boards over. They should be covered with slugs and other critters clinging to them. Move the boards to a spot where the birds will quickly spot the easy meal.

An hour later, or sooner if you see the birds attacking the slugs, move the boards back to their original locations, or near those locations, or to new spots where a slug reduction is wanted.

Continue the process until slug numbers dwindle. Although this is not a true method of pest control, it will have a gradual impact on the local slug population, if it's continued over a long period.

# Owl Indicators

OWLS PRETTY MUCH swallow their prey whole. They digest the soft matter of the mice, small birds, insects, and the like that they eat, and then regurgitate the hard and bony leftovers in small, dry balls or oblongs known as *owl pellets*. Only the most indigestible parts of the prey—usually about half of the skeleton—end up in the pellet. The size of each pellet generally coincides with the size of the owl hacking it up, and depending on the size of the owl the pellet might contain the remains of one or several prey critters.

The birds regurgitate most of their pellets onto the ground below the spots where they roost. Accumulations of pellets will build up, providing easily discernible evidence of the roost overhead. Setting up a watch with a view over that roost will pay dividends in observations of the usually secretive owls.

Dissecting owl pellets by carefully tweezing them apart is a fascinating activity on its own. The tiny bones and other undigested matter slowly reveal the species that the owl ate. It's a great activity for sharing between a parent and a child.

# Ratites: Southern Cassowary, a.k.a. Double-Wattled Cassowary (*Casuarius casuarius*)

238

THE SOUTHERN CASSOWARY is one of three species of cassowary, and the only one that lives in Australia; the other two are from nearby New Guinea. These large, flightless birds are in the same taxonomic order as ostriches (Africa), emus (Australia), kiwis (New Zealand), and rheas (South America). The cassowary is known for its defensive nature.

**PHYSICAL CHARACTERISTICS**: Standing as tall as 6.25' (1.9 m) and weighing as much as 176 pounds (80 kg), cassowaries are imposing, flightless birds, with females larger than males. Their large bodies are covered in glossy, drooping black feathers, and their wings are short stubs not used for flying. Atop the head is a brown, helmet-shaped growth, narrow and tapering in profile, called a *casque*. The white face grades into the bright blue of the featherless neck, from which drape two red *wattles*, or loose folds of skin. Skin color changes when the bird is aroused. If threatened, the bird will sometimes thrust both of its feet toward the attacker, potentially cutting the interloper with its dagger-like inner claw.

**RANGE**: The southern cassowary lives in a very restricted range in northeast Australia (Queensland) and New Guinea.

**HABITAT**: Tropical rainforests are the preferred habitat for the southern cassowary, and this is part of the reason the species is endangered.

Southern cassowaries sift through the rainforest leaf litter with their feet and casque for fallen fruits, insects, and dead animals. Fruits eaten are quickly passed through their digestive system, leaving behind many seeds to germinate. As a result, the cassowary is considered critically important to the survival of many rainforest plants.

Males are the nest builders and brooders of this species, and they may use the same nest site in multiple years. After the female lays the eggs, she leaves to find another mate. The male will sit on the eggs for fifty days, scarcely leaving the nest for food or water. Then he sticks by them for nine months or more.

**SONGS AND CALLS**: The cassowary has no songs, but it does have calls, of a sort. It communicates via extremely low booming grunts; it does this by bending its head low and inflating its wattle. Some calls are even too low for human hearing.

**CONSERVATION STATUS**: Habitat loss is the primary negative impact on the southern cassowary, but many adults are killed by cars, many young and eggs are destroyed by domestic dogs, and feral pigs are damaging the birds' habitat. It is estimated that there are only about 2,000 southern cassowaries left in the wild. Although it is illegal to transport them internationally, native New Guineans are still allowed to hunt them for food, and some end up in illegal international trade as zoo specimens or exotic pets, passed off as captively bred.

Double-wattled cassowary (*Casuarius casuarius*)

# Africa: Bwindi Impenetrable Forest, Uganda

BECAUSE OF ITS wide range of altitudes, large number of streams and rivers, varied forest habitats, and lack of glaciation, the Bwindi Impenetrable Forest in southwest Uganda has evolved into a hotbed of biodiversity, with more than 160 species of trees, 100 species of ferns, and 11 species of primates. Many tourists travel here to see the groups of habituated mountain gorillas in the park, but another real draw is the avian diversity, with nearly 400 species present. The highly diverse region of the Albertine Rift—the western slope of Africa's deep Rift Valley, formed by separating tectonic plates—forms the western border of the park; approximately twenty-three species of birds are endemic to this area.

Bwindi is truly a rainforest, with vines, orchids, and mistletoe covering the tall trees all struggling to find any light in the deep shade. The damp trails amid deep valleys, steep cliffs, and waterfalls make this park difficult to navigate. Visitors can explore the region via guided tours in Bwindi Impenetrable Forest National Park, a UNESCO World Heritage Site. However, the trip to the park is long, so fortune favors the bold.

**BIRDS TO SEE**: Most of the park's endemics are found at the higher elevations; these include Grauer's broadbill, dusky crimsonwing, strange weaver, yellow-eyed black flycatcher, handsome francolin, Ruwenzori turaco, Neuman's and Grauer's swamp warblers, stripe-breasted tit, and four species of sunbirds (Ruwenzori double-collared, regal, purple-breasted, and blue-throated).

In the lowland forest area around Buhoma, the park's entrance, visitors may spy choice birds such as the white-headed wood-hoopoe, bar-tailed trogon, dusky and olive long-tailed cuckoos, red-faced woodland warbler, white-bellied robin-chat, Archer's ground robin, and various sunbirds and starlings. White-starred robins, red-throated alethes, and equatorial aklalats can often be seen low in the forest, scanning the ground for ant swarms.

# Hand-Taming Birds

PATIENCE AND A handful of seed are the only things you need to encourage a wild bird to land on and feed from the palm of your hand. In prime wild-bird-feeding periods, such as late fall into early spring, when natural food sources are less abundant, the wait may be just ten to twenty minutes, and rarely more than a couple of hours.

Empty all your backyard feeders the night before you plan to attempt hand taming. Place a comfortable chair, with armrests, near your feeders.

The next morning, before full sunrise, sit in the chair with your arms resting on the armrests and a pile of seed in your upturned palms. Get comfortable and wait.

Your backyard regulars will soon begin to appear, flitting in and veering off at the last moment. Next, they might make a few tentative landings on the perches of the empty feeders or on the ground under them, only to dart nervously away after a few seconds.

If you're patient, soon one of the birds will make a pass at the seed in your hands. It may dart away but will soon return. And eventually a bird will land and eat from your hand. Don't react. Remain still. You will be rewarded for your patience!

- Some of the easiest birds to tame are chickadees, nuthatches, titmice, and small woodpeckers.

- Black oil–type sunflower seeds are the hand tamer's bait of choice; raw peanut meats also work well.

- Some people have had success taming bluebirds mealworms.

# The Magic of the Wryneck

BREEDING IN TEMPERATE regions of Europe and Asia and wintering in sub-Saharan Africa, the Eurasian wryneck (*Jynx torquilla*) is related to the Old World woodpeckers, yet it has many unique features distinguishing it from its relatives. The bird's ability to rotate its head 180 degrees from front to back, like a snake, in concert with a hissing noise that it utters when threatened, led to the bird being associated with witchcraft.

One belief was that, rather than its now-known habits of feeding on ants by hopping along the ground and digging into rotten wood, the wryneck lured ants into its mouth by playing dead on the ground near an anthill. This somehow led to the idea that the bird could lure lost lovers back to their mates.

From this spawned a cruel practice of nailing these birds to a wheel that, when spun and special phrases recited, would accomplish the task of drawing the wandering lover back home. In Greek mythology, a wryneck wheel made by Aphrodite was used to cause Medea to fall in love with Jason.

Another Greek myth inspired the bird's Latin name. When the nymph Inyx's voice was stolen by the goddess Hera to give to Echo, she retaliated by making Zeus fall in love with one of Hera's priestesses. Hera punished Inyx for this deed by turning her into a wryneck. Hence Inyx became *Jynx*, the genus name for the group of birds. The word *jinx* grew from the association of the bird with magic and curses.

# Quick Feeding Tips for Common Birds

For many common bird species, a combination of foods in feeders, food growing on plants, and types of habitat can be employed to attract them to a given spot.

For some species, however, one or more of these attrations may not apply– they are marked n/a.

| SPECIES | FEEDER FOODS | FOOD PLANTS | HABITAT |
|---|---|---|---|
| Blackbirds | Cracked corn, millet | Wild plants such as coneflower and ragweed | Marshland and adjacent backyards, meadows, agricultural fields |
| Bluebirds | Mealworms | Shrubs that bear edible berries | Nest boxes |
| Buntings | Millet, niger | Shrubs that bear edible berries; wildflowers that bear abundant small seeds, including aster, dandelion, goldenrod, and phlox | Hedges, shrubs, thickets |
| Cardinals | Safflower, black-oil sunflower, suet | Shrubs and vines that bear edible, elms (for their buds) | Evergreen trees and shrubs, thickets, hedges |
| Catbirds | Fruit | Shrubs and vines that bear edible berries and grapes | Thickets, hedges |
| Chickadees | Black-oil sunflower, suet | Bayberry | Nest boxes, deciduous trees |
| Crossbills | Black-oil sunflower | Alders, seed-producing deciduous trees, conifers for the seeds in their cones | Evergreen shrubs and trees |
| Doves | Cracked corn, black-oil sunflower, millet | Grasses, seed-producing weeds, pokeweed, elderberry | Evergreen shrubs and trees, birdbaths and mini ponds with shallow areas for wading |
| Finches | Black-oil sunflower, niger seed | Thistle, dandelion, fruit-bearing shrubs and trees | Tall, seed-producing wildflowers |
| Flickers | Suet, peanut butter, raisins | Fruit-producing shrubs | Nest boxes |
| Grosbeaks | Sunflower | Berry-producing shrubs, seed-producing deciduous trees | n/a |
| Hummingbirds | Nectar | Trumpet vine, fuschia, other plants with red flowers and downward-facing trumpet-shaped flowers | n/a |
| Jays | Black-oil sunflower, peanuts in the shell, corn | Nut-producing trees, berry-bearing shrubs and vines | n/a |
| Juncos | Millet, suet | Flowers and wildflowers with flower heads that produce abundant seeds | Weedy areas |

| SPECIES | FEEDER FOODS | FOOD PLANTS | HABITAT |
| --- | --- | --- | --- |
| Kingbirds | Killed insects, small fruits | Berry-bearing shrubs and vines | Weedy, insect-producing areas with low perches on the edge |
| Martins | Crushed eggshells | Weedy, grassy areas near water; colony nesting structures | n/a |
| Mockingbirds | Berries, suet | Berry-bearing shrubs and vines | Thickets, hedges |
| Nuthatches | Black-oil sunflower, shelled peanuts, cracked corn | Insect-attracting deciduous trees | Nest boxes, deciduous trees |
| Orioles | Fruit, particularly slices of orange; suet | Fruit-producing shrubs and trees | n/a |
| Pheasants | Corn on the ground, crushed eggshell | Agricultural crops | Standing agricultural and weed fields |
| Phoebes | Insect-attracting plants | Water source, nesting shelves | n/a |
| Robins | Suet | Fruit-producing shrubs and trees | Nesting shelves |
| Siskins | Black-oil sunflower | Seed-producing wildflowers | Coniferous trees |
| Sparrows | Millet | Seed-producing wildflowers and grasses | Weedy areas |
| Swallows | n/a | n/a | Nest boxes, white feathers for incorporation in their nests |
| Thrashers | Fruit | Berry-producing shrubs and vines | Thickets, hedges, fence rows |
| Thrushes | | Fruit-producing shrubs and vines | Thickets, hedges |
| Titmice | Black-oil sunflower, suet, shelled peanuts | Berry-producing shrubs | Nest boxes |
| Towhees | Millet, small fruits | Berry-producing shrubs | n/a |
| Waxwings | n/a | Trees and shrubs that produce small fruits and berries | n/a |
| Woodpeckers | Black-oil sunflower, suet | Rotting, insect-filled trees; fruit-producing trees and shrubs | Rotting trees, nest boxes |
| Wrens | n/a | Berry-producing shrubs, insect-attracting flowers and wildflowers | Nest boxes, weedy areas |

# Quick on the Draw

THE ABILITY TO quickly sketch the rough image of a bird is an important skill for birdwatchers. Fifteen seconds should be quick enough to capture the essence of the bird before it flits away.

The object is to get the shape of the bird down quickly, noting the highlights, areas of distinctive coloring, and critical field marks, so you can return to that sketch later and use it to make an identification that may have eluded you in the field.

1. Get a good look at the bird for your personal edification.

2. Create a fifteen-second sketch of the bird, with all the critical points noted and highlighted.

3. Take one or several photos, if you're so equipped.

4. Get a longer look at the bird for your own satisfaction, if it has not already fled.

Creating the sketch starts with a fast outline of the bird's general body shape, followed by shading and labeling of important areas of color and field marks, followed by written labeling around the image with arrows pointing to the areas being described or notated in words. If there is time, matching the colors of the birds by using a set of colored pencils can enhance the value for later use.

Practice, practice, and practice some more, when the pressure is off, perhaps while observing the birds of your backyard from the comfort of a lounge chair. Then, when the pressure is on and that rare bird you've never seen before shows up in the field, you'll be ready.

# Songbirds: Common Redpoll
## (*Carduelis flammea*)

COMMON REDPOLLS move in large flocks and are considered very numerous across their range. They are one of several northerly breeding species that are prone to irruptive movements. During years when there is a low seed production in their preferred tree species, spruce and birch, the birds move south out of their normal range in search of food. For those birdwatchers normally out of their range, having these little jewels visit your feeder is a treat indeed.

**PHYSICAL CHARACTERISTICS**: This diminutive finch may not be as showy in color as other North American finches, but neither is the bird's plumage subtle. Male common redpolls have a bright red cap over a back covered with brown feathers edged in white, while the underside is white with broad brown streaks on the flanks. The most diagnostic feature of the males is a pink or red wash over the breast and cheeks. Females lack this wash but still have the red cap, the black chin and *lores* (bare skin between the eyes and bill), and the small, conical yellow bill.

**RANGE**: This species of finch is normally found in the tundra and taiga regions of the world, across North America and Eurasia.

**HABITAT**: Low, scattered trees and shrubs of the taiga and the open tundra are the habitat preferences of the common redpoll. This is where the bird can find the small seeds of trees and weeds that it enjoys. It will flit about among the branches, even hanging from the branch to extract the seeds.

The common redpoll builds a small cup-shaped nest of twigs, roots, and grasses, which it then lines with a thick layer of downy feathers from ptarmigan and spruce grouse.

**SONGS AND CALLS**: Several different calls are uttered by the common redpoll, with the most common being the chattering *che che che tschrrr* call. Other calls are more trill- or buzzlike.

**CONSERVATION STATUS**: This species' population reaches millions worldwide, but local cases of salmonella poisoning have decimated large numbers of birds in some years.

Common redpoll (*Carduelis flammea*)

# Asia: Eilat, Israel

SITUATED AT THE confluence of three continents in a natural geographic funnel between the Mediterranean Sea and the Jordan Mountains, Israel is one of the best spots in the world for migrating birds. And the Red Sea resort town of Eilat, at the far southern tip of the country, is the focal point for activity, with half a billion birds passing through here in spring and fall. These birds are drawn to the well-watered oasis of the town and rest up here before continuing their journey across the deserts. Within this group is the largest collection of migrating raptors in the world, with nearly a million birds. Even outside of migration periods, birders will find many, many unique birds in Eilat to add to their life lists. The International Birding and Research Centre in Eilat and the Israeli Ornithological Center host an annual birding festival during the spring migration.

**BIRDS TO SEE**: Most visitors to Eilat will not have to travel far from their hotels in North Beach to see a dizzying array of seabirds such as brown booby, white-eyed gull, slender-billed gull, gull-billed and whiskered terns, and striated and Western reef herons. Even rarer birds such as streaked shearwater, red-billed tropicbird, lesser frigatebird, white-cheeked and bridled terns, and sooty and gray-headed gulls may make an appearance. Some of these birds can also be seen at the salt pans, in addition to greater flamingo, pied avocet, black-winged stilt, red-throated pipit, citrine wagtail, desert and Isabelline wheatears, as well as a smorgasbord of gulls; Heuglin's, lesser black-backed, Armenian, and yellow-legged are just a few of the species.

The ponds, salt pans, and scrub at the International Birding and Research Centre's bird sanctuary play host to many species, including the green bee-eater, an iridescent green bird with a cobalt blue face. Also found here are various species of warblers, flycatchers, and shrikes. An area known as the North Fields supports songbirds such as Dead Sea sparrow, desert finch, and Oriental skylark. Palestine sunbird, Tristram's starling, white-crowned black and hooded wheatears, and many other species can be found at the Elot Kibbutz. Where fresh water can be found, birdwatchers have a chance of seeing Lichtenstein's sandgrouse, crowned sandgrouse, and sand partridge.

Some of the more common raptors that pass through Eilat include black kite, honey buzzard, and common buzzard, but other species such as lesser spotted and Eastern imperial eagles; griffon vulture; marsh, pallid, and Montagu's harriers; northern goshawk; Levant sparrowhawk; steppe buzzard; osprey; lesser and common kestrels; Northern hobby; and Lanner and Barbary falcons can also be seen.

# Cleaning Out the Pantry

THIS IS A FUN PROJECT to share with the young birdwatchers in the family.

Many of the items that most of us have in our pantries and cupboards can be mixed to produce interesting new blends of food for the birds in the backyard. And it's really not critical how you deploy those extra foods. Cast them about on the ground, drop them into a bin feeder, spread them on a boulder; the birds won't worry over the method in which they've been offered these items.

Here's a list to get started, but use your own creativity and imagination on this project. The only caveat is this: If you are including flours in your mixture, plan to also add egg whites, oil, and water or juice, and then to bake the final product.

Pantry ingredients for the birds:

Bread and other baked goods

Peanuts

Peanut butter

Raisins, currants, and other dried fruit

Dates

Berries and cherries

Nutmeats

Apples

Oranges

Lard and solid shortening

Molasses

Oatmeal (including instant)

Cream of wheat

Snack crackers, graham crackers, and pretzels

Bread crumbs

Flour

Cornmeal and cornbread mix

# Some Common Modern Bird Myths

MYTHS DON'T EXIST only in ancient history. Several float around even today, and many people still believe them.

One of the predominant modern bird myths is that they mate for life. Several species do mate with the same bird in successive years, but this doesn't mean they don't also mate with others as well. Also, if one bird in a pair dies, the living one will seek out a new mate.

Two very popular myths involve causing harm to birds after feeding them something. The first is a commonly repeated childhood story that throwing a particular kind of dissolvable tablet of cold/flu medicine in the air for gulls to catch and eat will cause the bird to explode from the released gases as the tablet dissolves.

There is no evidence that this is true, nor is there evidence that rice thrown at weddings will be picked up by birds and cause them to die after the rice has swollen inside them. Birds eat dried seeds and rice all the time in the wild and no harm comes to them from it.

Another enduring myth, one constantly battled by wildlife rehabilitators and bird conservation groups, is that baby birds that have fallen out of their nests and are returned there by concerned people will be abandoned by the birds' parents. This is an utter falsehood, disproved countless times. Birds do not have a highly developed sense of smell, and therefore cannot tell and would not care if a human touched their baby. It is important, however, to not visit a nest you have discovered too often, as this may cue predators in to the nest location.

# A Dash of Salt

SALT AND MINERAL blocks are generally thought of as feeding features for mammals, such as members of the deer family that are of interest to hunters. However, other groups of animals, including birds, also will come to take salt and other minerals from the blocks.

Blocks are available at many animal feed, farm supply, and sporting goods stores. The most difficult part of obtaining one is getting it to your car and home; they are relatively heavy and bulky.

Keep in mind that in the backyard, a salt or mineral block can do a great deal of damage to your lawn or garden. As rain and snow fall on the block, some of the salt or minerals will leach out of the block and into the soil.

If the soil area is not contained, the salt or mineral leachate will spread out across a considerable area. The zone will not support many species of grass and other plants.

Before you place the salt or mineral block on the ground, dig a circle about 3' (91.4 cm) in diameter and 6" (15.2 cm) deep. Line the hole with a mini-pond liner or several layers of industrial-strength garbage bags, laid flat and unopened. Place 3" (7.6 cm) of medium gravel on top of the liner or garbage bags, and 3" (7.6 cm) of wood-chip mulch on top of the gravel.

With that protection in place, position your salt or mineral block at the center of the circle, atop the mulch. Replace the block once it has degraded.

# Sneaking Up on Birds

BIRDS ARE GENERALLY not inclined to allow too close an approach by humans, which they perceive as threats to their continued well-being. Anything birdwatchers can do to lessen the threat they pose in those little avian imaginations can help to decrease the distance between bird and birdwatcher.

• Use the elements to your advantage whenever you move through field or forest. Intermittent wind is a near constant in the outdoors on most days. And in those gusts lies a sound camouflage. Move when the wind blows and much of the underfoot crunching you might cause will be masked.

• Similarly, a bird that is singing is not listening. Take your steps while it is singing and it likely will not hear the sounds generated by your movements.

• Move slowly, at a pace that will not increase your heart rate or the interference with your hearing by blood flowing through your arteries. A slower pace also causes less disruption of the natural cadence of the wild and requires less time for the wild things to adjust after you move.

• Carry water and take frequent sips as you move along. That will keep your mouth and throat from getting parched, which often leads to coughing and hacking.

• In nature, staring is something that predators do. They maintain a constant watch on their prey as they slowly creep in for the kill. Squinting or otherwise partially closing your eyes will reduce the appearance of staring and the likeness of a predator.

# Hummingbirds: Calliope Hummingbird (*Stellula calliope*)

NOT ONLY IS THE calliope hummingbird the smallest hummingbird in North America, but it is also the smallest bird on the continent. In addition, it makes one of the longest migrations for a bird its size. This secretive bird has been difficult to study; thus, little information on its habits exists.

**PHYSICAL CHARACTERISTICS**: As it measures only 2.75" to 3.25" (7 to 8 cm) from the tip of its long, slender bill to the tip of its tail, the word *diminutive* is even too large to describe this bird. The rich metallic bronze-green of the bird's back contrasts with the pale undersides and dark wings. The male's *gorget*, or patch of color on the throat, is magenta-red and splayed in ray lines, atypical of the solid-colored gorget of most male hummingbirds.

**RANGE**: The calliope hummingbird can be found from southwestern Canada down into California in the United States during breeding season. Migration takes this bird to southwestern Mexico.

**HABITAT**: Seemingly odd for such a small bird, the calliope hummingbird breeds in cool mountain environments, preferring young, post-fire or post-logging growth.

The bird's Mexican winter habitat includes dry thorn woodlands and humid pine-oak forests. Like other hummingbirds, this species feeds on nectar from tube-shaped flowers and on aerial insects that it takes by darting from its perch and plucking from the air.

The calliope hummingbird often makes its nest in pine trees, sometimes on top of the base of a dead pine cone, thereby making the nest look like a pine cone. It covers the outside of the nest with dead bark, lichens, and mosses.

**SONGS AND CALLS**: Twittering and bickering sounds common to other hummingbirds have been noted for this species. Some researchers believe they utter a *pzzt-zing* sound during territorial diving display.

**CONSERVATION STATUS**: With little data on this species, population trends are difficult to determine, but the numbers appear to be stable.

Calliope hummingbird (*Stellula calliope*)

# Asia: Keoladeo Ghana National Park, Rajasthan, India

KNOWN MORE COMMONLY as Bharaptur, Keoladeo Ghana National Park is a spectacular wetland reserve where wading birds, waterfowl, and raptors abound. Almost half of the 11-square-mile (29 square km) park is wetland, with the rest being savanna and scrub woodland. It owes its protection to a former maharajah, who built dams and canals to expand the natural wetlands, creating a game hunting reserve. Combining travel to this park with an excursion to nearby Agra, the home of the Taj Mahal, makes for an excellent trip. Fortunately, the best time to visit is during the more comfortable winter months (summer is unbearably hot), November to March, when the resident birds are joined by the migrants. Travel to the park is easy, and within the park visitors can utilize bike, rickshaw, boat, or feet.

Nearly 400 species of birds can be found in the park. Perhaps because of its long protected status, birds here are both plentiful and relatively easy to approach, so you can get good views and pictures.

**BIRDS TO SEE:** The entertaining wading birds are numerous at Keoladeo, with herons, egrets, spoonbills, ibises, jacanas, and storks hunting the shallow waters. Species include Sarus crane, Eurasian spoonbill, black bittern, Indian pond heron, gray heron, Asian openbill, black-necked stork, and intermediate egret. Waterfowl include ducks (comb, spotted, and white-headed), whistling-ducks, shelducks (ruddy and common), teal (falcated, Baikal, and common), geese (greylag and bar-headed), pochards (common, red-crested, and ferrugionous), and scaups. The park is also a good site for raptors, with reports of kites (black-eared and Brahminy), eagles (short-toed snake, crested serpent, greater spotted, steppe, Bonelli's, and Pallas' fishing), harriers (hen, pallid, and pied), accipiters (shikra and besra), vultures (Eurasian griffon, red-headed, and white-rumped), and falcons (Oriental, Sakar, and Lagger). There are also many, many songbird species in the adjoining thickets and scrub growth, including flycatchers, starlings, mynas, wheatears, stonechats, bushchats, nuthatches, tits, swallows, martins, bulbuls, prinias, babblers, larks, sparrows, flowerpeckers, pipits, and many species of warblers.

# Wading Birds and Mini Ponds

MANY OWNERS OF backyard mini ponds enjoy the presence of wading birds, such as great blue herons, only slightly more than most backyard bird feeders enjoy the presence of squirrels. And you can take that enthusiasm down a notch for mini-pond owners who maintain expensive koi in their ponds.

Another way to look at that completely natural predator–prey situation that arises around backyard mini ponds is to consider the small bodies of water as another type of bird feeder. It's a specialized feeder, to be sure, but if properly filled with food it will attract birds to feed from it.

The food to fill a mini-pond feeder includes feeder goldfish from pet shops, minnows captured in local creeks or purchased from fishing bait shops, and small frogs raised in the pond from egg masses collected in local ponds and puddles. Feeder goldfish and bait-shop minnows are inexpensive to purchase. Gathering minnows and frog eggs from the wild is an acceptable practice when done in moderation from streams and ponds with preexisting abundance, with proper licensing, and never involving habitat of any endangered or threatened species.

Providing the goldfish, minnows, frogs, and other aquatic edibles with proper hiding cover will stretch the amount of attraction they provide for the wading birds. Plants covering the surface of much of the mini pond, underwater logs and brush, and similar impediments to too-easy pickings by the wading birds will allow the small fish and frogs to escape more often than they become quick meals. That will keep the wading birds interested enough to return again and again, and will provide them with occasional rewards for their visits and efforts, but also will help to keep your replacement costs down to the manageable range.

# Cuckoo, the Lustful Bird

OF THE MANY MYTHS surrounding the cuckoo, the most prevalent might be the association of the bird with the return of spring. Farmers in Europe timed their plantings with the return of the bird to their area. Many festivals were celebrated to commemorate the cuckoo's arrival, heralding a time of plenty.

Equally fascinating are the myths about where the cuckoo went for the rest of the year. Some cultures speculated that the birds hibernated in hollow logs, while others believed they turned into hawks for the winter.

One of the most interesting myths about the cuckoo, however, addressed the species' proclivity for laying its eggs in the nests of other birds. This tactic, called *brood parasitism*, is practiced by several other species, either exclusively or occasionally.

Bohemian peasants believed the Virgin Mary punished the cuckoo for working on the holy day of Sunday by cursing the bird to a life of homelessness, never having a nest of its own. People in Denmark believed the cuckoo was too busy answering children's questions to build a nest. (This may be related to various children's rhymes to the cuckoo, in which the bird was asked questions.) Because the male cuckoo sometimes eats its own eggs, the northern English believed the female bird would hide them in other birds' nests.

This strange behavior may have caused the cuckoo to be the source of the term *cuckold*. The word was originally assigned to the male cuckoo, which was believed to seduce the female birds of other species in order that his eggs may be laid in their nests. The term eventually became applied to the female cuckoo, with the idea that she would mate with any bird before laying her eggs in his nest.

**Guira cuckoo eating a mouse**

THE BIRDWATCHER'S DAILY COMPANION

254

# A Decoration for the Birds

As THE FALL HARVEST season bursts abundantly onto the scene, handy backyard birders can find an array of natural, food-rich plant materials that they can incorporate into bird-friendly landscape decorations.

Dried sunflower seedheads are the heavy hitters of the bird decor world. They form the base layer for everything from wreaths to swags to individual hangings—all aimed at providing natural food sources for birds in an attractive design.

Using light-gauge wire, you can attach to the sunflowers as well as to decorator forms a variety of other natural elements, with dried stems and seedheads of coneflowers, foxtails, grasses, wheat, sorghum, and a range of garden flowers and wildflowers being among the most readily available. Small mesh sacks filled with bird seed or seed-filled suet rolled into small balls also can be affixed to the decoration.

Traditional fall decorations also can be repurposed as components in the decorations. Indian corn, strawberry corn, and similar elements often are tossed into the trash, however, there's plenty of bird-attracting nutrition there.

The bottom line in making decorations for birds is this: The dried seedhead of nearly any plant will provide some level of feed to some bird species.

# Gobble Up the Evidence

THERE'S NO MISTAKING the signs of a flock of turkeys having passed through a mixed-oak forest. Wide swaths of the forest floor have been scratched clear of leaves as the large birds moved along on their constant search for fallen nuts, fruits, and insects.

The scratchings are mostly V-shaped, like a hole dug in the backyard by a dog, with the point of the V showing the direction in which the birds were traveling. The pattern is produced as the turkey scratches the leaves backward. Following the path of scratchings backward, toward the open ends of the Vs, can lead back to the spot where the flock roosted the previous night.

The number of scratchings in a given area reveals something about the amount of time the flock spent there and the relative abundance of food on the ground there. An interrupted area between areas of scratchings can mark the spot where something disturbed the birds, causing them to temporarily halt their feeding to hide, run, or even take flight. Such a collection of signs might signal where the path of the turkey flock intercepted that of some predator.

Scratchings also can reveal something about how recently the turkeys passed by. Fresh scratchings are moist, with nearly no leaves in them, whereas older ones are dried up and have begun to be covered by falling leaves. Windy periods or periods of heavy leaf drop will make the scratchings look older much more quickly.

Turkeys scratch less when the forest's nut and fruit crops are abundant and easy to reach. Scratching generally increases from late October into November, as the covering of fallen leaves increases.

# Cuckoos and Relatives: Yellow-Billed Cuckoo (*Coccyzus americanus*)

THE YELLOW-BILLED CUCKOO is known for its songs, one of which is responsible for the bird's name, and for its habit of eating large numbers of caterpillars. Unfortunately, the species seems to be in decline in at least parts of its range.

**PHYSICAL CHARACTERISTICS**: A large songbird with a long tail and curved bill, the yellow-billed cuckoo, along with its close relative, the black-billed cuckoo, has a distinct shape. The yellow-billed cuckoo has a grayish-brown back and white underside. The dark eye is set within a yellow orbital ring, and the curved bill has a black upper mandible and a yellow lower mandible (along with the tail, the major distinguishing feature between this species and the black-billed cuckoo). The undertail feathers are alternating black and white. These feathers can be seen along the edge of the grayish-brown upper tail when the bird is in flight. The grayish-brown wings are edged with rusty-colored feathers.

**RANGE**: The breeding range for the yellow-billed cuckoo comprises most of the middle and eastern United States with individuals noted in other parts of the country. The bird's range also extends into northern Mexico. Birds travel through Central America to South America for winter, settling east of the Andes in northern and central parts of the continent.

**HABITAT**: Optimal habitat for yellow-billed cuckoos includes open woodlands with dense low shrubs near waterways. They also occupy abandoned farmland and orchards.

Their primary food is large insects, including caterpillars, grasshoppers, and cicadas. In fact, research has shown that cuckoos may lay more eggs when numbers of these insects are abundant. They hunt mostly by gleaning insects from leaves and branches, but they occasionally catch them on the wing.

Cuckoos build their nests in trees relatively low to the ground. The nests are loose constructions of twigs covered with leaves and bark. They also lay their eggs in nests of other birds (brood parasitism). The birds of other species raise the young.

**SONGS AND CALLS**: The most common call of the yellow-billed cuckoo is a guttural, knocking *ka-ka-ka-ka-ka-kow-kow-kowlp-kowlp-kowlp-kowlp*. The call for which the bird is named, *coo-coo-coo-coo-coo-coo-coo*, is uttered only by the male just prior to the breeding season.

**CONSERVATION STATUS**: The yellow-billed cuckoo has experienced a dramatic decline in population levels in both the west and east coasts of North America. Birds are now considered *extirpated* (locally extinct) in Washington, Oregon, and Nevada. The state of California recognizes its existing Western population as a distinct subspecies, but federal designation for listing as endangered has been under review for years. Other than degradation of riparian habitats, no other causes have been discovered for the decline.

Yellow-billed cuckoo (*Coccyzus americanus*)

# Asia: Goa, India

THE state of Goa, on India's western coast, is a tropical getaway that just happens to have excellent birding. Wide, sandy beaches invite relaxation, and the surrounding mangrove estuaries, bays, plantations, and forests invite exploration. The varied habitats—from the foothills of the Ghat Mountains in the east to the beaches in the west—in a relatively compact area ensure that many different types and species can be seen. Visitors can compile an impressive list without venturing far from their hotel, but further exploration is easy and many hotels and tour operators offer guided trips as well. The state is home to six wildlife sanctuaries and one national park.

**BIRDS TO SEE**: Various gulls (Heuglin's, slender-billed, and brown- and black-headed) and terns (lesser crested, gull-billed, Sandwich,

and swift) are common, while plovers (Kentish, lesser and greater sand, and gray) scamper along the beaches.

Trips along the rivers can yield several species of kingfishers (black-capped, pied, stork-billed, and white-throated) and bee-eaters (green and blue-tailed).

Just a few of the dizzying array of species seen in the surrounding forests include white-breasted drongo, Malabar grey hornbill, heart-spotted woodpecker, pompadour green pigeon, Oriental magpie-robin, and Nilgiri blackbird.

The well-known and species-rich Carambolim Lake supports garganey, lesser whistling duck, cotton pygmy goose, purple swamphen, pheasant-tailed jacana, marsh harrier, and Asian openbill.

# Choosing a Field Guide

BEGINNING BIRDERS are often overwhelmed by the number of species and the similarities between many of them. This is where a good field guide comes in handy. But which one to choose? The number and variety seem as wide as that of the bird species we seek to learn about.

Beginners are often recommended to start with Peterson's guides, as these have been the gold standard for many years. They are illustrated with Roger Tory Peterson's detailed paintings of each bird, and the species are grouped on pages with similar birds, to help readers identify confusing species.

A newer guide that many seasoned and novice birders have flocked to since its publication

in 2001 is the National Audubon Society's *The Sibley Guide to Birds*. These guides have the advantage of more detailed illustrations and several different views of the same bird, as well as immature, male, and female forms. However, the illustrations are relatively small and the size of the book is large compared to the smaller field guides.

*Birds of North America* in the Kaufman Focus Guide series is organized similarly to the Peterson guides, but the illustrations are created using the best photographs of each species. These are then digitally edited to accentuate diagnostic features.

**Water birds in Goa, India**

# Evolution of Birds IV: Teratorns

THE TERATORNS WERE a group of predatory birds, much like today's hawks and eagles, but much larger in size—so large, in fact, that scientists have been long confounded by how the birds could actually get airborne.

The oldest known teratorn fossil has been dated to the late Miocene, between six and eight million years ago. All are native to North and South America. Several species have been found in the La Brea Tar Pits of Los Angeles. Scientists suppose that the birds were drawn from far and wide by the struggling mammals that were caught there, only to be trapped themselves.

The largest of the teratorns was *Argentavis magnificens*, fossils of which have been found in Argentina. This gargantuan bird stood up to 6' (1.8 m) tall, weighed between 158 and 172 pounds (72 and 78 kg), was nearly 12' (3.7 m) in length from tip of bill to tip of tail, and had a wingspan of between 21 and 24' (6.4 and 7.3 m).

One of its flight feathers alone may have measured 59" (1.5 m) long. Despite its large size, *Argentavis* was thought to feed on small mammals, lizards, and birds using its long, hooked bill.

Because of its weight, paleontologists don't believe that *Argentavis* could generate enough lift to get itself off the ground. Instead, they have created computer models that suggest the bird acted like a hang glider, running downhill or off a ledge to catch the wind, which would carry it high enough to glide, perhaps up to speeds of 150 mph (240 kph).

# Repurposing Fall Gourds

YOU CAN GIVE THOSE old gourds from your Halloween and fall decorations a second life as suet feeders in your backyard.

Allow them to dry completely, which often means using last year's gourds now dried to the point that seeds are rattling around inside and giving this year's gourds another ten to twelve months to reach that same state. Gourd drying is best accomplished by hanging the gourds in a dry, cool, dark, out-of-the-way spot, and checking them every month or so to head off problems with insects, rodents, mold, and the like.

With a dried gourd in hand, drill a 1" (2.5 cm) -diameter hole in what you intend to be the top of your feeder, the part of the gourd from which you will attach the hanging apparatus. Dump out the seeds and debris from inside the gourd. Carefully scrape the inside to remove any debris still sticking to the interior.

Render a batch of suet or suet-seed mixture as explained on pages 147 and 153. When the suet has cooled a bit but still can be poured, pour some of it into the hollow gourd until the gourd is nearly half full. Stand the gourd upright in your refrigerator for a couple of days.

Remove the suet-filled gourd from the refrigerator. Drill two 1" (2.5 cm) -diameter holes into the bottom of the gourd—the part of the gourd opposite what you previously determined will be the top. These holes should be on opposite sides of the gourd. Drill right through the shell of the gourd—slowly, so as not to crack the shell—until you fully expose the hardened suet inside.

Attach your hanging apparatus, which might be as simple as a wire with one end twisted around the gourd, to the top and your suet feeder is ready for hanging in the backyard.

Depending on damage to the gourd by birds, rodents, and the elements, you can refill the gourd with suet and hang it in your backyard several times.

# Birds by Habitat: Forest

THE BOREAL FOREST is the most northern of forest types in North America. It's a dense habitat of alder, birch, fir, pine, poplar, and spruce. It also includes bogs and grass-sedge areas.

Birds commonly found in the boreal forest include black-capped chickadee, black-throated blue warbler, Blackburnian warbler, blackpoll warbler, brown creeper, Cape May warbler, dark-eyed junco, evening grosbeak, fox sparrow, great gray owl, great horned owl, hermit thrush, northern goshawk, pine grosbeak, pine siskin, red-breasted nuthatch, red crossbille, ruby-crowned kinglet, ruffed grouse, spruce grouse, Swainson's thrush, Tennessee warbler, white-winged crossbille, winter wren, and yellow-bellied sapsucker.

More than 300 species of trees and shrubs, as well as diverse herbaceous plants, comprise the eastern deciduous forest, but broadleaf trees are the dominant species.

Among the birds found in the eastern deciduous forest are the Acadian flycatcher, American redstart, American woodcock, black-and-white warbler, black-billed cuckoo, blue-gray gnatcatcher, blue jay, broad-winged hawk, brown thrasher, cedar waxwing, Cooper's hawk, eastern towhee, eastern wood peewee, hairy woodpecker, hooded warbler, Kentucky warbler, pileated woodpecker, prairies warbler, red-eyed vireo, red-headed woodpecker, rose-breasted grosbeak, scarlet tanager, sharp-shinned hawk, whip-poor-will, white-breasted nuthatch, wild turkey, wood thrush, worm-eating warbler, yellow-breasted chat, and yellow-throated warbler.

Although pine trees exist in good numbers in the eastern deciduous forest, they become the dominant species of pine barren and pineland habitats.

Among the birds that thrive among the pines are Acadian flycatcher, American robin, American redstart, black-and-white warbler, blue-gray gnatcatcher, blue jay, brown creeper, brown thrasher, brown-headed nuthatch, Carolina chickadee, downy woodpecker, eastern towhee, gray kingbird, hairy woodpecker, hooded warbler, Kentucky warbler, northern parula, northern saw-whet owl, northern cardinal, ovenbird, painted bunting, pine warbler, prairie warbler, red-bellied woodpecker, red crossbill, red-shouldered hawk, ruby-throated hummingbird, ruffed grouse, summer tanager, tufted titmouse, whip-poor-will, white-breasted nuthatch, white-eyed vireo, white-throated sparrow, wild turkey, wood thrush, yellow-breasted chat, yellow-throated vireo, and yellow-throated warbler.

# Kingfishers and Relatives:
# Hoopoe (*Upupa epops*)

THE HOOPOE IS A very distinctive bird, for its plumage as well as its behavior. It is considered a sacred bird in the mythology of some cultures, and it was named as the state bird of Israel in May 2008.

**PHYSICAL CHARACTERISTICS**: The size of a robin, the hoopoe bears little resemblance to any other species. Its rusty, cinnamon-colored head and upper body are topped by an elaborate crest with feathers tipped in black. This crest fans out to be quite large during display. The long, strong bill is used for probing insects from the ground. The wings are broadly striped black and white, which may help the bird to blend into grassland foliage. The tail is long and black, with a broad curved white band in the middle. The wing pattern is extremely beautiful when the bird is seen in flight.

**RANGE**: Very widespread, the hoopoe can be found in most of Europe and southern Eurasia, as well as much of Africa and Madagascar. Northern populations move south into tropical Africa and India for winter.

**HABITAT**: The hoopoe's main habitat requirement is patches of open or sparsely vegetated ground, but this can be in a variety of habitats, from savanna to forest. These openings are where it hunts for insects, its main prey. The bird also hunts in the air, hovering with its rounded wings to capture flying insects.

Nests are made in tree cavities or in holes in walls, banks, or cliffs. When brooding, the female hoopoe's *preen gland* (which most birds have; it emits an oil used for preening, or waterproofing their feather coat) emits a liquid with a smell like rotting meat, which is thought to deter predators. The preen glands of the young also do this.

**SONGS AND CALLS**: The call of the hoopoe is onomatopoeic, described as a three-noted *oop oop oop* or *hoop hoop hoop*.

**CONSERVATION STATUS**: The species' broad habitat preference and wide distribution have allowed populations to be large and stable.

Hoopoe (*Upupa epops*)

# Asia: Limithang Road, Thrumsing La National Park, Bhutan

BHUTAN HAS UNTIL recently been an undiscovered country ornithologically. Closed to the rest of the world for centuries, the country recently had its first democratic elections. Its policy of Gross National Happiness keeps the intrusion of Western influences and technology somewhat limited. Much of Bhutan's environment is wholly unspoiled, thanks to the tenets of Tibetan Buddhism, the country's main religion. Bhutanese appreciate the value of the environment and do a good job protecting it. Tourism is allowed but limited to tour parties. For these reasons, Bhutan is a birding paradise, with almost 700 species recorded so far.

The country is bisected by one major road that climbs high into the Himalayas, with many twists, turns, and switchbacks. It is this route, the Limithang Road, which birders travel to gain access to the moist evergreen and broadleaf forests at higher elevations that harbor some choice species. The road and the surrounding forests are contained within the Thrumsing La National Park.

**BIRDS TO SEE**: Despite the protections, many species are considered threatened, such as the rufous-necked hornbill, a species that prefers the subtropical and warm broad-leaved forests at lower elevations up to 4,000' (1,200 m). Chestnut-breasted partridge, yellow-vented and broad-billed warblers, rufous-throated wren, beautiful nuthatch, and several species of babblers and laughing-thrushes also occur here. Wood snipe and Blyth's tragopan, a threatened species globally, prefer the cool broad-leaved forest at higher elevations. Satyr tragopan, blood pheasant, fire-tailed myzornis, and maroon-backed and rufous-breasted accentors can be seen in the evergreen forests above this. Rivers and streams below 4,600' (1,400 m) support kingfishers, fork-tails, dippers, and wagtails, while lucky birders may catch glimpses of the rare Pallas's fish eagle and white-bellied heron in broader rivers and lakes.

# Where Did All That Seed Go?

IF YOU'RE NOT plagued with a squirrel problem, and you see your seed disappearing more quickly than usual, you can probably chalk this up to those birds that like to cache, or store, their food.

Nuthatches and chickadees are well-known cachers. They will carry away seeds or nuts to a nearby tree, log, or house and wedge them into a crevice, to be visited at a later, leaner time. Some species of woodpecker are known for caching nuts or acorns into holes they've bored into trees or even the exposed wood of houses.

Although not regular visitors to feeders, shrikes also cache their food. Primarily predators, shrikes, both the northern and loggerhead species, will capture their prey, such as insects, lizards, rodents, and small birds, and impale the larger ones on thorns and barbed wire. They can more easily tear the prey apart there, eating what they need at a given time and returning later for more.

# The History of Bird Protection and Conservation IV: The Spotted Owl Debate

ALMOST NO OTHER bird became as well known during the 1990s as the northern spotted owl of northwestern North America. This bird nests and hunts in the old-growth forests of the Pacific Northwest, a habitat preference that has placed the bird at odds with the very profitable logging industry of the region.

Plummeting populations of the northern spotted owl in the 1980s caused a great deal of alarm in the conservation community. In 1987, these groups petitioned the U.S. Fish and Wildlife Service (USFWS) to include the bird on the Endangered Species List, thereby affording it legal protection. The agency rejected the petition but was later forced to reconsider it by a U.S. district judge. The owl was eventually listed as threatened in 1990, an act that allowed the USFWS and researchers to begin planning habitat protection for the species. The vast acreage that was being proposed sparked much enmity in the working class towns of the region, many of which were dependent on the logging industry for their livelihoods.

After the USFWS failed to come up with a plan for the owl's protection, most old-growth timber logging in the Pacific Northwest was halted. By 1993, the owl's numbers were still declining, prompting then President Clinton and Vice President Al Gore to get involved, leading to the creation of a Northwest Forest Plan, which significantly reduced the amount of timber that could be removed from old-growth forests in the region.

The media framed the spotted owl controversy as a conflict between environmentalists and loggers, but the issues were much larger. The events sparked much-needed debate in government and conservation circles about how species should be protected, and a move toward habitat protection as an integral component of endangered species protection became more prominent than ever before. Also, the ethical issues of choosing the welfare of other species over that of human communities became a hotly debated topic.

All because of a cute little owl.

# Citizen Science

BACKYARD BIRDWATCHERS can contribute to the current knowledge of bird species and help scientists keep track of bird populations by volunteering to participate in backyard bird counts. Having a network of volunteers keeping track of birds has helped scientists amass amazing amounts of data on bird populations and movements. These projects have the added benefit of the participants not having to leave the comfort of their homes to get involved.

The Cornell Lab of Ornithology in Ithaca, New York, runs Project FeederWatch from November through April. Participants pick two days of each week to count the birds at their feeder locations; the site chosen needs to be visible from one spot, no matter how many feeders are used. The highest number of birds seen at one time is the number that participants record. So, if three goldfinches are seen on the first day, but then eleven are seen at one time on the second day, only the eleven birds are counted. At the end of each two-day period,

the information is tallied on a form and sent to the lab, or information can be entered on the lab's website, www.birds.cornell.edu/pfw.

The Great Backyard Bird Count (GBBC) operates on similar principles, yet it runs for just four days each year during winter. GBBC is a joint project of the Cornell Lab, the National Audubon Society, and Bird Studies Canada. Volunteers can record for as little as fifteen minutes on one day, or record throughout the whole four-day period. As with Project FeederWatch, the highest number of birds seen at the feeder at one time is the number that should be reported for GBBC. Tallies are recorded on the downloadable form at the GBBC website, http://birdsource.org/gbbc, where volunteers can also keep track of what other participants are seeing during the count.

Both of these projects are great ways to get involved with helping scientists monitor these fascinating animals.

# Birds by Habitat: Grasslands

GRASSLANDS, WHETHER naturally occurring or maintained for agricultural uses, are characterized by thick but low vegetation, areas of dense shrubs, and scattered deciduous trees. They might be under active management or they might be reverting to a natural state after being removed from agricultural uses. They also are the initial growth that follows clear-cutting in forest areas.

Among the birds to be found in grasslands are goldfinches, kestrels, bobolink, common nighthawk, eastern bluebird, eastern meadowlark, field sparrow, Henslow's sparrow, horned

lark, loggerhead shrike, northern harrier, red-winged blackbird, ring-necked pheasant, and various sparrows.

Birds regularly found in farmlands are crow, kestrel, robin, barn owl, barn swallow, brown thrasher, cedar waxwing, chipping sparrow, common grackle, eastern bluebird, eastern meadowlark, European starling, gray catbird, house sparrow, house wren, northern cardinal, northern mockingbird, northern oriole, orchard oriole, red-tailed hawk, ring-necked pheasant, and yellow warbler.

Eastern meadowlark

# Woodpeckers and Relatives: Coppersmith Barbet (*Megalaima haemacephala*)

BARBETS ARE MEMBERS of the same family as toucans, woodpeckers, and honeyguides. There are four different families of barbets: two in South America, and one each in Africa and Asia. Most barbets have colorful plumage, stout bodies, large heads, and thick bills. The coppersmith barbet is in the Asian family, and it is considered the most common barbet there.

**PHYSICAL CHARACTERISTICS**: This brightly colored bird has a rich green back, rump, and upper tail feathers, with a cream-colored, green-streaked underside. Its large eyes sit in a circle of yellow surrounded by black. The throat is the same yellow with a red patch separating the throat from the breast. The stout bill is surrounded by bristly feathers nearly as long as the bill.

**RANGE**: This small barbet is a resident of South Asia from Pakistan east through India, China, and south into Southeast Asia in western Indonesia and also on the Philippine Islands.

**HABITAT**: Unlike other Asian barbets that prefer denser forests, the coppersmith barbet prefers open woodlands and scrublands of foothills and lower elevations. It will also come to gardens around human habitations.

One requirement for its breeding habitat is trees with dead wood for creating nesting cavities, which it excavates with its large bill. It breeds from December through July, during the rainy season when food is abundant.

Coppersmith barbets feed on fruits primarily; figs are a prized item, and the normally solitary bird may be seen in groups where figs are abundant. The birds will also catch insects on the wing.

**SONGS AND CALLS**: By inflating their throats and exhaling air, they create a *tuk tuk tuk...* call, repeated for long periods. The sound has been likened to a hammer pounding on a copper sheet, hence the bird's name.

**CONSERVATION STATUS**: Because of its tolerance and in some cases even preference for urban areas, the coppersmith barbet is the only species of Asian barbet whose numbers are not declining. The population is considered stable and increasing.

THE BIRDWATCHER'S DAILY COMPANION

Coppersmith barbet (*Megalaima haemacephala*)

# Asia: Sinharaja Forest Reserve, Sri Lanka

LOCATED JUST 19 miles (31 km) off the southwestern coast of India, the island nation of Sri Lanka is known for its exports of tea, coffee, and cinnamon. However, the island is also a hotbed of biodiversity. Most of Sri Lanka is lowland coastal plain, with montane habitats appearing only in the south central region. It is the western and southwestern flanks of these mountains that receive the greatest amount of precipitation, and as a result, some of the richest tropical forests grow here.

Most of the twenty or so endemic bird species on Sri Lanka can be found in the rainforest reserve of Sinharaja Forest, in the country's highlands of the south. Named a World Heritage Wilderness Area in 1988, this reserve, by virtue of its inaccessibility, protects about half of the country's remaining wet zone lowland forest. Several tour companies operate in the area, and there are lodges and guesthouses nearby.

**BIRDS TO SEE**: Some of the threatened endemic species found at Sinharaja include white-headed starling, ashy-headed babbler, green-billed coucal, red-faced malkoha, and the Sri Lanka blue magpie, known locally as *kehilbella*, which translates as "beautiful damsel of the forest." This latter species is particularly brilliant, with a bright red bill, a brown head and wings, a bright blue back, and a very long tail of the same blue.

There are also several interesting groundfeeding birds, specifically the Sri Lankan junglefowl, much like a domestic chicken, Sri Lankan spurfowl, and Sri Lanka scaly thrush.

Somewhat unique to this area is the phenomenon of mixed feeding flocks made up of as many as forty species of birds. This behavior both increases protection from predators and improves feeding efficiency. Lucky birders who see this phenomenon can sight birds such as greater racket-tailed drongo and orange-billed babbler, which tend to "lead" the flocks, as well as lesser golden-back woodpecker, velvet-fronted nuthatch, scarlet minivet, and dark-fronted babbler.

# Trash into Treasure

MANY HOUSEHOLD ITEMS that we discard can be repurposed into magical feeding devices in the backyard.

Holes can be cut into any sizable plastic container, from a milk jug to a detergent bottle, creating a depository for seed. The handle can be left intact to serve once again as the handle for hanging the newly created feeder.

The twelve hollows of an old muffin tin might be filled with suet and the entire tin then hung vertically on a post or tree trunk.

Old pie pans, skillets, and the like can be laid flat and filled with water for an extra birdbath. They also could be filled with sand for a dust bath and source of grit.

Cookie cutters no longer used for baking can be filled with suet or with bird cookies baked right into them and hung outside as feeders.

Cans, bag ties, wire hangers, and the like can be put to thousands of uses in any active backyard bird-feeding effort.

# Geese in Mythology

THE GOOSE IS A prominent animal in the myths and history of many cultures. This is likely attributable to the ease with which the birds are domesticated. They were even kept by the ancient Egyptians. Kept geese are purported to have saved the Romans from an invasion by the Gauls in 390 B. C. E. The Roman goddess Juno, the protector of the state, was associated with geese.

Creation myths from both Egypt and India feature the goose, with the former believing that from a goose egg hatched the sun, while the latter believed that Brahma, the Hindu god of creation, hatched from a goose egg.

Geese also often represented fertility. They were used as marriage gifts from the groom to the bride in the Far East, and there are accounts of ancient Earth Mothers being accompanied by geese in other cultures. Also, Mother Goose, from whom the children's rhymes are known, has been portrayed as both a human and a goose.

One of the more fantastical myths surrounds a species of goose that is often found in coastal areas around the British Isles, where the myth was hatched in the twelfth century. Writers have described the barnacle goose spontaneously generating from driftwood or other rotting wood along the shore. They were thought to begin life as a gelatinous white mass attached to the wood by the tips of their beaks. They slowly developed into an egglike form and within that into a goose, until with a full plumage they were large enough to drop into the sea and swim away or fly away.

The myth may have been spawned by the fact that the bird was never seen during the summer in the British Isles, as it breeds in the Arctic. However outrageous it may seem, it was so accepted as fact in the twelfth century that many Irish clerics dined on barnacle geese during fast days because they believed the birds were not born of flesh. It took a papal edict to stop this practice.

# Recycled Mesh

Larger mesh bags can be cut into shorter sections and tied off at both ends to produce multiple feeders.

Most mesh sacks will last through only a few uses as a feeder. The birds will reach through the openings for the food inside at first, but later the traces of food left on the strands of the mesh will attract their attention and they will begin to pull those apart.

In addition, larger birds and animals such as squirrels and raccoons will be less dainty about their use of the sack feeders. You can dissuade those larger creatures from using the sack feeders by hanging the sacks from long strings.

And the first few holes can be closed with the judicious use of string or wire, but eventually what's left of the sack will be ready for the trash.

THE MESH SACKS into which grocery stores package things such as onions and oranges should never be sent to the landfill without first being recycled through at least one reuse as bird feeders. After the original contents have been used or emptied from the sack, refill the sack with something such as suet, tie the sack shut, and hang with string or wire in a likely feeding location.

# Birds by Habitat: Waters and Wetlands

RIVERS AND STREAMS, usually bordered by stands of large, mature trees, areas of dense shrub growth, and grasslands, are areas of abundant food for birds.

Avian species commonly found along rivers and streams include the American dipper, bank swallow, belted kingfisher, eastern phoebe, great blue heron, green-backed heron, little blue heron, Louisiana waterthrush, mallard, semipalmated sandpiper, warbling vireo, and yellow-crowned night heron.

Lakes and ponds share many habitat qualities with rivers and streams, but their large still waters attract additional bird species.

Among the species regularly spotted along and on lakes and ponds are the American black duck, American coot, bald eagle, belted kingfisher, blue-winged teal, bufflehead, Canada goose, canbasback, common goldeneye, common merganser, common pintail, common tern, great blue heron, greater scaup, green-backed heron, green-winged teal, hooded merganser, horned grebe, lesser scaup, little blue heron, mallard, osprey, pie-billed grebe, red-throated loon, redhead, ring-necked duck, shoveller, snow goose, and yellow-crowned night heron.

They were known as swamps and marshes in the not-too-distant past. Today they are called wetlands. Regardless of the name, they are areas of reeds, rushes, and cattails.

Birds found in wetlands include American bittern, American coot, bald eagle, barred owl, belted kingfisher, blue-winged teal, bufflehead, Canada goose, canvasback, common goldeneye, common merganser, common pintail, common tern, common yellowthroat, coot, gadwall, great blue heron, greater scaup, green-backed heron, green-winged teal, hooded merganser, horned grebe, lesser scaup, little blue heron, mallard, osprey, pie-billed grebe, pileated woodpecker, prothonotary warbler, red-bellied wood pecker, red-throated loon, redhead, red-winged blackbird, ring-necked duck, ruddy duck, shoveller, snow goose, sora rail, Swainson's warbler, swamp sparrow, wood duck, yellow-crowned night heron, and yellow rail.

**An American dipper fishing**

# Songbirds: Skylark (*Alauda arvensis*)

THE SKYLARK'S EBULLIENT sound has been celebrated in literature and song for centuries, by everyone from Shakespeare to Hoagy Carmichael. Unfortunately, the bird is declining in much of its range.

**PHYSICAL CHARACTERISTICS**: A medium-size songbird, the skylark is brown-streaked above and white below with brown streaks amid a buffy wash on the breast and flanks. The feathers on the underside of the wings are pale gray. A streaked crest is prominent when raised, and brownish-gray cheeks are encircled in white, including the white eyebrow.

**RANGE**: The skylark has a wide range throughout Eurasia and North Africa, with some populations moving farther south for the winter months.

**HABITAT**: Open country suits the skylark best, because of its nesting requirements and courtship displays. They can be found, but only after concerted searching, as they blend in well with their surroundings, in agricultural fields as well as heathlands, where they feed on seeds and insects. They make their nests of grasses on the ground.

During courtship, the skylark males display for the females by rising straight into the air with much flapping and gaining significant altitude, singing all the way. They then hover for several minutes before dropping back to Earth.

**SONGS AND CALLS**: The often heard and lengthy song of the skylark is associated with the male's flight display. The call has been described by David Allen Sibley (author of the popular *Sibley Guide to Birds*) as a "spectacular varied warble of high, liquid, rolling notes in long series; often including mimicry of other species."

**CONSERVATION STATUS**: The Royal Society for the Protection of Birds (RSPB) in England lists farmers' switch from spring-sown cereal crops to autumn-sown ones as the primary reason for the skylark's decline in the British Isles. Autumn-sown cereal crops are taller and less useful as breeding habitat for the birds. Also, the overgrazing of pastureland has impacted habitat. The RSPB has helped to devise a scheme for leaving some habitat for the skylarks to stem the population decline.

Skylark (*Alauda arvensis*)

# Asia: Woolong National Nature Reserve, Sichuan Province, China

LOCATED IN CENTRAL Sichuan Province in southwestern China, Woolong National Nature Reserve is home to one of the largest populations of the endangered giant panda. The government, with the help of the World Wildlife Fund, has set up a research facility to study them and breed them in captivity. Woolong also happens to support an amazing diversity of birds, with a species list topping 300. The 2,700-square-mile (7,000 square km) park encompasses both mountain slopes and lower valleys, and it is governed by a relatively subtropical humid climate.

Just 83 miles (134 km) from the city of Chengdu, the provincial capital, Woolong has become one of China's more popular nature reserves, because of the giant pandas for the general public, but birders have come to know it as well, especially for the diversity of pheasants. A hotel in nearby Sawang serves as a base for many visitors.

**BIRDS TO SEE**: Vibrantly plumed pheasants are what birders flock here to see, and species such as Temminck's tragopan and the Chinese monal do not disappoint. Other less showy but no less exciting species are also present, including golden, koklass, blood, white-eared, and common pheasants. Other gamebirds found here include snowy, Tibetan, and Verreaux's monal partridge, and wood snipe. Two species of vultures, lammergeier and Himalayan vulture, can be found at the higher elevations.

# Feeding beyond Winter

EXCEPT IN AREAS where bears and similar large, dangerous animals might become a problem as a result, continuing a backyard feeder program right through spring and into summer can open new windows into the world of the birds in and around your backyard. That's the time of year when many of the birds molt into their most brilliant and colorful plumage of the year. Maintaining a feeding program into that season will bring many of those brightly colored birds into prime viewing locations.

Spring and summer feeding also can make things easier for the birds at a time of year when they are spending huge amounts of energy—periods when they are defending territories, trying to attract mates, brooding clutches of eggs, and raising their nestlings. Easily available food will provide a welcome boost through all that demanding activity.

In addition, in early spring, when the migration is underway for many species of birds, feeders maintained outside the normal late fall through winter period can provide a boost to returning birds and those just passing through an area. At that same time, the individual birds that just barely eked through the harsh winter months might make it into a period when they can recover off the fat of the land in spring and summer because of some later than normal feeder availability.

Golden pheasant (*Chrysolophus pictus*)

# Mythical Birds: Chickcharney

Deep in the pine forests of the Bahamian island of Andros dwell fiery-eyed, elfin creatures who, when angered, can bring bad luck or even twist your head around so that it faces backward. This is the legend of the chickcharnies.

Many local legends say the creatures are birdlike, very similar to an owl, but in addition to having only three toes on each foot, they apparently also have slender arms with three fingers on each. Their long tails enable them to hang from trees. They nest in the tops of tall pine trees, specifically two that are drawn together and secured.

Chickcharnies are said to be capricious in nature. When encountered by people, if the creatures are treated well they will bestow good luck on the people.

However, bad treatment could result in bad luck, and perhaps even the forcible twisting backward of the badly behaved person's head, as this snippet of a local rhyme alludes to:

"So be careful! Watch your back!
An don cha do no wrong,
Cause when Chick Charney ready,
He sure could do you harm!"

Some people believe the origin of this mythic creature springs from an extinct species of burrowing owl that lived on the island until the sixteenth century. A *Time* magazine article from 1947 likened chickcharnies to tiny, leprechaun-like creatures.

# Maple-cicles, Yum

Maple trees are a popular landscaping tree in many regions. Nearly all of us are familiar with them and probably give them little thought. They are simply the trees in our yards.

However, they also are a potential natural feeder. Inside their twigs and branches flows a natural sugar that is attractive to a wide range of common bird species. It's not only the famed sugar maples, with their metal spouts and buckets attached, that will produce a sugary flow. All maple sap has a high concentration of sugar.

In late February and into March, that sugary sap is flowing. Any injury to the tree will result in an oozing drip to the outside world. And if that injury is at the end of a twig or branch during periods of freezing temperatures, that ooze and drip will form icicles filled with maple sugar.

Those maple-flavored icicles have multiple uses, including delicious consumption by us homeowners. They also will be tapped by various species of birds, particularly when they begin to melt and drip.

Many small breaks in maple twigs and branches occur naturally every year, but we can add to that by strategically breaking off the tips of twigs that are planned for pruning anyway. You might want to place a few of the breaks strategically low for easy access, if you intend to sample the icicles yourself.

# Invasion of Privacy

NONE OF US OWNS all the places where we want to watch birds. Public lands greatly expand our list of potential birding spots. However, our hobby will lead us onto, or at least next to, lands owned by others. We'll be peering into others' backyards, their farm-yards, and the like. We'll be spying on what many consider to be their private spaces, and we'll often be doing that with powerful and obvious optical devices.

Although we may be looking at feeders or shrubs, from the perspective of the property owners, we appear to be looking at spots much more private and much more human.

We can readily come off as well-equipped Peeping Toms. And if we're birding in a group, even a group of two, a resident having his or her morning coffee in his or her dining room will have the sudden shock of being watched by a "crowd" of strangers.

A knock on a front door, an introduction, and an explanation of your intentions will go a long way toward circumventing any problems that might arise. However, nobody wants such an impromptu meeting at the door before 8:00 a.m. Be courteous at all hours and on all visits.

# Songbirds: Sedge Warbler (*Acrocephalus schoenobaenus*)

THE SEDGE WARBLER is a conspicuous songbird of Europe during breeding season. Although it may not often be seen in its densely over-grown habitats, it can often be heard singing. This species is a member of the Old World warblers, unrelated to the wood-warblers of the New World.

**PHYSICAL CHARACTERISTICS**: This small song-bird blends in well with its brushy surround-ings, as its back and wings are streaked light and dark brown. Its undersides are a creamy white. A dark cap and white eyebrow sit above the eye and a narrow bill.

**RANGE**: Found throughout Europe and into Central Asia during the breeding season, the sedge warbler migrates to sub-Saharan Africa for the winter months.

**HABITAT**: Any wet area with dense growth, including marshes, swamps, rivers, and even

ditches, can be a home for the sedge war-bler, where it hunts for insects and feeds on berries in season. The bird constructs its nest of grasses and mosses just a few feet above ground in thickets.

The sedge warbler makes impressive flight displays, lifting off vertically from a perch, rising into the air with rapid wing beats, and then spiraling downward for the finale.

**SONGS AND CALLS**: Its flight display is ac-companied by its varied song—musical trills interspersed with harsher, grating notes—which can continue uninterrupted for several minutes.

**CONSERVATION STATUS**: The sedge warbler is common and widespread, but it presumably would be affected by alteration of wetland habitats in its breeding and migratory range.

Sedge warbler (*Acrocephalus schoenobaenus*)

# Asia: Mai Po Marshes, Hong Kong, China

TRAVELERS TO Hong Kong who seek to escape the intensity of the city and have an interest in birdwatching can do no better than to visit Mai Po, a wetland area for migratory birds in the northwest corner of the city. Traditionally used as a shrimp farming area, in which ponds, known as *gei wai*, were filled to support the growth of shrimp and then drained after the harvest to capture any fish that also ended up in the ponds, the area became a regular stopover for a multitude of wading birds and seabirds.

The Mai Po marshes have been designated as wetlands of international importance and are now managed by the World Wildlife Fund (WWF) Hong Kong. Aquaculture is still practiced here, and the area is a model of sustainable fishing. WWF continues to drain the gei wai on a rotational basis from November to March to maintain the food resource for migrating birds. Spring is the best time to visit. Permits are required to access some of the viewing areas, and guided tours are also available.

**BIRDS TO SEE**: As many as 60,000 waterbirds have been documented to winter at the Mai Po marshes, including waterfowl, waders, gulls, herons, and cormorants. During migration in spring and autumn, up to 30,000 wading birds pass through or use the marshes as a stopover. These species include pied avocet, marsh sandpiper, curlew sandpiper, common redshank, and spotted redshank.

The Mai Po marshes have been a reliable area to see the endangered black-faced spoonbill, as well as the endangered Saunders's gull. The extremely rare spoon-billed sandpiper has also been sighted here, causing flocks of birders to come from far and wide for a chance to see it. Other rare species found at Mai Po include spotted greenshank, Asiatic dowitcher, and gray-tailed tattler.

# Microclimates in Action

EVEN IN OUR little backyards, birds and other creatures can find wide swings in climate that they will use to their benefit.

Microclimates—localized zones where climate differs significantly from the surrounding area—explain the differences we notice many times every day in our lives, from the warmer areas of our homes generally being on the south and west sides, to grass growing along a sidewalk needing more water than the same species of grass growing in the middle of the backyard.

A *microclimate* can be anything from a few feet (or centimeters) to several miles (or kilometers) in size. Within the microclimate, temperatures might be lower or higher than the surrounding area, precipitation might be more or less than in the surrounding area, and frosts might be more or less common.

Larger microclimates might result under the influence of large bodies of water, topography, soil type, vegetation covering the area, and urban areas, all which can moderate temperatures, provide extra shelter from prevailing winds, and engage unnatural heating and cooling effects, such as radiation of stored heat into the night. Large paved areas also can significantly impact the available groundwater in a given area, another potential influence on local climate elements.

# Birds of Prey in Myth and Culture

BECAUSE OF THEIR impressive abilities as hunters, birds of prey have become partners and competitors with humans as well as inspiration. These birds—hawks, falcons, and vultures—have been chosen to represent gods and royalty, as well as the baser natures of men. For example, the lanner falcon served as the inspiration for the Egyptian god Horus, god of the sky, war, and protection. The Egyptian royalty held falcons in such high regard that the birds were often buried in their tombs to accompany them to the next world.

The original peoples of the Americas also have a rich cultural and mythological use of raptors. The Inca of South America appreciated the hunting qualities of raptors, or *waman* (in Quechua, their language), especially the sharp-shinned hawk, *k'illi*, the caracara, *quoriquenque*, and the eagle, *'anka*. Their mythology, like that of many other Native American cultures, features a winged, hawklike deity called the Thunderer or Thunderbird.

Using the parts of birds of prey was believed to confer their power to the user. The Amahuaca of Peru boiled hawk talons and then smeared the juice on their bodies before hunting. This use of raptor parts extends into modernity, such as in Mexico, where the feet of hawks and owls are hung in trucks and buses to ward off evil and bad luck.

This respect and admiration doesn't always carry through to all members of a culture. Raptors were seen as both a commodity and even a pest by nineteenth-century settlers of North America. The birds were viewed as competition for game animals, or worse, as predators on livestock, a claim repeatedly disproved. Tens of thousands of birds were killed before migratory bird laws were enacted in the early twentieth century. Birds in general became more respected in the late twentieth century, and events such as hawk watches during migration and even festivals to honor eagles, hawks, and owls have become annual events and a big tourist draw.

# Corn Times Two

A SPECIAL FEEDER to offer dried cobs of corn is another simple do-it-yourself project.

Start with a 24" (61 cm) length of one-by-twelve lumber. Cut the piece in half so you have two 12" (30.4 cm) pieces. From one piece, cut two triangles that are 2" (5.1 cm) tall by 4" (10.2 cm) long. The 4" (10.2 cm) side should be cut with the grain. From that same piece, cut a 4" (10.2 cm) wide by 11½" (29.2 cm) shelf.

With two wood screws through the back of the 12" (30.4 cm) -long piece, and a line of wood glue, attach the 4" (10.2 cm) -long piece as a shelf to the front of the 12" (30.4 cm) piece, about 3" (7.6 cm) from the bottom.

With one wood screw through the back of the 12" (30.4 cm) piece into each triangle, and a line of wood glue, attach the triangles as supports for the shelf.

Turn two wood screws through the center of the shelf, from bottom to top, with the heads of the screws flush with the bottom of the shelf and most of the screws extending out the top of the shelf.

Drill a hole at each of the top corners of the 12" (30.4 cm) piece to attach wire for hanging the feeder.

When the feeder is in position, turn whole, dried cobs of corn onto the exposed screws.

The birds, and squirrels, will gradually strip the kernels off the cobs. When they're empty, the cobs can be replaced with more. Or the denuded cobs can be turned off the screw, dipped in suet or peanut butter, and returned to the screw as a new source of food.

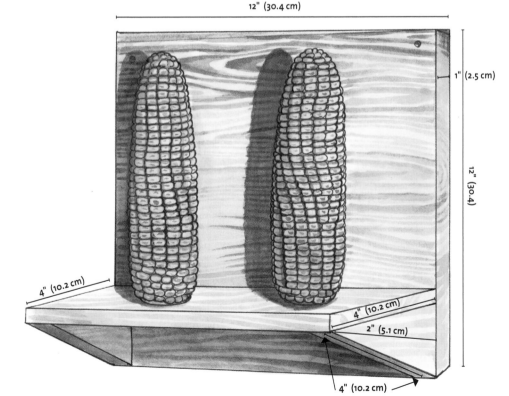

# Behavior: Getting Around on Foot

VISUAL CLUES ARE the first and foremost details that new birdwatchers look for when starting the practice. Field guides perpetuate this preference for morphological character-istics by focusing primarily on field marks. But there are many other details to watch for when attempting to identify a bird, especially when conditions prevent seeing these distinc-tive visual clues.

Behavior is equally as important for the begin-ning birder. It gives a clue to the bird's feeding habits, nesting locations, and other informa-tion. One of the most obvious behaviors is locomotion. Different birds move differently when in trees or on the ground.

One of the most distinctively locomotive groups is the climbing birds, such as wood-

peckers, creepers, and nuthatches. Nuthatches are able to climb up or down a tree trunk, while the brown creeper climbs only upward in a spiral around the tree trunk. This may be frustrating for a birder trying to get a view of it, but the behavior, size, and general brown coloring, when taken together, are immediate clues as to the brown creeper's identity.

Like brown creepers, woodpeckers also use their tails as props to stabilize them as they climb a tree. Woodpeckers have zygodactyl feet to aid them in climbing. The two rear-facing toes can be moved forward if needed for greater purchase on a tree trunk. These birds will climb a trunk, searching for insect holes to bore into. This foraging behavior is often accompanied by their distinctive *peet* calls, especially when flying from tree to tree.

# Songbirds: Black-Throated Magpie-Jay (*Calocitta colliei*)

ONE OF THE MOST flamboyant jays in the world because of its extremely long tail and showy crest, the black-throated magpie-jay lives in a very small region of Mexico.

**PHYSICAL CHARACTERISTICS**: This showy jay displays similar blue colors to other jays, but the long tail and other markings make it very distinctive. The rich, blue back and upsides of the wings and tail are contrasted with an all-white underside. Pale blue eyebrow and cheek patches sit within an all-black face and crown, topped with a showy, forward-arching crest of black feathers.

**RANGE**: These birds live in a very restricted range of northwest Mexico in the southern Sonora, Jalisco, and Colima states.

**HABITAT**: Frequenting mostly dry, lowland country in thorn forest and open woodlands near rivers, the black-throated magpie-jay can be seen perched atop low shrubs and within trees. Like other jays, they move in small, noisy groups, feeding on insects, seeds, and fruits. Their nests are built in thorny shrubs and are made of twigs lined with mosses and lichens.

**SONGS AND CALLS**: This magpie-jay has an extremely rich vocal repertoire, including barks, whistles, clicks, rattles, and yelps, many repeated rhythmically.

**CONSERVATION STATUS**: The black-throated magpie-jay population is considered stable. Deforestation and excessive grazing may have impacted their numbers.

Black-throated magpie-jay (*Calocitta colliei*)

# Asia: Arasaki District, Izumi City, Japan

IF CRANES ARE your bird of choice, one of the best sites in Asia to see them is in the agricultural fields of the Arasaki District in far southern Japan on the island of Kyushu. This region of rice paddies and wetlands plays host every year during winter to thousands of migrating cranes of several species. Designated a natural treasure, the area encourages visitors with a Crane Observation Center, museum, and park, which provides information and allows viewing opportunities. Visitors can stay in nearby Izumi.

**BIRDS TO SEE**: Cranes, cranes, and more cranes. The most common species are hooded and white-naped cranes, although common and sandhill cranes return reliably as well, in lesser numbers. Some of the rare crane species to look out for include Siberian, demoiselle, and red-crowned.

The wetlands also attract a wide variety of other water birds, including herons (black-crowned night-heron and intermediate egret), the rare black-faced spoonbill, Kentish plover, northern lapwing, and several species of ducks (eastern spot-billed duck, northern pintails, Eurasian wigeons, and northern shovelers).

# Tempting Bluebirds

IT'S COMMON KNOWLEDGE in modern birding circles that the key to attracting bluebirds lies in offering nest boxes to supplement the ever scarcer natural cavities. However, many other attractions can be brought to the backyard to enhance the attraction to one of the most sought-after of birdwatching species.

Bayberries, red cedars, sumac, and Virginia creeper are among the ornamentals whose berries the bluebirds relish. Blueberry bushes are another favorite source of berries, but generally one of much shorter duration. And for those willing to take a more adventurous tact, allowing some poison ivy plants to vine up the trees in some out-of-the-way area of the backyard will generate another favorite type of berries for bluebirds.

A handful of mealworms are a certain attraction, when bluebirds are known to be in proximity to the feeders. Placing live mealworms at other times will only result in escaped mealworms, which are among the most expensive of foods for backyard birds.

Those bluebirds that do come to feeders have shown a preference for chopped peanut meats and chopped fruits, dried or fresh.

Suet feeders may hold some attraction for bluebirds in winter, particularly if stocked with fruit-laden cakes of suet.

# Mythical Birds: Alerion, or Martlet

OF THE MANY fantastical creatures devised or created from misunderstandings of the natural sciences, the martlet is surely one of the more curious. The bird was considered similar to a swift or swallow, and its endless time on the wing hunting insects is likely to have birthed this association. Martlets were thought to have either no legs with just feathers in their place or very short, rudimentary legs, not useful for walking. Thus, they spent most of their time in the air and making their nests on cliffs. Some legends say that there are only two of these birds living at a time. The birds live for sixty years, at which time they lay two eggs. After the eggs have hatched, the parents fly to the sea where they drown themselves.

The bird was a symbol of the restless nature of industrious people, and a symbol for the unquenchable thirst for knowledge. Thus, the bird has been used as an emblem by many institutions of learning, such as Westminster School and Worcester College at Oxford in England, and McGill University and the University of Victoria in Canada. It was also a commonly used symbol in heraldry.

One version of the explanation of the mythic bird's derivation is from the bird of paradise. The natives of New Guinea who sold the dead birds to Westerners for their feathers were thought to cut off the birds' feet since they thought they were of no use. The Westerners thus thought the birds had no feet.

# Insects on the Menu

IN OUR BACKYARDS, we can do much to attract various insect types that will provide fodder for a variety of birds. Here are some of the favorite insect foods of some of the most common backyard birds:

- **Red-winged blackbird**: beetles, cankerworms, grasshoppers, gypsy moth caterpillars, mayflies, moths, spiders, and tent caterpillars

- **Eastern bluebird**: beetles, crickets, grasshoppers, and katydids

- **Western bluebird**: beetles, crickets, and grasshoppers

- **Northern cardinal**: aphids, beetles, various caterpillars, crickets, grasshoppers, moths, scale insects, and spiders

- **Black-capped chickadee**: various caterpillars, moths, and spiders

- **Flicker**: ants

- **Grackle**: ants, beetles, various caterpillars, earthworms, grubs, grasshoppers, and spiders

- **Grosbeak:** bees, beetles, cankerworms, various caterpillars, flies, grasshoppers, spiders, wasps, and yellow jackets

- **Jay**: beetles, gypsy moth caterpillars, grasshoppers, spiders, and tent caterpillars

- **Junco**: ants, beetles, various caterpillars, spiders, and wasps

- **Northern oriole**: ants, beetles, various caterpillars, crickets, grasshoppers, mayflies, and tent caterpillars

- **Robin**: beetles, earthworms, grasshoppers, leafhoppers, and spiders

- **Chipping sparrow**: ants, beetles, various caterpillars, grasshoppers, and spiders

- **Song sparrow**: ants, beetles, grasshoppers, and wasps

- **Thrasher**: beetles, earthworms, grasshoppers, leafhoppers, and spiders

- **Thrush**: beetles, earthworms, grasshoppers, leafhoppers, and spiders

- **Titmice**: various caterpillars

- **Woodpecker**: ants, beetles, various caterpillars, moths, spiders, tenet caterpillars, and weevils

# Behavior: Perching Birds

MOST BIRDS THAT birdwatchers will encounter at their feeders and even in the field are songbirds, or passerines, such as sparrows, chickadees, finches, jays, robins, wrens, and warblers. These small, agile birds use their slender but strong feet to grab hold of twigs and branches for momentary rest as well as for overnight roosting. But they can also grasp onto the sides of tree trunks or other vertical objects, aided by their very sharp claws. Since they spend most of their time in trees, hopping from branch to branch, they can't walk easily, so they get around on the ground by hopping.

The perching skills of birds are legendary, and this is aided by the very effective anatomical structure of the bird's legs and feet. The tendons in a bird's toes automatically lock onto a perch when they alight on it. As soon as pressure is applied to the feet and the legs bend, the tendon tightens and the toes curl around the perch. This is how birds are able to sleep on a perch. The tendons release only when the weight is taken off the feet, as when a bird begins to take off in flight from the perch. The toes straighten out when this happens, releasing the bird's hold.

# Songbirds: Wood-Warblers

WARBLERS ARE A fascinating, colorful, and often vexing group of birds for the novice and even sometimes the experienced birdwatcher to identify. The North American species are called wood-warblers to distinguish them from Old World warblers. The number of species (115 species worldwide and most of them in North America) and their similar behavior and plumages (feather coats) contribute to this difficulty in identification.

**PHYSICAL CHARACTERISTICS**: Wood-warblers are small songbirds. They can be solid-colored or streaked on their backs and chests, depending on the species. Many species are very colorful during breeding season but molt to a more drab feather coat during non-breeding season.

These examples refer to adult plumage.

*Solid backs and wings, solid chests:*

- Prothonotary warbler (olive back, blue-gray wings, bright yellow breast)
- Black-throated blue warbler (blue back and wings, white breast with black face and flanks)

*Streaked backs and wings, streaked chests:*

- Yellow warbler (olive back, yellow breast with red streaks)
- Cape May warbler (olive back with black streaks; wings with white, olive, and black; breast yellow with black streaks; chestnut mask)

*Streaked backs and wings, solid chests:*

- Hermit warbler (gray back with black spots; white and black wing bars; white breast; black chest; yellow face)
- Bay-breasted warbler (black and olive-streaked back; white wing bars; "bay," or chestnut-brown cap, throat, and flanks; black mask)

The bills of wood-warblers are narrow, effective at ferreting insects from flowers, leaves, and bark.

**RANGE**: Most wood-warbler species can be found from the Great Lakes region east to the Canadian Maritimes and then south along the East Coast. However, other species breed as far south as the mountainous regions of Central America and northern South America.

**HABITAT**: Many of these small songbird species spend most of their time in the upper branches of tall trees in spring and summer, flitting quickly from branch to branch in search of insects. This makes them especially difficult to spot.

Other species of wood-warblers, such as the Swainson's warbler, the ovenbird, and the waterthrushes, stay close to the ground and feed by turning over dead leaves in search of insect prey. The black-and-white warbler is unusual in that it often climbs up and down tree trunks, rooting out bugs from the bark.

**SONGS AND CALLS**: Wood-warblers' songs tend to be very complex and include buzzes, trills, and long rising and dropping whistles. Call notes are short and sharp.

**CONSERVATION STATUS**: Like many other songbird species, warblers are very sensitive to habitat degradation. The species with more specific habitat preferences have been impacted most significantly. Kirtland's warbler, for example, was in significant decline until recently. Their preferred breeding habitat of large stands of jack pine maintained by fire was being logged intensively. Now with better habitat management, the bird is making a recovery. The common yellowthroat, by contrast, prefers almost any stand of dense growth for breeding, as long as it is near a wetland. Consequently, its numbers are strong.

Prothonotary warbler (*Prontonotaria citrea*)

# Asia: Taman Negara National Park, Malaysia

IT'S RARE TO FIND conservation land that hasn't been altered in some way by human hands— some wetland habitats have even been created by people, for example. Taman Negara National Park, nestled within the mountains of Malaysia on the Malay Peninsula about 190 miles (300 km) northeast of Kuala Lumpur, is just such a protected place. Considered one of the world's oldest tropical lowland forests (130 million years old), the area has never been altered by significant forces, geological or anthropomorphic. This has preserved some exceptional biodiversity, especially plant and insect life, within Taman Negara, which translates as "national park" in the Malay language.

More than 350 species of birds can be found in this 1,677-square-mile (4,340 square km) park. They can be difficult to see among the dense vegetation, but they are well worth the effort. Most of the park is undeveloped, and visitors need a permit to traverse the miles of well-tended trails. Several very comfortable lodges can be found in the area of the park's only official entry point at the Kuala Tahan headquarters.

**BIRDS TO SEE:** One of the most remarkable groups that visitors to Taman Negara are sure to encounter is the unusual and beautiful hornbills, including the great, black, and white-crowned. Several species have a prominent *casque*, or horned protrusion on their upper bill. Another showy and omnipresent group is the ground-dwelling pittas—garnet, banded, giant, and blue-winged are a few of note. These songbirds hop around rooting through the litter for insects and other fare. Pheasant species are also well represented, and many of the park's species are brightly colored, such as great and crested arguses, and the Malayan peacock-pheasant. Rich-hued kingfisher and lesser fishing eagle can be seen along rivers. Other commonly seen species include babblers, broadbills, drongos, bee-eaters, trogons, and woodpeckers.

# Yule Log for Birds

THE YULE LOG has seen many incarnations since its medieval origins among the pagans of central Europe, from a burning celebration of or introduction to the season to an ice cream confection to an annual Christmastime feature on some local television stations. And now, here's a plan for a yule log for birds.

Select a log at least 8" (20.3 cm) in diameter and 2' (61 cm) long, with the bark still in place (a rough bark with lots of cracks and crevices offers the most possibilities). Drill several holes, each 2" (5.1 cm) in diameter and 2" (5.1 cm) deep, into the log, irregularly spaced along the length of the log and on all sides, except the side you've chosen to be the bottom (usually the flattest side).

Prepare a suet-seed mixture as explained on page 153. Allow it to begin cooling and, when it's the consistency of pudding, spoon it into holes drilled into the log. Also spread lines of suet-seed mixture into the cracks and crevices of the log. As an alternative to suet, the holes, cracks, and crevices may be filled with peanut butter or a peanut butter–seed mixture.

Using heavy thread or fishing line on a heavy needle, thread cranberries, peanuts, and popcorn into a long garland to be wrapped around the log. Place it anywhere in your backyard where you'd like to draw more guests.

# Bird Sayings, Part IV: Ducks

DUCK METAPHORS seem to pepper the English language like buckshot. The phrase "sitting duck," in fact, has been attributed to hunting, as a duck at rest is an easy shot, since it takes a bit of energy for the animal to get aloft. The term is also used to refer to the game of billiards when a ball is set up right in front of a pocket.

Associating a hurt animal with an ineffective politician may seem an odd metaphor, but that is the source of the phrase "lame duck." It refers to any elected official who, because of term limits, is due to leave office. The period during which he or she does not have to seek reelection is considered a lame duck session.

However, the phrase was originally used within the London Stock Exchange in the eighteenth century to describe a broker who couldn't pay his debts. Similarly, a person is a "dead duck" when his or her unfavorable fate is assured.

People who have all their affairs in order before embarking on a project are said to have all their "ducks in a row." The origin likely simply refers to the duck family's habit of floating in an orderly line.

Duck metaphors are also used to indicate how easily something is accomplished. An expression for an easy task is "duck soup." If a person easily sloughs off insults or difficult tasks, these are said to pass off him or her "like water off a duck's back," referring to the ability of ducks and other waterfowl to easily shed water from their feathers.

# A Clean Birdbath Is a Healthy Birdbath

BIRDS ARE FILTHY BATHERS. There's an incredible amount of dirt in their feathers, and they're not too careful about where or when they leave their droppings.

In addition, a birdbath is a closed, noncirculating aquatic environment, which is the perfect breeding ground for everything from bacteria to algae to mosquitoes.

It's essential from both an aesthetic and a health perspective to clean every birdbath often and hard. A strong, rough scrubber is the essential tool for the job. Something with wire bristles is a good start. Combine that with a strong but environmentally safe cleanser that will not leave any residue behind in the clean bath.

Empty the bath, scrape it clean, and then scrape it with cleanser, rinse it, and repeat. After the surface appears clean, allow the bath to dry in the sun before filling it with clean water.

Another way to keep a birdbath clean is to equip the bath with a small aquarium-type pump that will continuously move the water. With just a bit of plastic tubing, the pump can be the powerhouse for a small fountain effect in the birdbath.

# Behavior: Birds in Flight

MORE OFTEN THAN NOT, new birders will see birds in flight rather than see them sitting perched at a close distance. When birds are in flight, those prized field marks become all but useless for identification, except in species with striking plumages more visible in flight than at rest. It's important to become acquainted with the general kinds of flight for groups of birds, as well as with some of the more idiosyncratic flight patterns of certain species.

Observe birds at rest so that you can identify the species, and then carefully observe them as they take off in flight. How do they take off: by dropping down from a branch, or lifting up from the ground? Do they fly in a straight line, an undulating pattern, or by zigging and zagging? All of this information provides excellent clues to group identification.

For example, finches and woodpeckers use an undulating flight pattern. A few quick beats of their wings before folding them to their bodies create this up-and-down movement. The sine wave pattern of the woodpecker is flatter than that of the finch, as members of the latter group rise up more when the wings are folded.

Other small songbirds, such as wrens and warblers, fly in a straight line with steady wing beats, usually directly away from an inquisitive birder. Crows also have this pattern, but obviously they are much bigger and generally fly much higher than songbirds. Their relatives, the ravens, on the other hand, often soar and perform somersaults or circles in the midst of their glides.

Raptors are large soaring birds, and each species has a distinctive flight style. Buteos such as red-tailed hawks can often be seen gliding for long distances separated by periods of flapping. They, as well as other raptor species, can also often be seen rising in circles, riding on columns of warm air called *thermals*. Turkey vultures fly in a very characteristic manner, with their wings held in a V pattern, or *dihedral*, tipping side to side as they glide along. Other smaller raptors, such as Cooper's hawks or sharp-shinned hawks, fly with a few rapid wing beats, and then glide.

Kestrels (a small species of falcon) and ospreys will hover, hanging motionless in the air held aloft by winds as they scan the ground and water for prey, respectively. Hummingbirds are also a hovering species, but these much smaller birds do this while beating their wings nearly one hundred times per second as they sip nectar from flowers.

The elusive woodcocks and snipes, our land-based sandpiper species, will dart from cover with a zigzag, serpentine pattern to elude potential predators.

Flocks of birds assume their own collective diagnostic patterns. Species such as geese, ducks, and cranes fly in a group V pattern, while seabirds such as pelicans, cormorants, and sea ducks may fly in a straight-line pattern.

Careful observation of these patterns will add to your growing knowledge of the behavior of birds, a valuable addition to any birder's skills.

# Songbirds: Sparrows

SOME NEW TO BIRDWATCHING experience sparrows as others react to warblers: with crossed eyes and exasperation. With hundreds of species and numerous subspecies, some birdwatchers feel they may never identify individual species of sparrow because of their similarity in plumage color and patterns. Some may learn to recognize the most common species—the house sparrow (a species introduced to the United States from Europe, and not in the same family as American sparrows)—or other species found at their bird feeders, such as the chipping sparrow, American tree sparrow, song sparrow, white-throated sparrow, and fox sparrow. These New World species are more closely related to the Old World family of buntings rather than the Old World sparrows.

**PHYSICAL CHARACTERISTICS**: Like the warblers, the sparrows can be more easily deciphered if you break them down into groups. The broadest division is between the streaked sparrows and the clear-breasted sparrows.

Examples of clear-breasted sparrows include the American tree sparrow, chipping sparrow, white-crowned sparrow, and clay-colored sparrow.

The group of streak-breasted sparrows includes these species: fox sparrow, song sparrow, savannah sparrow, and grasshopper sparrow.

**RANGE**: Sparrows are found all over the world. Buntings are found mostly in Eurasia and Africa, and Old World sparrows are found in Europe.

**HABITAT**: The stout bills of sparrows can easily crack open a variety of seeds, their preferred food. Thus, sparrows can be found both in forested habitats (fox sparrows and song sparrows) and open habitats such as meadows and agricultural fields (grasshopper sparrows and vesper sparrows).

But many species are commonly seen at the edge between these two habitats (white-throated sparrows, white-crowned sparrows, and chipping sparrows). In this predilection for seeds, sparrows are similar to the finch family and can easily be confused with those species.

**SONGS AND CALLS**: With so many species in these families, you would rightly expect that there would be a wide variety of calls. Many are distinctive and can be easily learned with practice. The song sparrow's song seems random and wild at first, but after repeated hearings, one can pick out a pattern. The white-throated sparrow's "Sam-Peabody-Peabody" (or "pure sweet Canada Canada" if you're from the great north) is one many people can recognize. Many sparrow calls are single notes, in a variation on the classic chip or tweet.

**CONSERVATION STATUS**: As a group, the populations of sparrow species are generally stable. However, some species with specific habitat needs, such as the Cape Sable Seaside sparrow, are endangered. Their degraded wetland habitats in the Florida Everglades caused the extinction of this bird's close relative, the Dusky Seaside sparrow, in 1990.

In contrast, species generalists (those species who can tolerate a wide range of habitats), such as song sparrows and white-throated sparrows, have fared much better. Both are also tolerant of human-created landscapes, such as suburban neighborhoods and parks.

House sparrow (*Passer domesticus*)

# Australia: Kakadu National Park, Northern Territory

COVERING ALMOST 7,700 square miles (20,000 square km) in the far north of Australia's Northern Territory, Kakadu National Park is a rich cultural and ecological treasure. The world knows the area mostly for its distinctive rock formations, but other sites, such as impressive waterfalls, are also found here. This is a good site for seeing a large number of Australian birds, as the park is home to 30 percent of the country's species.

The park features several habitats. The plateau is the high stone country, perched above the lowlands and wetlands, separated by a sinuous line of steep cliffs that stretches for 310 miles (500 km). The floodplains of the Alligator rivers drain water to the coast and are tidally influenced. Vast areas of savanna are also present. December to March is the true wet season, so travel is recommended at other times throughout the year. The town of Jabiru has accommodations, but campsites are also available, scattered throughout the park.

**BIRDS TO SEE**: Visitors will go away staggered by what they've seen here. Australia is home to so many distinctive bird families that it expands a birder's horizons significantly. The grasswrens are endemic to Australia, and the white-throated grassrwren can be found around some of the park's waterfalls. Some of the waterbirds seen along the floodplains are kingfishers (azure and little), rufous nightheron, green pygmy goose, and comb-crested jacana. A species of stork known as the jabiru (a.k.a., Asian black-necked stork) is also present, but this is a wholly different species than the jabiru from South America. Kakadu is also one of the most important breeding areas for the magpie goose. Other species found in the park include barking owl, blue-winged kookaburra, bush thick-knee, rainbow bee-eater, Toressian crow, whistling kite, and white-bellied sea eagle.

# In a Family Way

Birds offer a near theatrical production of different behaviors throughout the year, especially when it comes to starting a family.

Courtship is a highly varied and individualized behavior among bird species. Male goldfinches spend long hours on feeding forays with females in which they're interested. Male woodpeckers set their drumming on dead tree trunks and limbs into a frenzied pace. Male buntings flutter over weedy areas, singing loudly.

Nest-building is another widely varying behavior, with every species building in its preferred habitat, at its preferred elevation, and with its preferred materials. Most observers wonder how the loose tangle of twigs into which mourning doves lay their eggs holds together at all. The American robin expends huge effort and energy to build adobe-like cups of mud and grass.

Hatching, rearing, and fledging the next generation is a fast-paced period for all species. In some, both parents will work at a fever pitch to supply the babies. In others, it's completely left to the female. And in still others, such as the cowbird, the female lays her eggs in the nests of other birds, and then both parents abandon parental duties.

Regardless of parental arrangements, there comes a time when any bird with babies in the nest will gradually show less urgency in gathering food for them, react negatively to the young birds' constant begging, and encourage the fledglings to begin fending for themselves.

# Evolution of Birds V: Australia's Mihirungs

As WITH MUCH other life on isolated islands or continents, Australia's current and prehistoric fauna tend to be quite unique creatures. Many species are found nowhere else. Such is the case with the mihirungs, which are better known scientifically as Dromornithids and are described from the fossil record as far back as the Oligocene Epoch, thirty-four to twenty-four million years ago.

These were large, flightless birds, similar in size to the terror birds of the Americas. The last know species, *Genyornis newtoni*, lived as recently as 50,000 years ago, so they overlapped with humans, and possibly went extinct because of it. Australian aboriginal people have legends of giant emus that they called *mihirung paringmal*. Researchers believe these may be the Dromornithids, which they say are more likely related to today's geese rather than emus. (Hence the bird's nickname, "Giant Demon Duck of Doom.")

The most well known and earliest of these giant birds—*Dromornis stirtoni*, or Stirton's Thunder Bird—weighed up to 1,200 pounds (500 kg) and stood up to 10' (3 m) tall. The bird's huge head, large bill, and strong, thick legs caused some scientists to believe *Dromornis* and other mihirungas were fast runners. There is much disagreement among paleontologists over the diet of these birds. Many claim they were vegetarian, citing Genyornis's hooflike feet and noncurved bills, while those positing carnivorousness cite the large size of the beaks.

# A Rockin' Birdbath

HAVE YOU EVER THOUGHT about incorporating a natural birdbath into your backyard? It's rare that the perfect rock with the perfect birdbath shape occurs exactly where we want it in the landscape. You may have to sculpt an existing rock to meet your design vision.

Rock carving is easier than generally assumed, although there is always potential for injury. Safety gear, including heavy leather work gloves, completely enclosed safety glasses, a long-sleeved shirt or jacket, and a head covering, is mandatory. A clear work area that is void of people who might be injured from flying rock particles and of objects that might be damaged by the same also must be assured.

Evaluate the contours of the rock and locate where you will create your natural birdbath. With a mallet and rock chisel, slowly and gradually remove a layer of rock in the spot where the depression will serve as a natural birdbath. Clear the dust and particles, and remove another layer. Continue layer after layer until the desired depth and contour are achieved. Keep in mind that few birds want to wade in water deeper than a few inches (or centimeters).

Many rocks will hold water nicely. However, if the rock you'd like to carve is highly porous, you might want to apply a liquid sealant to the surface before filling it with water.

# Putting All the Pieces Together

So, NOW YOU MAY KNOW how to tell the difference between a chickadee and a titmouse, or even a song sparrow and a house sparrow, but can you tell the location of the supercilium on these birds, or which feathers on the wing are the primaries and which are the secondaries? Although perhaps beyond the very basics of birding, learning the different parts of a bird will not only help you interpret a wider variety of field guides, but it will also help you communicate with other birders more easily.

As you've no doubt learned from your observations, the variety of plumages among species can be dizzying. Once you start seeing the parts comprising a bird, you'll start taking more notice of these features, their colors and shapes, and it will take you into the level of advanced birding.

The diagrams on this page shows the important features of a generalized bird's head, body, and wings.

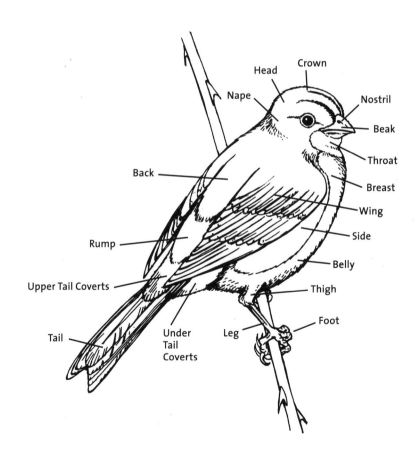

# Woodpeckers

THE WOODPECKERS are a fascinating, colorful, and entertaining group of birds. Also, many species are not shy around people, so it makes watching them easier and more enjoyable.

**PHYSICAL CHARACTERISTICS**: The main common physical attribute of all woodpeckers is a long narrow bill that they use to excavate holes in trees and/or penetrate ground insect nests. Nearly all species also have zygodactyl feet, which means that two toes point forward and two point backward, an adaptation for clinging to the bark of trees.

Many species are brightly colored, usually with red and mostly around the head. Some large South American species, such as the red-necked and the crimson-bellied woodpeckers, also have red undersides and lower backs, in addition to nearly all-red necks and heads. Ground-active woodpeckers tend to be more drab-colored in browns, greens, and grays, with no head markings; this may be to make them less obvious to predators. This camouflage concept may extend to the ladder-backed species, such as North America's downy, hairy, red-bellied, and red-cockaded woodpeckers and the yellow-bellied sapsuckers. The mottled black-and-white pattern may echo the dappled sunlight that plays across tree trunks in the forest. Moustache stripes are also common in many species.

**RANGE**: Woodpeckers are present worldwide except in Australia, Madagascar, and many islands.

**HABITAT**: Woodpeckers are found in forests and woodlands, where they nest in trees and feed on insects rooted out from live and dead trees; in the months when insects are not active, as in the temperate and northern winters, they will feed on seeds, fruits, and the sap from trees.

Flickers as a group specialize in ground insects. The Andean flicker lives above the tree line in the Andes Mountains of South America. A few species of woodpeckers are found in grasslands and savannas.

**SONGS AND CALLS**: Woodpeckers' calls can be loud and prolonged. Some are used for territorial demarcation while others may be used to communicate with mated pairs. Many calls, such as those of North America's pileated and red-bellied woodpeckers, can be likened to a laugh. Their calls are usually diagnostic of species, with a little work. Although not a song or a call, the pounding these birds do on trees is usually rhythmically idiosyncratic. The yellow-bellied sapsucker in North America, for instance, is known for drumming on metal, such as on roofs, mailboxes, or stovepipes, to attract mates and establish territory in spring.

**CONSERVATION STATUS**: Woodpeckers are in decline wherever habitats that hold the characteristics these birds prefer for nesting and feeding areas are damaged or degraded. Many larger species, such as pileated and ivory-billed, need large trees in which they can excavate their relatively large nesting cavities. Both species decline with intensive logging. The pileated has returned, while the ivory-billed may or may not be extinct (see Day 131).

Other smaller species, like the downy, hairy, and red-bellied woodpeckers, can tolerate a wider range of conditions and are less affected by habitat alteration.

**Red-bellied woodpecker (*Melanerpes carolinus*) feeding a chick**

# Australia: Wet Tropics of Queensland

A VISIT TO THE northwest coast of Australia, in the Queensland province, gets the ecotraveler not only the Great Barrier Reef just offshore, but also the magnificent Wet Tropics of Queensland, a World Heritage Site. This 3,475-square-mile (9,000 square km) region contains Australia's largest remaining extent of wet tropical rainforest and encompasses several national parks, including Daintree, Barron Gorge, and Wooroonooran. A range of accommodations and tour operators can be found in the area, as well as boat, bike, and car rentals.

From coastal mangrove stands to lush montane rainforest and drier scelerophyll woodland, the area hosts a staggering number of endemic plants, and more families of primitive plants than anywhere else on Earth. Forty percent of Australia's bird species can be found here.

**BIRDS TO SEE**: This area is home to the endangered southern cassowary, as well as two species of bowerbird: tooth-billed and golden, the former of which is endemic to this region. Other endemic species include bridled honeyeater, Macleay's honeyeater, Atherton scrubwren, fern wren, mountain thornbill, gray-headed robin, northern longrunner, Bower's shrike-thrush, pied monarch, Victoria's riflebird, and lesser sooty owl, in the barn owl family. The Australian brushturkey and orange-footed scrubfowl are two of several ground-nesting birds common in the rainforest.

# Looking Back, Looking Ahead

TAKING A LOOK BACK over the past year in a review of what you wanted to achieve and what you actually did can be a great starting point for the coming year. For those of us wanting to attract birds into our backyards, a few specific questions will guide this process to a more thoughtful and reasoned conclusion, with better guidance for the new year.

Did you attract the birds you were hoping to attract into your backyard? Which of your efforts did they respond to most readily? Was there one particular species you were hoping for, but failed to attract? What might you try differently with that species still as your target? Is there a different species you really want to achieve in the coming year?

Did you encounter any problem birds? What species were they? Why were they a problem? What might be done to lessen or eliminate their impact in your bird garden?

Were the plants you added to your bird garden successful in your setting? Why, or why not? Did you notice any patterns among the successes or failures in your plants? Did you notice any spots that could stand to have some new plants installed?

What about your hardscape features, such as mini ponds, bird feeders, birdbaths, nest boxes, and the like? Is the placement of those features working out, both for the birds and for your viewing pleasure? Are any repairs or replacements needed? Any additions or alterations?

What were the top three things that happened in your bird garden last year that most pleased you? What caused those events to happen? How can those circumstances be replicated in the coming year, if you want the same to happen again?

# Extinction in Birds II

Some estimates put the number of bird species officially considered extinct since 1500 at almost 200 species. Islands are the sites of the greatest number of extinctions; the Hawaiian chain is a well-known example, with numerous species lost and many currently at risk of extinction. These are just a few more of the well-known recently extinct species.

The great auk, a flightless bird related to penguins and razorbacks, was once widespread across the North Atlantic and the population may have numbered as many as a million birds at its height. Like other related birds, great auks bred on islands, usually rocky shores, and fed in the sea. Ironically, this bird may have met its fate because it was so numerous. The bird was killed for food, for its skin, and for its feathers, which were used as down for pillows. Its eggs were gathered for food and collections. Merchant and exploratory vessels knew the locations of colonies and would stop there to provision their ships with food. The two last recorded birds met an awful end, being strangled to death by collectors on Eldey Island off the coast of Iceland.

The passenger pigeon was also a numerous species that gathered in large flocks, a strategy that made this bird easy to kill. These flocks numbered in the hundreds of thousands during migration periods, and the birds nested colonially as well, with an estimated total population of three billion to five billion at the time of the initial European colonization of America. Some estimates indicate that at its height in recorded history, the population of passenger pigeons accounted for 25 to 40 percent of the total number of birds in the United States. It would take days for a single flock to pass overhead. In the nineteenth century, the birds were harvested in large numbers for sale in markets, where they would fetch fifty cents per dozen. Public outrage was late and ineffective, with laws being passed when the populations were too low to sustain themselves. The last wild birds were captured in Pike County, Ohio, on March 24, 1900, and the last captive bird, Martha, passed away at the Cincinnati Zoological Garden on September 1, 1914, at age twenty-nine.

The only parrot species native to North America north of Mexico, the Carolina parakeet was a bright green and yellow bird that made its home in the eastern United States. It gathered in flocks outside the breeding season, feeding on cultivated crops, including grains and fruits, which made it a serious enemy of farmers. Unfortunately, this spelled the bird's demise, and the species became extinct in the 1920s.

# Extending Holiday Cheer

IN THE DAYS after the holiday season, you can gather discarded Christmas trees that have been dumped on the curb for the week's trash pickup. They provide an awful lot of prime wildlife habitat that you can bring back to your own property.

Old conifers—overlapping one another in a brush pile, slanted singly against a fence, or laid on the ground in a corner of the backyard—provide many small creatures with shelter from wind, snow, and ice, as well as escape cover from predators.

Cardinals, chickadees, juncos, wrens, and other birds, as well as rabbits, squirrels, and the like, will make frequent and regular use of the "discarded" trees, even long after they have lost all their needles. The many nooks and crannies created by the abundant twigs and branches of a conifer provide a great deal of safe refuge.

If the tree is placed near a bird feeder, it will become a windbreak where the birds can take a break from their feeding without moving far from the food source. That helps them to conserve energy, a critical concern for all wildlife in winter.

# Bird Songs

SOMETIMES ALL BIRDERS ever see is nothing at all when out for a bird walk. Most birds are hidden by the foliage of trees or dense grasses (for meadow species). This is why it is so important to learn the vocalizations of birds. It not only clues you into the type or even the exact species, it can also tell you where the bird is.

The best way to get started is just by listening. It may be hard at first, especially if several species are singing at once. Focus on a single song and its characters, rather than memorizing the entire song, so as not to get overwhelmed and discouraged.

Try repeating the song to yourself using your own translation. If you can listen and remember the calls and songs being made by the birds you are actually seeing, that association will begin to stick in your mind.

Go birding with experienced people. Many can instantly tell what a particular song is, and they can help you understand the song.

Some calls are complex, and the best way to learn these is by picking apart the song, even writing down the phrases you hear. Is there a particular rhythm that repeats? Or is there no rhythm at all? Is the sound nasal, rasping, whistling, or fluty? Well-traveled birders may even notice regional differences in songs within the same species.

Recordings are a valuable resource, and many are available in CD-ROM form, but a few online libraries are also available.

Bird songs can be challenging, and some require a bit of work to learn. However, the most important thing to do is to keep listening. Once you do, you'll find that it opens up an entirely new facet of bird "watching."

# Resources

Armstrong, Edward A. *The Life and Lore of the Bird in Nature, Art, Myth, and Literature*. New York: Crown Publishers, Inc., 1975.

Arnott, Michael. *The Aberdeen Bestiary, Folio 57r Translation and Transcription*. University of Aberdeen, Scotland, www.abdn.ac.uk/bestiary/translat/57r.hti.

Australian Museum, "Australia's Extinct Animals," www.australianmuseum.net.au/Australias-extinct-animals.

Avibirds European Bird Guide Online, www.avibirds.com.

Bird Guides Ltd., www.birdguides.com.

BirdLife International, www.birdsofbritain.co.uk.

Byers, Clive, John Curson, and Urban Olsson. *Sparrows and Buntings: A Guide to Sparrows and Buntings of North America and the World*. Boston: Houghton Mifflin, 1995.

Chappell, Jackie. "Living with the Trickster: Crows, Ravens, and Human Culture." PLoS Biology 4, no. 1 (2006): e14. www.ncbi.nlm.nih.gov/pmc/articles/PMC1326277.

Cornell Lab of Ornithology, www.allaboutbirds.org.

Cornell Lab of Ornithology and the American Ornithologist's Union, Birds of North America Online, www.bna.birds.cornell.edu/bna.

Cornell Lab of Ornithology, "The Search for the Ivory-billed Woodpecker," www.birds.cornell.edu/ivory.

Department of Vertebrate Zoology, National Museum of Natural History, "Encyclopedia Smithsonian: The Passenger Pigeon," www.si.edu/encyclopedia_si/nmnh/passpig.htm.

Dunn, Jon, and Kimball Garrett. *A Field Guide to Warblers of North America*. Boston: Houghton Mifflin, 1997.

Estók, Péter, Sándor Zsebök, and Björn M. Siemers. "Great tits search for, capture, kill and eat hibernating bats." Biology Letters 2009: rsbl.2009.0611v1-rsbl20090611.

Feduccia, Alan. *The Age of Birds*. Cambridge, MA: Harvard University Press, 1980.

Ferguson-Lees, James, and David A. Christie. *Raptors of the World*. *Boston*: Houghton Mifflin, 2001.

Fleming, Samantha. "Ravens in Mythology," 1998, www.ravenfamily.org/nascakiyetl/obs/rav1.html.

Fuller, Errol. The Great Auk: *The Extinction of the Original Penguin*. Charlestown, MA: Bunker Hill Publishing, 2003.

Great Seal of the United States, www.greatseal.com.

Hamori, Fred. "The Legend of the Turul Hawk," www.stavacademy.co.uk/mimir/turulhawk.htm.

Harrison, Colin, and Alan Greensmith. *Birds of the World*. London: Dorling Kindersley, 1993.

Harrison, Peter. *Seabirds: An Identification Guide*. Boston: Houghton Mifflin, 1985.

Hulme, F. E. *Myth-Land*. London: Sampson Low, Marston, Searle, and Rivington, 1886.

Lok, A. F. S. L, and T. K. Lee. *Barbets of Singapore Part 2: Megalaima haemacephala indica* (coppersmith barbet), Singapore's only native, urban barbet. *Nature in Singapore* 1 (2009): 47–54.

Louis Agassiz Fuertes www.louisagassizfuertes.com/growing_up.htm.

Madge, Steve, and Hilary Burn. *Crows and Jays: A Guide to the Crows, Jays, and Magpies of the World*. Boston: Houghton Mifflin, 1994.

Mission San Juan Capistrano, www.missionsjc.com.

National Audubon Society, Waterbird Conversation, www.audubon.org/bird/waterbirds/index.html.

New South Wales government, www.environment.nsw.gov.au.

Newton, Ian (Ed.) *Birds of Prey*. San Francisco: Fog City Press, 2000.

Norris, Scott. "Largest Flying Bird Could Barely Get Off the Ground, Fossils Show," *National Geographic News*, July 2, 2007, http://news.nationalgeographic.com/news/2007/07/070702-biggest-bird.html.

PBS, "Harriman Expedition Retraced: Louis Agassiz Fuertes, 1874–1927," www.pbs.org/harriman/1899/1899_part/participantfuertes.html.

Peterson, Roger Tory. *A Field Guide to Western Birds: A Completely New Guide to Field Marks of All Species Found in North America West of the 100th Meridian and North of Mexico.* Boston: Houghton Mifflin, 1990.

Peterson, Roger Tory, Guy Mountfort, and P. A.D. Hollom. *A Field Guide to Birds of Britain and Europe.* Boston: Houghton Mifflin, 1993.

Peterson, Roger Tory, and Virginia Marie Peterson. *A Field Guide to the Birds of Eastern and Central North America*, 5th edition. Boston: Houghton Mifflin, 2002.

Pickrell, John. "Terror Birds: Predators with a Kung-fu Kick?" *National Geographic News*, August 1, 2005, http://news.nationalgeographic.com/news/2005/08/0801_050801_terrorbirds.html.

Quammen, David. *The Song of the Dodo.* New York: Scribner, 1996.

Roger Tory Peterson Institute of Natural History, www.rtpi.org.

Royal Society for the Protection of Birds, www.rspb.org.uk.

San Diego Zoo, Animal Bytes, www.sandiegozoo.org/animalbytes.

*Science Illustrated*, "When Giant Birds Reigned Supreme." January/February 2010.

Sibley, David Allen. *National Audubon Society The Sibley Guide to Birds.* Boston: Houghton Mifflin, 2000.

Smithsonian National Zoological Park, www.nationalzoo.si.edu.

Species Information Network, www.species.net.

Tate, Peter. *Flights of Fancy: Birds in Myth, Legend, and Superstition.* New York: Delacorte Press, Random House, 2007.

*Time*, "The Bahamas: Chickcharnys at Munich," March 24, 1947, www.time.com/time/magazine/article/0,9171,887342,00.html.

University of Michigan Museum of Zoology, Diversity Web, http://animaldiversity.ummz.umich.edu.

U.S. Fish and Wildlife Service, Southeast Region, "Ivory-billed Woodpecker Recovery Starts Here...," www.fws.gov/ivorybill.

Vermont Center for Ecostudies, www.vtecostudies.org.

Warhol, Tom. *Hawks* (Animalways). Tarrytown, NY: Marshall Cavendish Benchmark, 2005.

Warhol, Tom. *Owls* (Animalways). Tarrytown, NY: Marshall Cavendish Benchmark, 2008.

Welch, Craig. "A Brief History of the Spotted-owl Controversy," *Seattle Times*, August 6, 2000, http://community.seattletimes.nwsource.com/archive/?date=20000806&slug=4035697.

Wet Tropics Management Authority, www.wettropics.gov.au.

Winkler, Hans, Davis A. Christie, and David Nurney. *Woodpeckers: An Identification Guide to the Woodpeckers of the World.* Boston: Houghton Mifflin, 1995.

# Index

# Photographer Credits

# About the Authors

**TOM WARHOL** is a naturalist, writer, and photographer living in Vermont. He holds a master of science degree in forestry from the University of Massachusetts, and he has worked as a conservation professional for eight years, with the Massachusetts Riverways Program, The Nature Conservancy, The American Chestnut Foundation, and the New England Wild Flower Society. He is also the author of several books for Benchmark Books, including *Biomes of Earth* (2007), a six-volume series, and three volumes in Benchmark Books' Animalways series—*Eagles, Hawks,* and *Owls* (2004–2007).

**MARCUS H. SCHNECK** is the outdoor and nature editor at the *Patriot-News* in Harrisburg, Pennsylvania, and a regular contributor to a range of outdoor, travel, nature, and general-interest magazines. He has written more than two dozen books on subjects including backyard birds, nature and the outdoors, travel, pets, and gardening. He lives and gardens to attract birds in historic Berks County, Pennsylvania